AF449245

THE *ARS COMPONENDI SERMONES*
OF RANULPH HIGDEN, O.S.B.

DAVIS MEDIEVAL TEXTS AND STUDIES

UNIVERSITY OF CALIFORNIA, DAVIS

General Editor: Daniel Silvia
Managing Editor: Kevin P. Roddy
Editorial Board: Sydney R. Charles, Gerald Herman, Dennis Dutschke, James J. Murphy, Neal W. Gilbert, David A. Traill
Production Editor: Kathleen Cifra-Peck

VOLUME SIX

Margaret Jennings

The *ARS COMPONENDI SERMONES* OF RANULPH HIGDEN, O.S.B.

THE *ARS COMPONENDI SERMONES*
OF RANULPH HIGDEN, O.S.B.

BY

MARGARET JENNINGS

E.J. BRILL
LEIDEN · NEW YORK · KØBENHAVN · KÖLN
1991

The paper in this book meets the guidelines for permanence and durability of the Committee on Production Guidelines for Book Longevity of the Council on Library Resources.

Library of Congress Cataloging-in-Publication Data

Higden, Ranulph, d. 1364.
    [Ars componendi sermones. English]
    The Ars componendi sermones of Ranulph Higden, O.S.B. : a critical edition / by Margaret Jennings.
        p.   cm.—(Davis medieval texts and studies, ISSN 0169-7994 ; v. 6)
    Bibliography: p.
    Includes index.
    ISBN 90-04-06862-7 (pbk.)
    1. Preaching—Early works to 1800.   I. Jennings, Margaret.
II. Title.   III. Series.
BV4209.H5413   1987
251'.009'023—dc19   87-23925
                                           CIP

ISSN   0169-7994
ISBN   90 04 06862 7

PRINTED IN THE NETHERLANDS

For Lawrence

CONTENTS

FOREWORD ix
INTRODUCTION...xi
    I. The Changing Concept of "Art"
    II. The Influence of Medieval Logic
    III. The Pastoral Movement in England
    IV. Ranulph Higden's Life and Works
    V. The *Ars componendi sermones*
    VI. Manuscripts
    APPENDIX. SCHEMA OF PASTORALIA...........................xlviii
Ars Componendi Sermones 1
    I. Prefacio ad hanc artem
    II. De intencionis rectitudine
    III. De conversacionis sanctitudine
    IV. De prolacionis aptitudinc
    V. De dicendi circumspeccione
    VI. De thematis congruitate
    VII. Quod them congruat materie proponende
    VIII. Quod thema sit de biblia
    IX. Quod thema sufficienter dividatur
    X. Quod thema concordancias admittat
    XI. De prothematis extraccione
    XII. De oracionis premissione et gracie imploracione
    XIII. De auditorum alleccione
    XIV. De thematis introduccione
    XV. De thematis divisione
    XVI. De clavibus divisionis
    XVII. De sermonis dilatacione
    XVIII. De membrorum subdivisione
    XIX. De dilatacione facienda per auctoritates
    XX. De regulis dilatacionum
    XXI. De coloracione membrorum
APPENDIX
    Outline of the *Ars componendi sermones* and of the major sources
    from which it was compiled 73
GLOSSARY 81

FOREWORD

Since the publication of Th. Charland's *Artes Praedicandi* in 1936, several significant studies of the rise and development of Arts of Preaching have appeared, most notably Chapter VI in James J. Murphy's *Rhetoric in the Middle Ages*. I do not wish to restate here what has been so ably presented by others. There are, however, a few aspects of both classical and medieval tradition surrounding these *artes* which have not been featured in earlier critiques and which contribute to an appreciation for this form, namely: the changing concept of "ars," the dialectical/logical emphasis of the schoolmen, and most importantly, the great pastoral movement of the high Middle Ages which can be posited as the ultimate impetus for their composition. It is this last point which separates the *artes praedicandi* from their medieval rhetorical counterparts, the *artes dictaminis* and the *artes poeticae* and which enhances one's understanding of the shaping influences in this genre. Finally, the specifically Higden material focuses attention on his singularly well-made manual for the construction of a thematic sermon, the *Ars componendi sermones*.

The edition of the Higden text would not have been possible without the encouragement and help of Myra Uhlfelder, the constructive criticisms of Leonard Boyle, O.P., and Siegfried Wenzel, and the advice of Consuelo Wager Dutschke. Many other scholarly debts have been acknowledged throughout the Commentary but one, that to James J. Murphy, must be singled out. His generosity, concern, and assistance over several years are the real reasons (both philosophically and practically) for this edition's appearance.

INTRODUCTION

The Art of Preaching is a literary form which has roots in antiquity
but which remains a medieval phenomenon as distinctive in its own way
as the Gothic cathedral and the song of the troubadour. Built on the
foundation of classical rhetoric,[1] the *artes praedicandi* expounded several
of the tenets of Ciceronian composition for use in the now-Christian
pulpit.[2] So timely was the mold and so successful the effort that
thousands of manuscripts and early printed books survive from the thirteenth through the fifteenth centuries, when this type of manual was
most popular throughout Europe;[3] these texts spell out, for all who care
to learn, the intricacies of sermon design available to a preacher who
had mastered the art.

I

The Changing Concept of "Art"

By proclaiming the title "ars" the medieval preaching manuals
immediately invite comparison to the ancient oratorical styles, and it is
certainly demonstrable that with political oration in abeyance and with
legal exhortation having little scope, sermonizing practically monopol-
ized the third field distinguished by Aristotle—that of epideictic or occasional oratory.[4] But the "art" in the *ars praedicandi* reflects the particular filtration of classical concepts which the Middle Ages effected, and
like the genre itself, is a curious blend of the Greek *techne*, the Latin *ars*,
and the matrix of fifteen hundred years out of which the medieval usage

---

[1] Harry Caplan's "Rhetorical Invention in Some Medieval Tractates on Preaching," *Specu-
lum*, 2 (1927), 284-95 and "Classical Rhetoric and the Medieval Theory of Preaching,"
Classical Philology, 28 (1933), are pioneer studies. Further bibliography is available in
James J. Murphy, *Medieval Rhetoric: A Select Bibliography*, 2nd ed. (Toronto, 1989).

[2] James J. Murphy, "The Arts of Discourse, 1050-1400," *Mediaeval Studies*, 23 (1961),
194-205 and "Cicero's Rhetoric in the Middle Ages," *Quarterly Journal of Speech*, 53
(1967), 334-41.

[3] Harry Caplan's *Medieval Artes Praedicandi: A Handlist, Cornell Studies in Classical Philology*, 24 (1934), and the *Supplement* in volume 35 (1936) are standard. Th. Charland's
Artes Praedicandi (Ottawa, 1936) annotates most of Caplan's entries. More recent studies,
editions, translations are noted in Murphy's *Medieval Rhetoric: A Select Bibliography*.

[4] Charles Sears Baldwin, *Medieval Rhetoric and Poetic* (New York, 1928), p. 230. A similar
statement is contained in Robert E. Curtius, *European Literature and the Latin Middle
Ages*, tr. William Trask (New York, 1953), pp. 154-55, where it is noted that even in the
Rome of the Empire, judicial oratory had sunk to the level of a rhetorical exercise and political oratory had become fictitious deliberative speech, while epideictic exercised the
strongest influence.

took shape.[5] Plato in the *Gorgias* had defined "techne" by allowing Socrates to deny this title to the craft of rhetoric because a "techne" had to be based on knowledge and aim at what is good.[6] In the *Phaedrus*, Plato insists that the possessor of a "techne" be able to conceptualize and define the subject with which he is working to structure it and to mold its scattered parts according to the Form of Idea of the Whole. Hence, he must have the capacity to analyze in a logical manner, and he must possess that dialectical power which not only studies the object of its concern and divides it into parts but also knows how it acts on other things and is affected by them.[7] Cicero enlivens the question of whether rhetoric is or is not an "ars" by presenting the argument of the *De Oratore* through a clash of opinions and personalities. Crassus maintains that rhetoric is an art; Antonius, who poses as a self-made orator, denies it. The question is settled by a compromise: rhetoric is not an art in the scientific sense which demands that its rules cover all cases and be infallible; but it is an "art"—like to the Greek "techne"—in the sense that general principles can be established which apply fairly consistently.[8] Cicero's solution was not original; it is found in germ in the initial section of Aristotle's *Rhetorica* and negatively applied to the work of Philodemus who classified rhetoric, or the art of persuasion, as no "techne" at all, for the persuasion to him was sheer guesswork.[9]

From a different angle, Horace also endeavors to establish a definition for "ars," although his major concern is whether good poetry can be attributed to *natura* or to *studium*. He certainly exhibits a broader vision of the nature of the problem than that betrayed by the earlier Roman critics who agreed with the Alexandrians in putting emphasis on what they called "ars" or "techne"—to poetry as hard work, as technical proficiency requiring special knowledge and training rather than as

---

[5] Some understanding of "art's" extensive history can be gleaned from James J. Murphy, ed., *A Synoptic History of Classical Rhetoric* (New York, 1972), and in James J. Murphy's *Rhetoric in the Middle Ages* (Berkeley, 1974), pp. 9-10, 59, 74, 171, 173. Extraordinary variations in usage are apparent in the citations to the term in the *Thesaurus Linguae Latinae*, Vol. II (Leipzig, 1906), cols. 656-673.

[6] 460 a-b

[7] 269c.

[8] The question of whether or not oratory is an art is raised by Antonius in *De Oratore* I, 92-3 and further discussed at 109-110, 145-46, and II, 28-33, and 232.

[9] See Aristotle's *Rhetoric* I, 1 (1355 a 12) in the translation for Loeb Classical Library made by John Henry Freese (Cambridge, Mass., 1959), p. 11: "Scientific discourse is concerned with instruction; our proofs and arguments must rest on generally accepted principles. . ." Philodemus maintains that the art of speech is not a "techne" in the same sense as an exact science; its principles and general rules do not apply without exception, but it does have principles and rules that generally apply though a certain amount of contingency will remain. An exact science, he says is a "pagia techne," a fixed art, but sophistic is a "Stoxastike techne," a guessing or approximate "techne" (in I, 68-77 of his *Rhetorica*). Persuasion as sheer guesswork is discussed in II. 116. See also G. M. A. Grube, *The Greek and Roman Critics* (London, 1965), pp. 201-2.

native creative genius.[10] The *Letter to the Piso's* counsels that both are needed:

ego nec studium sine devite vena;
nec rude quid prosit video ingenium: alterius sic
altera poscit opem res et coniurat amice. (ll. 409-411)

But Horace's vision is not Plato's and it is very possible to discern here that the lofty ideal of the ancient Greek "techne" of that innate knowledge of the principles of ordering and of their many interrelationships, is largely lost. Indeed, Lucan's *Parasite* illustrates the word's pejorative connotation when his protagonist argues whether the art of getting free dinners is a true art, on the basis of the definition that an "ars" is a "complex of concepts exercised towards an end which is useful to (human) life." In affirming his point, Lucian uses many illustrations which for centuries had been employed to prove that rhetoric was an "ars" or "techne."[11]

The problem in defining an art and classifying subjects as *artes* was further complicated by Quintilian's excessively boring treatment of the matter in the second book of the *Institutes of Oratory*. There is little doubt, however, that in Quintilian's mind "ars" and sheer technical skill were equated and that *nudae artes* were simply dry textbooks which showed extreme subtlety, killing whatever was noble in eloquence, draining away the live sap, and leaving nothing but the bare bones.[12] Servius, too, apparently found that an "ars" was a mere technical skill, and the medieval grammatical textbooks often were classified only under this term.[13] The word was used more favorably when coupled with "liberales" or when it denoted a university faculty. These instances, though quite different from the singular sense, seem to affect its total definition as the Middle Ages progress. In fact, assisted by theological speculation, such amelioration advances the signification of "art" in some circles towards that of *facultas movendi* and *vis* or *potentia*.[14] In the twelfth century, Hugh of St. Victor seems influenced by both

---

[10] Ibid., p. 152.

[11] *The Parasite*, 4 and 9, edited by A. M. Harmon for Loeb Classical Library (Cambridge, Mass., 1913), pp. 247-8 and 255.

[12] Vol. I, *Praefatio*, 24: "Nam plerumque nudae illae artes nimia subtilitatis adfectione frangunt atque concidunt quidquid est in oratione generosius, et omnem sucum ingenii bibunt et ossa detergunt. . ."

[13] Servius, *Aeneid* I, 748 (*In Vergilii Carmina Commentariorum*, vol. II, ed E. K. Rand *et al.* [Lancaster, Pa., 1946]. p. 307), shows that he considered "ars" very much in the line of a technical skill: "*Nec non et vario* arte poetica utitur ut praemittat aliquid quo sequens liber videatur esse coniunctus quod in omnibus servat." The first reading of DuCange's *Glossarium Mediae et Infimae Latinitatis*, vol. I (Paris, 1840), p. 416 is telltale: "Ars, Artes, Grammatica."

[14] The *Thesaurus Linguae Latinae*, vol. II (Leipzig, 1900-1906), col. 656 ff. and the *Mittellateinisches Worterbuch*, vol. II (Munich, 1967), pp. 982 ff. offer broader definitions and permit "ars" to signify a *facultas movendi* and a *potentia* or *vis*.

viewpoints in that he first calls knowledge an "ars" when it compromises the rules and precepts which deal with verisimilitude and opinion, and secondly when he shows that the ultimate concern of any art is with the changeless archetypal patterns in the divine Wisdom to whose likeness each art endeavors to help restore man.[15] "Ars" in the latter section is directed toward a more universal goal; while remaining predicable to the technical definition, it can also be a part of human ordering toward the Divine and hence involves a conceptual grasp of a segment of reality and a teleologically ordered scheme.[16]

In a more practical vein than that in which Hugh was philosophizing, Geoffrey of Vinsauf discussed the scope of "ars" in the initial section of his *Poetria Nova*. Since, he maintains, the *materia* of the poem will be its contents, the author must plan it out with great care—a long and laborious process. Geoffrey's comparison of poetic creation with the planning of an architect stresses the importance of this step in the poem's total composition; like an architect the poet must consider carefully what will go into his creation.[17] But in conjunction with determination of his *materia* the poet must also establish the order of his poem, that is, fix the beginning, middle, and end of his *materia*:

> Certus praelimitet ordo
> Unde praearripiat cursum stylus, aut ibi Gades
> Figat. Opus totum prudens in pectoris arcem
> Contrahe, sitque prius in pectore quam in ore.[18]

Here Geoffrey asserts that the order of the poem predetermines the limits and principal divisions of that piece; a few lines later, order will mean something different and will signify the way to begin, the disposition of the poem's contents, the first of its sections, which is to be

---

[15] "Ars dici potest scientia, quae artis praeceptis regulisque consistit ut est in scriptura disciplina, quae dicitur plena, ut est in doctrina. Vel ars dici potest quando aliquid verisimile atque opinabile tractatur, disciplina quando de his, quae aliter se habere non possunt, veris disputationibus aliquid disseritur . . . hoc ergo omnes artes agunt, hoc intendunt, ut divina similitudo in nobis reparetur, quae nobis forma est, Deo natura, cui quando magis conformamur, tanto magis sapimus."

[16] Hugh's is probably the most sophisticated definition of "ars" that can be found in the twelfth century. John of Salisbury devotes Chapter II of Book I of the *Metalogicon* to this subject, but art here remains a system, albeit a system that reason has devised in order to expedite our ability to do things within our natural capacities. He contends that the Greeks might have called it a "methodon," that is, an efficient plan which avoids nature's wastefulness and straightens out her circuitous wanderings, so that man may more easily and correctly accomplish what he is to do. The citation from Hugh of St. Victor is taken from the *Didascalicon—De studio legendi*, ed. Charles H. Buttimer (Washington, D.C., 1939), p. 23. The translation of John of Salisbury which is presented above is from the edition of the *Metalogicon* by Clement C. I. Webb (Oxford, 1929), p. 28: "Est autem ars ratio que compendio sui naturaliter possibilium expedit facultatem."

[17] An excellent treatment of the nature of Geoffrey's discussion in this section of the *Poetria Nova* can be found in Douglas Kelly, "The Scope of the Treatment of Composition in the Twelfth- and Thirteenth-Century Arts of Poetry," *Speculum*, 41 (1966), 271-77.

[18] Verses 56-59.

followed by the middle and the end. In both cases, though, the ordering of the poem demands a conception of the whole, a delineated mode and process of presentation, and a direction which greatly enhances the earlier medieval definitions of the scope of "ars." For when the content of the future poem has been planned, unified, and arranged, then only may the poet begin to write: "Mentis in arcano cum rem digresserit ordo/ Materiam verbis veniat vestire poesis" (60-61).

Throughout, the poem's "oneness" remains the most important consideration; all ornamentation ought to be adapted to the total plan and fit organically into the completed work. Therefore, the *materia* must be constantly considered before and during embellishment.[19] This initial stress on the scope of "ars" in the *Poetria Nova* is not, however, meant to deny the existence of technical rules of procedure in the text which, frankly, abound. It is intended solely as a reminder that they are not all that is contained in this thirteenth-century treatise on the craft of creating poetry. Rather there is a certain orientation in Geoffrey that reminds one of the larger definition of "techne" which was recognized in the fourth century, B.C., and which comes to its fullest medieval expression in the *ars praedicandi*. Here, teleological determination in both celestial and terrestrial spheres, provisions for organic growth, and a continuum of division and dilation allow to "ars" a good deal of the significance presaged in its classical heritage.[20]

II

The Influence of Medieval Logic

As augured by the investigation of "ars," analyses of thematic sermon manuals reveal that classical rhetorical principles have been enveloped in medieval thought and that the pristine dispositional pattern of a text

---

[19] Cf. verses 69-70 and Kelly's treatment of this subject on p. 273. The text of the *Poetria Nova* has been edited by Edmond Faral in *Les Arts Poétiques du XIIᵉ et du XIIIᵉ Siècle* (Paris, 1924), pp. 197-262. A translation appears in James J. Murphy, ed., *Three Medieval Rhetorical Arts* (Berkeley, Los Angeles and London, 1971).

[20] At the risk of laboring the point I will briefly summarize: the arts of preaching are very much concerned with the technical qualities and rules which insure a finished and acceptable product. However, they are constantly ordered to a general end—to bring man closer to God—and the design of these treatises commands that the specific end of each sermon as developed from the theme be always discernible in the divisions and dilations which are prescribed for the sermonizer. Although Hugh of St. Victor sees "ars" in a philosophic sense as a part of the continuum of learning and growth which ultimately leads man to the most perfect knowledge of God of which he is capable in this world, the *artes praedicandi*, in a more practical vein, see the precepts of the thematic sermon as a part of the living organism whose function is ultimately akin to that of Hugh's "ars." Man's perfectibility in God is more proximate through Hugh's conception of "ars," more remote through that presented in the arts of preaching—but evident in both and functioning in both.

like Cicero's *De Inventione* is no longer a primary consideration. Such overlays are particularly discernible in the rules and conventions which govern the development of the university-style sermon. Having chosen a biblical text or theme, and having strengthened it in the "protheme" and the "introduction," a preacher could advance to division—the statement of subtopics derived from the theme which explains some meaning or meanings contained in it. Whatever method of division was adopted, the sermonizer was advised to avail himself of such useful devices as distinction and acceptance of plurality. Distinction involved the separation of species from a genus; e.g., duty might become particularized as duty to God, to one's neighbor, to oneself and so forth. Acceptance of plurality meant envisaging several things under one head without the formal enumeration of division and distinction, as in "the supreme law involves love of God and love of other." In drawing up his division, a preacher was also admonished to follow some definite order: either the order of words as they occurred, or better the order of grammatical construction or the best logical order of ideas.

Confirmation of the division by authorities might accomplished in three ways. When the words of the material being divided and those of the divisions appeared in the authorities and when the meaning of no word was distorted to make the authority apply, the authorities were said to be in verbal and real concord with the division. When the ideas of the theme and the division appeared in the authorities but the words did not, the authorities were said to be in real concord only. And when the words of the theme and division were used but their meaning were in some way violated to make authority applicable, the authority was said to be in verbal concord. This last concordance was thought practically valueless, and a preacher was warned against its use in any part of his *confirmatio*.

A further refinement of the rules for division and confirmation could be found in those *artes praedicandi* which discussed intrinsic and extrinsic modes of division. The former (*divisio intra*) implied an artificial division of the theme into its constituent parts and provided for the straightforward use of the rules for division as indicated above. The latter (*divisio extra*) described a division sought for outside of the theme and subsequently applied to it. A *divisio intra*, which was sometimes difficult to grasp and therefore suitable for the clergy, might employ the text: "So run that you may obtain" (I Cor. 11:24) and immediately open with the statement: Here we are invited to the race by the words, "so run." A *divisio extra*, which was perhaps better for a popular audience, might begin with a discussion of the three types of law (natural, written, evangelical) and focus the division thus: Here the preacher of the evangelical law instructs us in what we must do by his use of the word "run"; in how we must do it by "so"; and to what end in the phrase "that you may obtain."

After their presentation of the structure and style of the division, the *artes praedicandi* proceed to give the sermon's skeleton flesh through a great variety of dilationary methods. So many were these that some scholars have concluded that the thematic sermon form offered amazing opportunities for the juggling of words and ideas.[21] But this statement must be understood as unfairly critical of such preceptive pieces. Their authors thought of them as a usable tool, and, other things being equal, the halting and indifferent speaker whose sermon is at least constructed on some definite and intelligible plan is likely to preach better than the "sayer of a few words." Especially in their favor were the requirements that the entire sermon be based on scripture, that a theme be repeated, that accurate quotation be the norm, and that a text be *bene concordatum*. A tripartite division was also sound pedagogical method and the stressing of rhythm and cadence in an age of memory and oral learning should not be minimized.

Especially in their emphasis on words and word constructs were the *artes praedicandi* more than self-taught juggling acts, since it is here that they best illustrate how the three customary rhetorical questions (whether a thing is, what it is, and of what sort) merged readily with the questions of dialectic.[22] Indeed, a disposition to reason about facts instead of just observing them—a disposition which can be traced in Carolingian authors—was made stronger in the twelfth century when controversies concerning logic and metaphysics profoundly influenced the teaching of grammar.[23] Such philosophic probing was channeled realistically by the *moderni* who professed a concern for practical issues and effective application, that is, with actions and words.[24]

The practice of using the procedures of dialectic within the arts of discourse can be traced with some certainty as early as William of Conches, who criticized the *grammatici antiqui* for failing to discuss the *cause inventionis*. [25] The *Summa* of Petrus Helias follows the advanced

---

[21] Woodburn O. Ross, ed., *Middle English Sermons*, EETS, O.S., #209 (London, 1940), p. li.

[22] Richard McKeon, "Rhetoric in the Middle Ages," *Speculum*, 17, (1942), p. 32.

[23] M. Charles Thurot, "Notices et extraits de divers manuscrits latins pour servir à l'histoire des doctrines grammaticales au Moyen Âge," *Notices et Extraits des Manuscrits de la Bibliothèque Nationale et Autres Bibliothèques*, 22 (Paris, 1874), p. 117.

[24] McKeon, "Rhetoric," p. 26: "Gradually in the course of the twelfth and thirteenth centuries they limited their statements to figures and forms of words, accomplishing their practical objectives by that device in a fashion which met with little effective opposition from logicians and theologians, and since they were unhampered by the need to consider things or thoughts, they were prolific in production of the 'new' methods—they were fond of calling themselves 'moderni'—which constituted one of the important guises in which rhetoric entered the fourteenth century." A lucid treatment of the members of this so-called Drogonic sect is given by McKeon on pp. 26-7.

[25] William felt that when the cause of invention (the reason for the coining of a particular word) had been found, it could be used as a criterion for determining the proper grammatical function of the word. Further, the principal or proper purpose of its invention is the criterion by which we ought to judge a word, not its syntactic function. Cf. Richard W. Hunt, "Studies on Priscian in the Eleventh and Twelfth Century," *Medieval and Renais-*

program outlined by William and systematizes these *cause*, providing a paradigm whereby the student can discern how preoccupied the twelfth-century glossators on Priscian were with questions of logic.[26] They are concerned to show what sort of argument Priscian was using and to set it out formally. Only theoretically did they reserve the investigation of truth and falsity for dialectic; immediately after a declaration of this attitude they might discuss the substantial and accidental significations of a verb. Priscian's own method might, of course, account for the early glossators' lack of success in separating grammatical and dialectical uses of such terms as substance of a noun and accidents of various other parts of speech. Petrus Helias did make a determined effort to free himself from questions that did not belong to grammar, but dialectic still remained the dominant partner.[27] The newer contributions made by the glossators of the school of Ralph of Beauvais were the applications of logical analysis to the meaning of words.[28] Later glossators, moreover, refined many of the dialectical distinctions made by Petrus Helias with regard to genus and species of grammatical terms, substance and accidents with regard to the *potestas* of a letter—a recognition of the *modi essendi intelligendi,* and *significandi* which was later to become the foundation of speculative grammar. However, in the organization of syntax, the interest in logic of the later twelfth century grammarians found its most profitable outlet. In this process the emphasis is on logical analysis and the examples are imaginary.[29] In the anonymous gloss *Promisimus* the task of the grammarian is defined as follows: "Hec duo, certa regularum assignato et subtilis circa iudicium constructionum inquisitio et solutio perfectum faciunt gramaticum."[30] Truly, the assimilation of the new Aristotle and the works of the Arabic logicians led to a new speculative grammar where discussions of syntax were conducted on rigorously logical lines, with little room for the use and appreciation of

---

sance Studies, 1 (1941), 212.

[26] Petrus Helias systematizes the *cause inventionis* and extends their use. He distinguishes a *communis causa inventionis omnium dictionum* and a *propria causa inventionis cuiusque partis orationis*. He also gives a *causa inventionis* for each of the accidents of each part of speech. See Hunt, ibid., p. 214. Petrus Helias, however, "usait encore sobrement le peripatetisme" (Thurot, p. 118).

[27] Hunt, p. 220. Petrus is conscious that he is an innovator in the task of freeing himself from the shackles of questions which are not properly grammatical.

[28] For example: "Nota improprie ponitur hoc loco hoc adverbium 'quasi' cum dicit 'quasi consonanti' (I, 25, p. 19, 20), quia hec est differentia inter 'ut' quod est adverbium similitudinis et 'quasi' quod est nota similitudinis, quia per 'ut' notatur similitudo existentie, per 'quasi' vero similitudo non-existentie, verbi gratia, 'Iste homo incedit ut sapiens' convenienter dicitur, si in te ita sit, ut dicitur, ut scil. sit sapiens" (L fol. 34ra) as quoted in Richard W. Hunt, "Studies on Priscian in the Eleventh and Twelfth Century, Part II," *Medieval and Renaissance Studies*, 2 (1950), 26.

[29] Hunt illustrates this process with ample quotation; see ibid., p. 36.

[30] *Promisimus*, fol. 21ra, as cited in Hunt, ibid., p. 37.

authors. The influence that dialectic, argumentation, and disputation had on all branches of learning was, of course, deeply felt in the study of terminology and method in grammar. In the thirteenth century each part of the text under discussion came into focus through a species of division by dichotomy: from the first phase of the text being explicated, each subdivision was motivated by a general consideration.[31] Also at this time, and perhaps largely as a result of the teaching of grammar by the arts masters who spent much of their time in disputation, philosophical analysis penetrated even into the forms of exposition, and grammar became a purely speculative science whose end was the explication of reasons for first principles. These speculative grammarians saw the relation between logic and grammar in a simple vein: by logic we arrive at truth and knowledge, and by grammar we are enabled correctly to express and communicate these in words.[32] Grammar is thus handmaiden to philosophy.

It is justifiable to state, consequently, that the thirteenth century gave a more logical thrust to the forms of exposition and introduced there the principles of Aristotelian philosophy which were unknown during the twelfth century and which remained current throughout the fourteenth. These tendencies can also be detected in the *artes dictaminis* and *praedicandi*. In the former, the rhetorical questions which have already been remarked can be discerned in their transmuted form. Konrad of Mure uses an extended categorization of them as the basis for his entire treatise: "quis, cuius, cur, quid, quo, quomodo, cui, ubi, et quando." Within these categories many logical innovations rear their heads: in the chapter "de cuius" the four Aristotelian causes are defined and illustrated for "in conmuni usu loquendi causa dicitur omnes res de qua agitur et que movet et facit ut aliquid sit vel fiat."[33] By far the longest section, however, belongs to *quomodo*, which is consistently arranged and divided into several sections which illustrate the varying definitions of the scope of "in what manner." Here occurs again the word *modernus* which is often attached to these modes of discourse and which may be connected with their dialectical bent, because the thirteenth century added to the *logica vetus* and *logica nova* the *logica modernorum*, a

---

[31] "Au xiiie siècle on appliquait à chaque partie du texte une méthode de division qui consiste à arriver, par une série de dichotomies, à la premiére phrase du texte que l'on veut expliquer, chacune des subdivisions étant motivée par une considération générale." Thurot, p. 106. There was more of an effort to give a logical appearance to the presentation than to get at the main proposition of the argument. Cf. p. 107.

[32] R. H. Robins, *Ancient and Mediaeval Grammatical Theory in Europe* (London, 1951), p. 89.

[33] See the *Summa de arte prosandi, compilata a magistro Cuonrado cantore ecclesie thuricensis. . . .* ed. Ludwig Rockinger, *Briefsteller und Formelbucher des eilften bis vierzehnten jahrhunderts* in *Quellen und Erörterungen zur Bayerischen und Deutschen Geschichte* (Munich, 1863), Vol. I, pp. 417-482, particularly pp. 421, 434, and 460.

systematic treatment of the properties of terms as found, for example, in the *summulae logicales* of Peter of Spain.[34] I have already mentioned the *moderni* who might borrow freely from dialectical rules without feeling obliged to the entire dialectical process, and the word is significant in other ways connected with dialectic. Thomas Aquinas in his discussion of Anselm's ontological argument for the existence of God is quite specific in naming the *moderni* as those who live in a world dominated by the Aristotelian philosophical viewpoint.[35] The word also provides a good transition to the *artes praedicandi*, whose mode of composing sermons is consistently called *modernus*.[36]

As grammar envisioned a universal structure beyond linguistic particulars which dealt with modes of signification, and as the logico-grammatical material formed the substructure for great speculative edifices, so the *artes praedicandi* came to illustrate in another manner that part of the structure of medieval thought which dealt with ways of speaking as well as with modes of being—of posing questions *in voce* as well as *in re*.[37] However, in discussing the influence of logic and dialectic in these *artes* I wish to emphasize with Lecoy de la Marche that "la scolastique n'a fait que donner à un vieux principe une extension nouvelle."[38] The old principle was, of course, rhetoric, but it was inevitable that analytical processes should become a quite noticeable part of the treatises since their inception is largely connected with the universities where dialectic remained tremendously important.[39] The difficulty which the modern student, fortified by an understanding of Aristotle's *Rhetorica*, might envision in the application of the syllogism rather than the rhetorical enthymeme in an art of discourse would probably not be apparent to the medieval preacher. If it were seen, he might perhaps reply: that sacred eloquence differs from the secular in that its subject matter lies not in the realm of opinion and probability but in truth and divine science; that it is as sound a procedure to use a dialectical

---

[34] Paul Vignaux, *Philosophy in the Middle Ages* (London, 1959), p. 70.

[35] Anton C. Pegis, "St. Anselm and the Argument of the *Proslogion*," *Mediaeval Studies*, 28 (1966), 264: "In the history of Christian thought, the thirteenth century begins the era *after* Aristotle. This is the era of the *moderni*, St. Thomas's contemporaries as seen by him, who could no more return to the world of the historical Augustine than they could undo the new world of Aristotle in their midst."

[36] Perhaps the most frequent allusions to the "modern" method are those of Robert of Basevorn in his *Forma Praedicandi*. The word is adopted by Ranulph Higden also; see below, pp. 22, 25, and so on.

[37] Vignaux, p. 71.

[38] A. Lecoy de la Marche, *La Chaire Française au Moyen Âge* (Paris, 1886), p. 298.

[39] Dialectic, in fourteenth century Oxford for example, remained a part of the largely pervasive "libri logicales." See James A. Weisheipl, "Developments in the Arts Curriculum at Oxford in the Early Fourteenth Century," *Mediaeval Studies*, 28 (1966), 151-167 and 185. Cf. R. J. Schoeck, "On Rhetoric in Fourteenth Century Oxford," *Mediaeval Studies*, 30 (1968), 214-225.

method in the demonstration of truth as with the investigation of it and further that in Aristotle, Cicero, and Quintilian he had precedents for the policy of adapting to overly rhetorical purposes the method of the allied art of dialectic.[40] Of all the disciplines which the Middle Ages received and appropriated for itself, dialectic became the essential technique, but its application to religious problems must not be considered a form of empty game; dialectic enchanted the men who discovered it. "And medieval reason, once it had a new technique at its disposal, applied it directly to the realm of religious concepts—the realm which was for the mediaeval mind the immediately given."[41] To have recourse to dialectic was similar to having recourse to reason, and consequently the triumph of dialectic is felt in the *artes praedicandi* which prescribe the procedures of argumentation and subsume under logical rules the modes of elocution and invention.[42] Innumerable treatises contend that preaching with simplicity does not imply preaching without art, and in order to be clear and convincing the medieval preacher often had recourse to the precise and rigorous rules of formal logic. Hence, these sermon-makers might justify the refined technique of the *artes praedicandi* by maintaining that they put philosophy into the service of an apostolate in much the same manner that doctors did in theological science.[43] Thus, a sermon theorist like Ranulph Higden was careful to spell out the four causes as they manifested themselves in preaching, yet he or his redactor was also careful to distinguish preaching from the *lectio* and *disputatio* in the schools. Logical analysis of words, an inheritance from grammar, becomes a key in the entire development of the sermon because the theme yields up its dispositional possibilities through this process. The laying down or *positio* of the theme (a phrase echoed again and again) is undoubtedly carried over from the *positio* of scholastic logic and underlies the infallibility of the scriptural text;[44] the analysis of this scriptural text through its several possible divisions parallels the dialectical method of the schools and even the chapter *De congruitate thematis* reflects the logico-grammatical emphasis on *congruitas* as the efficient cause of the construction.[45] Since the syllogism is the core and

---

[40] Caplan, "Classical Rhetoric," p. 88.

[41] Vignaux, p. 26.

[42] Jean Leclerq, *L'Idée de la Royauté du Christ au Moyen Âge*, (Paris—Unam Sanctum 32, 1959), p. 114: ". . .prescrivent des procèdes d'argumentation et soumettre à des règles logique l'invention et l'élocution."

[43] An example of the expression of this opinion within the *artes praedicandi* can be found in the anonymous treatise (Bibl. Nat. lat. MS 455, fols. 56-57ᵛ) which is treated extensively by Jean Leclerq in "Le Magistère du Prédicateur au xiiiᵉ siècle," *Archives d'Histoire Doctrinale et Littéraire du Moyen Âge*, 25 (1946), 111 ff.

[44] Philotheus Boehner, *Medieval Logic: An Outline of its Development from 1250 to 1400* (Manchester, 1952), p. 15. *Positio* seems to be the equivalent of the axiom in the modern sense of the word.

[45] See Thurot, p. 218.

center of medieval logic, it is not surprising that it receives extended treatment in the *Ars componendi sermones*, but it is not imposed as a *sine qua non* of sermon construction. If one were to review the logical writings of Albert the Great, one would find that most of the topics treated there appear in condensed form in the *artes praedicandi*; for example: the discussion of genus and species from the treatises on the predicables; the division of genus into species from the whole into its parts, the spoken word into its several meanings, the distinction of accidents on the basis of subjects and subjects by reason of their accidents and accidents according to accidents from Albert's *De Divisione*; deduction and induction as means of argumentation from his *Priora Analytica*; the possibilities of syllogistic reasoning and inference from the *Topica*; and even the method of illustration and example itself which may derive at least in some form from the various *sophismata Alberti* which served as illustration of the scholastic thought process.[46] It is indeed possible that the concern which compilers of the *artes praedicandi* felt about verbal and real concordance in the confirmation of a theme and its subdivisions was a reflection of the logical concern over the signification of a word—a concern which remained controversial from Abelard to William of Occham. Finally, there is an openly logical bent in one of the declarations of the chapter *De clavibus divisionis* in Higden's *Ars*: "Item fit declaratio logice secundum partes tocius diversimode sumpti vel prout sunt partes tocius virtualis vel tocius universalis vel tocius integralis."[47] But, to point out the logical and dialectical elements in an *ars praedicandi* is not to imply that the rules of a hard and fast analytical method were intended to govern the preaching of the Word. Like the precepts of ancient rhetorical tradition which are also found in abundance in the arts of preaching, the logico-dialectical elements were offered as a means of attaining clarity and precision in the preaching apostolate: "elle indique des limites dont il ne faut pas s'écarter: à cette condition chaque prédicateur exerce son talent en toute liberté.[48]

---

[46] For the works of Albert the Great see the *Opera Omnia* edited by A. Borgnet (Paris, 1890). A summary of their contents can be found in Boehner, pp. 2-5. Ranulph's *Ars* shows logical tendencies, particularly in the chapters *De clavibus divisionis*, *De membrorum subdivisione*, and *De dilatacione facienda per auctoritates* (third and ninth modes).

[47] See below, p. 53.

[48] Leclerq, *L'Idée*, p. 124.

III

The Pastoral Movement in England

Since the object of dialectic is to convince a hearer of truth, any discussion of its use in the *artes praedicandi* inevitably involves the pastoral attitude which both precedes and fosters this conviction. It has been convincingly and repeatedly demonstrated that the preaching function is ultimately and essentially pastoral activity; hence, canonical principles which came to govern its exercise made the right to preach dependent on the possession of a cure of souls.[49] Though for purposes of clarity this discussion will be principally confined to English sources, it may safely be said that the insular traditions are easily paralleled on the continent and often stem from or give flower to a facet of earlier and foreign legislation. In England itself, however, there was a long history of pastoral concern. At the Council of Cloveshoo in 747 it was ordered that priests in places and districts assigned to them by the bishops of the province should take care to discharge with great diligence the duty of the apostolic commission in baptizing, teaching, and visiting, and learn to construe in the native tongue the Creed, the Lord's Prayer, the Mass, and the baptismal rite; they must also teach the articles of faith, the doctrine of eternal life, and the other truths.[50] Actually, there is here a scheme for teaching which the parochial clergy might well have studied and pursued in those early centuries, and the canons issued under Dunstan's influence in 960 reiterated those of 747 and extended them in directing the clergy to preach to the people every Sunday.[51] It was, nevertheless, a good century afterward that the pastoral concern which was to become so widespread later began to show itself in earnest. It is possible to trace

---

[49] The main principle that underlay canonical legislation concerning who might preach appears again and again in both Latin and vernacular treatises. In the fourteenth century, for example, it can be discerned in a tract like the *Regimen Animarum*, a handbook of canon law and instruction which survives in several manuscripts, one of the more readable being Harley 2272. There, on fol. 9, the question "Who can rightfully preach?" is answered with sufficient clarity: priests, deacons, and subdeacons "si habent prelationem et curam animarum." The question apparently remained significant, judging by the frequency with which it appears in the manuals. For additional commentary see Reginald Ladner, "*L'Ordo Predicatorum* avant l'ordre des Prêcheurs," *Saint Dominique*, ed. Pierre Mandonnet, Vol. II (Paris, 1937), p. 28 and pp. 30ff.

[50] Charles Smyth, *The Art of Preaching*, 747-1939 (London, 1940), p. 11. The best survey of the rise and development of pastoral attitudes in the Middle Ages is contained in the unpublished D.Phil. Dissertation of Leonard Boyle, O.P., "A Survey of the Writings Attributed to William of Pagula," Oxford, 1956. Although this text is cited frequently below, my debt to Father Boyle's work and words is more pervasive than any series of footnotes might indicate.

[51] Henry Gee and William John Hardy, comp., *Documents Illustrative of English Church History* (London, 1896), pp. 20 ff. for the Cloveshoo decrees which became the model for others.

this burgeoning to the schools and to the developments in theology there which had ultimately to be made available to the ordinary curate; it is possible to see in the occupation with the care of souls a new conception of the imitation of Christ in conjunction with the reforms legislated by Gregory VII;[52] but whatever development is finally responsible, the fact is that the pastoral renewal of these middle centuries found both impetus and encouragement in canonical legislation provided from the Third and Fourth Lateran Councils and practical guidelines and implementation in the local fulfillment of the conciliar documents.

Besides extermination the remains of the schism and Waldensian heresy, the Third Lateran Council (1179) undertook to restore ecclesiastical discipline. Its third canon forbade the promotion of anyone to the episcopate before the age of thirty and provided that deaneries, archdeaneries, parochial charges and other benefices involving the care of souls were not to be conferred on anyone less than twenty-five years of age; canon five demanded ecclesiastical title for every ordinand; canon eighteen provided for the establishment in every cathedral church of a school for poor clerics.[53] Though these canons are not overwhelming in their provisions, the acknowledgement of pastoral problems which they represent was a new movement in ecclesiastical legislation, and its effects were to be felt and its ordinances reiterated and enlarged in 1215.

The concern manifested by the members of the Third Lateran Council about pastoral matters ran parallel with a movement to bring theology of the schools within reach of the ordinary clergy because of priests actively engaged in the *cura animarum* faced problems similar to those discussed in the schools, *summae* disputations, and glosses. Though the delineation of practical cases from the *cura animarum* had become a steady feature of the tracts on penance, matrimony and the eucharist, Robert Courson seems to have been in the vanguard in realizing the demand for popular works of theology when he produced his *Summa de sacramentis* between 1204 and 1207.[54] Subsequent compilations by Peter of Roissy,

---

[52] Ladner, p. 31, remarks: "la note la plus caractèristique de cette fin du xie siècle et du début du xiie fut d'être traversée par un souffle très rémarquable: un désir ardent de s'occuper des âmes." Leonard Boyle in his dissertation, pp. 189 ff., connects this phenomenon with the interest manifested in the schools about pastoral problems and the inevitable deepening of this concern under the influence of the evangelistic friars; he is, however, not satisfied with this formulation as a definitive answer. For the influence of the friars see M.-D. Chenu, "Evangelisme et théologie au xiiie siècle," in *Mélanges F. Cavallera* (Toulouse, 1948), 339-46. In Paris at the end of the thirteenth century Henry of Ghent would hold: "Audientium intelligo non tam praesentium quam etiam illorum ad quos per audientes doctrina illa poterit provenire"; for additional comment see Jean Leclerq, *Revue des Sciences Réligieuses*, 21 (1947), 136.

[53] *The Catholic Encyclopedia*, Vol. IX (New York, 1910), p. 18, gives a brief but useful survey of the decrees promulgated by this assembly. Commonly called in Canon Law the "Great Council of the Lateran," or just "Great Council," the 1215 gathering of a large number of bishops succeeded in publishing its declarations widely.

[54] Boyle, "A Survey." p. 193. For supplementary material on Courson see V. L. Kennedy, "Robert Courson on Penance," *Mediaeval Studies*, 7 (1945), 291-336, and "The Content of Courson's *Summa*," *Mediaeval Studies*, 9 (1947), 81-107.

Robert of Flamsbury, and Geoffrey of Poitiers were of wider import but definitely influenced by Courson. Though Courson's treatise and Roissy's *Manuale de Misteriis Ecclesiae* were manuals of general pastoral theology, the *Liber Poenitentialis* of Robert of Flamsbury seems to have been the first of the *summae confessorum* or manuals for confessors. It was, no doubt, inspired by the new alliance of theology and canon law which followed upon Gratian and Peter Lombard and which is evident in greater or less degree in all the treatises on pastoral theology for several centuries.

The movement towards pastoral awakening which had been taken up by the theologians had the seal of authority set upon it by the Fourth Lateran Council. The Council fulminated against all current abuses but with especial vigor against clerical ignorance which, it declared, was no longer to be tolerated.[55] "Moreover, by the decree *Omnis utriusque sexus* the Fathers emphasized the traditional doctrine that the sacrament of penance was the medicine that cured the moral sickness of sin."[56] However, if this obligation of annual confession to the parish priest and communion at Easter was to be carried out seriously, it meant that both priests and laity must be instructed—and primarily the priests who might then impart their advanced conceptions of moral theology to the souls entrusted to their care. The episcopal legislation inspired by the Fourth Lateran Council shows the same solicitude for priestly education and often attempts to provided the minimum of the theological and canonical knowledge required; but "if we are to connect the development of synodal statutes with this event in church history it must be with the knowledge that IV Lateran was the most universal expression of needs acutely felt by many churchmen of the day and because diocesan legislation was itself a response to those needs."[57]

Though Honorius III had officially charged the Dominicans with popularization of certain of the Lateran decrees—particularly that on confession—[58]these statutes had had publicity in England long before the arrival of the friars through the synodal constitutions of Richard Poore (1217-21), which give a simple exposition of the chief articles of faith and a summary of the seven sacraments.[59]   Other thirteenth-century

---

[55] Giovanni D. Mansi, ed., *Sacrorum Conciliorum Nova et Amplissima Collectio* (Paris, 1901-27), Vol. XXII, 998, 999, hereafter cited as Mansi.

[56] Ibid., 1007, 1010. The relevant portion of the decree is here quoted: "Omnis utriusque sexus fidelis, postquam discretionis pervenerit, omnis sua solus peccata saltem semel in anno fideliter confiteatur proprio sacerdoti, et iniunctam sibi poenitentiam pro viribus studeat adimplere, suscipiens reverenter ad minus in Pascha Eucharistiae sacramentum. . ." The comment is from F. Broomfield, *Thomas de Chobham: Summa Confessorum,* in *Analecta Mediaevalia Namurcensia,* 25 (Louvain and Paris, 1968), p. xxi.

[57] C. R. Cheney, *English Synodalia of the Thirteenth Century* (Oxford, 1941), p. 37.

[58] The official date for this charging is February 1221; see Boyle, "A Survey," p. 211.

[59] C. R. Cheney and F. M. Powicke, *Councils and Synods and Other Documents Relating to the English Church,* Vol. II: 1205-1313 (Oxford, 1964), p. 55.

bishops continue to deal with religious instruction and the technique of confession. The Constitutions ascribed to St. Edmund Rich and those of Alexander of Stavensby (1224-37) provided a set of general regulations for parish clergy, a model sermon to be preached by the priest on the seven deadly sins, and a treatise on confession, instructing the priest how to hear confession and how to examine penitents and dealing with satisfaction, excommunication and reserved sins.[60] Bishop Alexander ordered that these constitutions should be copied and kept by every priest, a prescription which Walter de Cantilupe, Bishop of Worcester, echoed in his own constitutions of 1240.[61] Robert Grosseteste of Lincoln gave great attention to his pastoral obligations, writing several treatises on confession and the manual *Templum Domini*, which provides a large amount of pastoral instruction in a short space and generally in a semi-diagram form. The *Instituta* of Roger de Weseham (ca. 1250) gives a series of *septenarie* (including sacraments, petitions of the Lord's Prayer, and gifts of the Holy Spirit), the eight beatitudes and the ten commandments, a rather detailed exposition of the Creed, and a fairly inclusive list of thing to be avoided at all costs.[62] Nevertheless, the most outstanding and elaborate example of episcopal legislation is the code issued by Archbishop Pecham from the Provincial Council of Lambeth in 1281 which, along with the subjects treated above, gives a section *De informatione simplicium* beginning with the words "ignorantia sacerdotum" and outlining a program of religious instruction. The topics treated are to be expounded to the people in the vernacular four times a year.[63] This tract and Bishop Quivil of Exeter's *Summula* became the standard works on the subject of medieval pastoralia; they were recommended and partially reissued by diocesan mandates or circular letters throughout the fourteenth century and were the inspiration for any number of longer and more complete manuals of instruction which were largely non-episcopal compilations.

The particular English genius which lay not in high speculation but in the adaptation of the master's teaching to life in the world insured a

---

[60] Mansi, Vol. XXIII, 415-428 and 429-442.

[61] Walter de Cantilupe's decrees are recorded in Mansi, Vol. XXIII, 523-548. His constitutions dealt with the administration of the sacraments and under the heading of confession gave a suggested parochial program: commandments, sacraments, deadly sins, creed, and also a treatise on confession which all priests were to possess and use. See W. A. Pantin, *The English Church in the Fourteenth Century* (Notre Dame, 1962), p. 192.

[62] This text, from MS Bodley 57, fol. 96ʳ-97ᵛ, is printed by Cheney (*Synodalia*), on pp. 149-152.

[63] D. Wilkins, *Concilia Magnae Britanniae et Hiberniae*, Vol. II (London, 1737), p. 54. For an evaluation of Pecham's influence, see Pantin, *English Church*, pp. 193-4. The *Summula* of Bishop Quivil of Exeter is primarily a diocesan manual for the examination and instruction of penitents, but incidentally covers some of the ground of Pecham's program, e.g. the Ten Commandments and the Seven Deadly Sins. For a discussion of this work, see Boyle,"A Survey," p. 258.

literature rich in the application of theology and law to daily affairs. Hence, shortly after the publication of the decrees of IV Lateran and possibly about the time of the Council of Oxford in 1222, Thomas Chobham published his *Summa de Poenitentia*,[64] a manual which like Richard Wetheringsett's *Summa qui bene presunt*, had great pastoral import.[65] Indeed, these two began a tradition of pastoral *summae* of English origin that kept apace of the best continental products. Whereas Grosseteste's entire *Templum* is simply a statement of what a priest is required to know before he can satisfactorily counsel and interrogate a penitent, for Wetheringsett the emphasis is on the *cura animarum* as a whole. And though Grosseteste and his contemporaries did not know Raymond of Pennafort's *Summa de casibus poenitentiae* when they wrote their treatises, the English manualists of the next generation allowed Raymond (largely through the redaction of John of Freiburg)[66] to exercise his remarkable influence in the field of pastoral care. Before this continental influx, however, possibly the greatest of all the English manuals of the thirteenth century was the *Speculum iuniorum*.[67] Written about 1250 it is a striking mixture of English and foreign sources coupled with the latest teachings from the schools under the ostensible organization of *bonum* and *malum*. The *Summa iuniorum* of Simon of Hinton and the *Signaculum apostolatus mei* are other entries in the English tradition which by 1260-70 was well-defined and closely knit. If this insular manual tradition does not prove that the English clergy were sufficiently educated, it does at least indicate that men of greater culture took an interest in their less well-educated brethren. Though English production of pastoralia languished a little in the last years of the thirteenth century, the *Oculus sacerdotis*, which appeared around 1320-28, reflected the new trend in continental manuals and provided a much broader base for the instruction of the local clergy.[68] Despite outside influence, the

---

[64] Broomfield, p. xx. Broomfield contends that this English contribution is a typical product of the intense concentration on practical matters that characterized English graduates on their return home.

[65] Wetheringsett's *Summa* was probably composed before the Council of Oxford; it enjoyed a considerable reputation in the thirteenth and fourteenth centuries. See Boyle, "A Survey," pp. 220 ff. Some 56 or more manuscripts of this text survive. In it the author sets out to cover the whole range of knowledge—canonical and theological—with which a priest who has the care of souls must be familiar (e.g. the Creed, Seven Sacraments, Ten Commandments, Gifts of the Holy Spirit, etc.).

[66] The *Summa de casibus* of Raymond was legalistic and casuistic; by introducing Aquinas's moral theory into it, John of Freiburg gave it "that balance of moral principle and legal canon which is so desirable in priests to whom the care of souls is entrusted," Boyle, "A Survey," p. 269. A good study of Raymond's work is A. Walz, "Sancti Raymundi de Pennafort auctoritas in re penitentiali," *Angelicum*, 12 (1935), 346-96.

[67] Leonard Boyle, "Three English Pastoral *Summae* and a 'Magister Galienus'," *Studia Gratiana*, 11 (1967), 133-44.

[68] Boyle, "A Survey," pp. 281 ff. Fr. Boyle has published a briefer introduction to William of Pagula in the *Transactions of the Royal Historical Society*, 5th Series, 5 (1955), 81-110.

setting of William of Pagula's work is thoroughly English, and its appearance was a harbinger of the new and vigorous stream of native manual production. Thus the tradition begun by Flamsbury, Chobham, and Wetheringsett in the first quarter of the thirteenth century, and which faltered a bit after 1270, had its renewal and continuation in Pagula, Higden, and de Burgh. In purpose, therefore, the *Oculus sacerdotis* was designed to embrace the main aspects of the *cura animarum* to which a parish priest was committed: the *Pars oculi* was a modest *summa de poenitentia*, the *Sinistra pars* dealt with sacramental theology, and the *Dextra pars* was canonical and largely oriented to the preaching office. It commanded much more than a casual circulation and had an established place in the pastoral care of the fourteenth and early fifteenth centuries.[69] Most of the subjects treated by Pagula and intimately connected with the development of pastoral theology in England came also to be treated in other treatises throughout the century, notably the *Cilium oculi*, the *Regimen animarum*, the *Memoriale presbiterorum*, and Higden's *Speculum curatorum*. Probably the most logical and clear-cut redaction of Pagula was the *Pupilla oculi* of John de Burgh, which appeared in 1385 and which presented a scientific and successful recasting of the *Oculus sacerdotis*.[70] Along with Archbishop Thoresby's *Instructions* and the *Instructions for Parish Priests*, the *Manuale sacerdotis*, and the *Festiall* of John Mirc,[71] the *Pupilla oculi* (the only one of the manuals to be printed at an early period) indicates that the tradition of pastoral theology which was to result in pastoral care remained a lively and constant consideration for groups and individuals within the Church who endeavored to implement the conciliar and synodal decrees.

But ultimately, the various manuals and the different conditions that had given them birth could be conveniently classified as pastoralia and within that term further specified under the headings general and particular.[72] The former would refer mostly to those writings which have absorbed our consideration up to this point as they dealt with more than a limited aspect of the *cura animarum*; particular pastoralia embraces only those works which concentrate on one of the many facets of the care of souls: for example, manuals on the vices and virtues, expositions of the commandments, *summae* of sacramental theology, *summae confessorum*, collections of moral *exempla*, tracts on the Mass, or *artes praedicandi*. It seems desirable, therefore, to turn now from the general

---

[69] Fr. Boyle makes periodic additions to his lists of manuscripts and informs me that the *Oculus* exists in more than eighty manuscripts from the fourteenth and fifteenth centuries.

[70] John de Burgh, *Pupilla oculi* (London, 1510). See also Pantin, *The English Church*, pp. 202-11.

[71] Bibliographical information and useful summaries may be found in Pantin, ibid., pp. 211-16.

[72] Leonard Boyle's schema of pastoralia has been appended to this introduction (p. xlviii).

to the particular with regard to the aspects of pastoral care which deal especially with the subject of this introduction: namely, preaching.

In the light of certain pieces of evidence some scholars have concluded that a sermon was a rare event for a fairly good part of the thirteenth century; that there was no regular Sunday preaching and such as there was remained spasmodic and incidental; that little preparation was made for preaching either in the training of the clergy or in the furnishing of churches; that it was only with the coming of the friars to England in 1221 and 1224 that any attempt at revival of the tradition of Wulfstan and Aelfric took place.[73] While it is indeed true that the friars made a great contribution to Church life in England, successfully invading the once sacred domain of the parish priest and, no doubt, stirring many to reconsider the whole question of their relationship to their flock, the friars did not operate in an ecclesiastical vacuum nor without a growing concern on the part of bishops and priests alike for the spreading of a pastoral renewal in English catholicism. It is curious indeed that scholars have credited the French church with such a renaissance in the early thirteenth century, that priests are thought to have delivered sermons there regularly on Sundays and holy days while denying to English ecclesiastical life anything even vaguely comparable. Happily, it has been shown that the hypothesis that the English parish priest did deliver sermons is not contradicted by the episcopal decrees usually adduced to prove that he did not.[74] Likewise, the ignorance of the parish clergy has been greatly exaggerated; when Bishop Poore asked his priests to teach the seven sacraments, he was not naming theological entities which were common knowledge; before 1145, the sacraments were thought of as a whole of several parts and their fixed number was only popularized after IV Lateran.[75] Between 1224 and 1327, when Bishop Alexander Stavensby of Coventry issued his tripartite constitutions, he gave a by no means simple enumeration of sins suitable for a primer but rather a relatively sophisticated treatise, complete with scholastic definitions and authorities. It is obvious that this was not the sort of thing which one would find in the homilies of the Fathers; a new sermon technique and

---

[73] These views are strongly expressed by John H. Moorman in his *Church Life in England in the Thirteenth Century* (Cambridge, 1945), pp. 77-81. H. S. Bennett, G. G. Coulton, and Margaret Deanesley have also set forth similar opinions.

[74] D. W. Robertson, Jr., "Frequency of Preaching in Thirteenth Century England, " *Speculum*, 24 (1949), 376 ff.

[75] H. Weisweiler, "Maître Simon et son groupe 'De sacramentiis'," *Spicilegium sacrum lovaniense*, fasc. XVII (1937), lxxv. The system of seven sacraments was popularized on the scholastic level by Peter Lombard in his *Sentences* and did not really reach the pastoral level until after the Fourth Lateran Council, which decreed as follows: "Cum sit ars artium regimen animarum, districte praecipimus ut episcopi promovendos in sacerdotes diligenter instruant et informent, vel per se ipsa, vel per alios viros idoneos, super divinis officiis, et ecclesiasticis sacramentis, qualiter ea rite valeant celebrare." See also Hefele and Leclerq, *Histoire des conciles* (Paris, 1907-38), Vol. V, 1356.

content had to be arranged and typified for the comparably unsophisticated parish priest. Possibly when Walter de Cantilupe used the expression "frequenter praedicent" in his constitutions he was demanding the
announcement of specified subjects with no real implication that the priests were not carrying out their duty to explain the Gospel of the Mass
and to discuss the virtues of the Saints.[76] Certainly no such systematic
analysis as that desired by the Bishop would have been available in
homily collections. In fact in its intent to educate the laity as well as the
clergy for confession, Walter's decree must have been regarded as essentially a progressive measure rather than a reform. In this same light one
ought to examine the *Instituta* of Roger of Weseham which indicate that
the holy Bishop did not desire just a simple enumeration of the articles
of faith but an illustrated and well-developed discussion of each one.
Considering the use made of the papal permissions for university study
designated *licet canon* and *cum ex eo*, it is indeed probable that Weseham was justified in believing that his priests were capable of composing
such discussions.[77] A similar consideration might also be bestowed upon
the decrees of Archbishop Pecham whose opening denunciation of
ignorance is theological in character and may refer to the extremely
recent introduction of the parish clergy to the theology of the schools
and their consequent befuddlement; moreover, the content of the decree
makes it clear that the author's concern was the theological inadequacy,
and both this inadequacy and the anxiety of the bishops must be
evaluated in light of contemporary theological progress. Finally, in two
pronouncements, the statutes of 1237 and those of Bishop Peter Quivil,
there is every implication that sermons were delivered on Sundays for
those who wanted to hear them.[78] The decrees reflect an effort to incorporate into sermons that fast-growing body of popular pastoral theology;
and although they do not state it, to achieve this, a new mode of preaching and preaching instruction had made its appearance on the English
scene.

Pioneered in England by such authors as Alexander of Ashby (ca.
1200), Thomas of Salisbury (ca. 1215), Richard of Thetford (ca. 1250),
John of Wales (ca. 1280), and Hugh of Sneyth (ca. 1290) in the thirteenth century, the sermon manuals gained added stature there through
the work of Robert of Basevorn (ca. 1322) and Thomas Waleys (ca.
1338).[79] They and many of their numerous continental colleagues in the
preaching manual tradition have been thoroughly treated in recent

---

[76] Robertson, p. 380.

[77] Leonard Boyle, "The Constitution 'Cum ex eo' of Pope Boniface VIII," *Mediaeval Studies*, 24 (1962), 263-302.

[78] The 1237 decrees are printed in the *Concilia* but for conjectures about them see M.
Gibbs and J. Lang, *Bishops and Reform, 1215-1272* (Oxford, 1934), p. 109.

[79] See Murphy, *Rhetoric in the Middle Ages*, pp. 310-363, and Charland, pp. 21-91.

studies. But to this worthy company Ranulph Higden has been only grudgingly admitted—a circumstance I propose to remedy.

IV

Ranulph Higden's Life and Works

Notes in MS Laud Misc. 619 in the British Library and in New College Oxford MS 152 indicate that Ranulph Higden entered the Benedictine monastery at Chester in 1299 and died there at a ripe old age in 1363 or 1365, possibly on the feast of St. Gregory.[80] What monastic records survived the Reformation indicate that he had no part in the internal or external dissension which troubled Chester abbey during the latter years of his life,[81] such aloofness seems entirely in keeping with his position as monk-scholar and probable head of the scriptorium.

Certainly Higden's greatest literary memorial is the *Polychronicon*, a universal history which gave to the learned people of fourteenth century England a clear and original picture of world history; the work is based on medieval tradition but with a new interest in antiquity and with the early history of Britain related as part of the whole.[82] The *Polychronicon* has been treated at some length elsewhere and so I will mention only those features in it which assist in our understanding the other works which occupied Ranulph Higden for at least as many years as those he spent on the universal history.

From the chronicle of Henry Knighton, canon of Leicester abbey, we learn that Higden brought his *Polychronicon* to an end in 1327 but later continued it to 1340.[83] Huntington Library HM 132 bears witness to this later composition, as it is generally considered the working copy of the last and fullest recension of the text, written most likely in 1340 and worked over and added to for several years afterwards.[84] The many

---

[80] I am indebted to John Taylor, *The Universal Chronicle of Ranulph Higden* (Oxford, 1966), p. 2, for the citation of these manuscripts.

[81] My study of conditions in Chester has appeared in the *Proceedings of the Leeds Philosophical and Historical Society*, 16 (1977), 149-58, under the title "Higden's Minor Writings and the Fourteenth Century Church."

[82] The complete Latin text of the *Polychronicon* was published for the first time in the Rolls Series in nine volumes: the first two in 1865 and 1869 under the editorship of Canon Hardwick and Churchill Babington and the other seven, edited by J. Rawson Lumby, in 1886. A few excerpts relating to British history had appeared in T. Gale's *Historiae Britannicae Scriptores*, *XV* (1961), Vol. I, 179-287. There is no satisfactory modern edition.

[83] V. H. Galbraith, "An Autograph MS of Ranulph Higden's *Polychronicon*," *The Huntington Library Quarterly*, 23 (1959-60), 1. See also Consuelo W. Dutschke, *Guide to Medieval and Renaissance Manuscripts in the Huntington Library* (San Marino, California, 1989), 175-177.

[84] Galbraith, p. 5.

years undoubtedly spent in the composition of the *Polychronicon* and its obvious thoroughness may be sufficient explanation for its pre-Reformation popularity; it has been estimated that before 1550, the numbers of copies extant in Europe may have run well into the thousands. From erasures in the holograph and from comparison of earlier and later recensions, it can be determined that the idea of an acrostic to identify the author and the work came as an afterthought to Ranulph, surely later than 1327 and probably not until 1340,[85] when he may have observed a similar practice in Basevorn's *Forma praedicandi*. Textual study also makes it possible to define Higden's practice in citing other authors; he does not usually copy their words verbatim, but gives the sense of his borrowings with an accuracy which makes corrupted reference easily discernible. The scope of the *Polychronicon* also prompts agreement with Taylor's conclusion that "Higden's mind was set chiefly on completeness and he is better described as an encyclopedist than a historian proper."[86]

The characterization "encyclopedist" applies with even greater accuracy to his other writings, more overtly religious than the *Polychronicon*, which were in Tanner's words "sui temporis laude digna."[87] Undoubtedly a reputation such as that which Higden enjoyed is responsible for the now demonstrably spurious attribution to him of works like the Chester Mystery Plays. Among those which are likely to be Ranulph's are lists of *distinctions theologicae*, expositions of Job and the Canticle of Canticles, an *Ars kalendarii*, and a *Pedagogium artis grammaticae*.[88] This last, unfortunately, is no longer extant although it did at one time form part of the library of Syon abbey, and its composition is certainly in line with the Benedictine emphasis on education which came into even greater prominence after the reforms of Benedict XII.[89] The other works, and an *Abbreviationes chronicorum*, are attributed to Higden by both secular and Benedictine bibliographers, and it is possible in the light of his historical and theological labors that these attributions or

---

[85] Galbraith, p. 17. Galbraith's minute analysis of the manuscript H.M. 132 is well worth additional study. Thanks to information supplied to me by James J. Murphy, I am, however, quite sure that none of the manuscripts that survive of the *Ars componendi sermones* is in the same script as the holograph copy.

[86] Ibid.

[87] Thomas Tanner, *Bibliotheca Britannica Hibernica* (London, 1748), pp. 402-3. The entry reads "Higedenus, (Ranulphus) also Higdenus, Hideden, Hygden vel Higedemus."

[88] Magnoaldo Ziebelbauer in his *Historia rei literariae ordinis S. Benedicti* (Vienna, 1754) Vol. IV, pp. 30, 40, 113, 162, 323, 334, 466, and 655 types Ranulph's work under categories such as "De theologia positiva et libris ad eam spectantibus," "De theologia scholasticae scriptoribus," "De scriptoribus historiae prophanae," and so forth. In Vol. I, p. 70, he called Ranulph an ornament to his age, even though it was bronze!

[89] In the *Catalogue of the Library of Sion Monastery*, ed. Mary Bateson (Cambridge, 1898), p. 2. It was part of MS Sion A.4. and is thus described: "Prima pars pedagogici compilati a Radulpho Higdon de Ordine sancti Benedicti." Tanner refers to this manuscript on p. 403.

references to similar works are substantially correct.[90] However, the long sermon manuscript which was originally attributed to Higden in the *John Rylands Library Bulletin*[91] must now be definitely taken from him and given to Father Ralph Acton, a decision which is supported by the opening lines of the text—the incipit being "cum in ecclesia mea quietus residerem et loquendi ad populum."[92]

The *Ars kalendarii* which forms part of Magdalene College Cambridge MS 23 is said to be Ranulph's composition, and there is nothing is style or content which militates against this assertion. The treatise begins almost immediately to justify its existence by a quatrefoil exposition of Genesis and the luminaries fashioned so promptly by the Creator;[93] it proceeds to explanations of the results of this creation: time ages, indictions, olimpiads, solar and stellar years, months, weeks, days, the movements of the heavenly bodies, and other technical subjects.[94] But the climax of the treatise and indeed its ostensible raison d'être is detailed instruction for the determination of the paschal feast, after which treatment and a warning against various errors the text rapidly concludes. Its *explicit* is particularly revealing of Higden's character:

> Constatus introducendus rudibus in artem kalendarii summarie compilavi maiora ficientibus dionisium exiguum, bedam, elpericium, ptolomeum, al-faraganum cum ceteris recencioribus inspiciendos derelinquo.[95]

The fact that the treatise preceding the *Ars kalendarii* in the manuscript as it now exists could readily be one from which Ranulph had "compiled" is curiously "right" to a student of his writings.

---

[90] A short résumé of the writings most probably Higden's can be found in Taylor, pp. 182-84.

[91] Moses Tyson, in his "Handlist of Additions to the Collections of Latin Manuscripts in the John Rylands Library, 1908-1928," *Bulletin of the John Rylands Library*, 12 (1928), 600, had attributed MS 367, a collection of sermons, to Ranulph by equating him with the author of this text, a "Radulphum de Attone."

[92] In a letter to me, dated May 9, 1969, Dr. F. Taylor, the Keeper of Manuscripts at the John Rylands Library, identified the author of MS 367 as Ralph Acton and supported his identification with the citation from the *incipit* which I have copied.

[93] Fol. 24[r]: ". . .enim legitur quod fecit deus luminariis [sic] et posuit ea in firmamento celi ut illuminarent terram. . ." Higden's tract extends from the very bottom of fol. 23[v] to fol. 36[r]. Tables follow on fol. 36[v], 37[v] and 38 (the recto of fol. 37 is blank). According to the flyleaf, this *Ars* is of the late fifteenth century, a dating which is borne out by the difficult, semi-cursive hand in which the treatise is written and which is most probably of that period.

[94] Discussion of these subjects forms the body of folios 24[v] through 34[v].

[95] Fol. 36[r]. The people that Ranulph mentions here had reputations for various computational ventures in the Middle Ages: Dionysius Exiguus was roundly criticized for errors in determining the duration of an era; Bede and Heiric of Auxerre were excerpted from and quoted in varying contexts; Ptolemy and al-Faragani were often cited for their determinations of the vernal equinox. See Charles Homer Haskins, *Studies in the History of Mediaeval Science* (Cambridge, 1924), pp. 82ff. for an outline of the growth of astronomical knowledge in the medieval period.

But the works which place Ranulph Higden truly in the widening
stream of fourteenth-century church life, and in the ever-developing pastoral renewal which was one of the mainsprings of its action are the
Speculum curatorum and the *Ars componendi sermones*. The *Speculum*
lies squarely within the handbook tradition which remained special facet
of English parochial life from the days of Richard Wetheringsett and
Thomas Chobham. Higden's *Speculum* is, as he himself indicates, a
compilation and it leans much on the common sources of all handbooks
in this vein.[96] It probably owes a little to the *Manipulus curatorum* of
Guido de Monte Rocherii (in quoting the *quodlibets* of Henry of Ghent
in imitation of other theologians),[97] but it is generally dependent on the
Summa confessorum of John of Freiburg which it quotes explicitly and
upon the *Oculus sacerdotis* of William of Pagula, which it uses without
acknowledgement for points concerning occasional preaching and
excommunications.[98] John Taylor's assertion that the work is taken
mainly from the *De universo* and the *De legibus* of William of Auvergne
and the note on the flyleaf of the Cambridge MS to the effect that the
manuscript is based on the *Sentences* of Peter Lombard are true only in
the most general sense; that is, the pastoral handbook is in origin much
indebted to the theological discussion which is crystallized in the *Sentences* just as the precepts of science and law which have filtered down
to the *Speculum* can be found in purer state in the writings of William
of Auvergne.[99] But even in his avowed copying, Ranulph is no slavish
imitator; he is obviously dissatisfied with the parroting of twelve

---

[96] The "compilavi" of the *explicit* to the *Ars kalendarii* is echoed in the acrostic of the
Speculum: "Cestrensis monachus frater Ranulphus compilavit hoc speculum. . ." A brief
glance through the second volume of Leonard Boyle's dissertation, which contains lists of
manuscripts, sources, and bibliography on the many pastoral manuals which stem from the
Middle Ages, shows how commonly used some sources, like John of Freiburg, were.

[97] An identifying characteristic of the *Manipulus curatorum* of Guido de Monte Rocherii is
the use it makes of the *quodlibets* of Henry of Ghent and other theologians, no doubt in
imitation of John of Freiburg's use of the *quodlibets* of Thomas Aquinas. Ranulph uses one
of these *quodlibets* on fol. 98ᵛ of the Balliol College MS (77) of the *Speculum curatorum*.
See the note in Boyle, "A Survey," p. 303.

[98] Higden specifically uses John of Freiburg ("secundum Thomam" is the general clue to
this citation) on folios 8ʳ, 45ʳ, 59ʳ, 64ᵛ, 78ʳ, 96ʳ, and other points in the Balliol College MS.
Higden gets his topics for occasional preaching from Pagula and also his listing of excommunications which can be found in the last chapter, "De sentencia excommunicationis."
Higden differs from Pagula (Balliol College MS 77, fol. 99ʳ for Ranulph and New College
MS 292, fol. 11ʳ for Pagula) in thinking that a penitent ought to be absolved before a penance was assigned him; see Boyle, "A Survey," pp. 304ff.

[99] See Taylor, p. 5. William of Auvergne's *De Fide et Legibus* treats a vast number of subjects: from the wholly immaterial structure of faith in human psychology to the very material aspects of belief in the form of sacrifices, from the devil and his wiles, to idolatry,
heretical practices, virtues and vices. The *De Universo* concerns itself with physical
phenomena and metaphysical concepts such as eternity, judgement, punishment, necessity,
and fate. It certainly seems that William of Auvergne might be more plausibly connected
with the *Speculum* through his *De Sacramentiis* and *De Poenitentia*, rather than through
the *De Universo*.

apostles, twelve credal statements, which was of fairly general currency in his day, and he is given at some length to straightening things out.[100] The work is studded with many gems—such as the chapter on *sortilegium*—but it cannot and must not be judged solely on this basis.[101] As the true stuff of John Bromyard's *Summa predicantium* is not in the lore or exempla which one may sift from it, so the nature of Higden' *Speculum* is apparent in its very title: *Mirror for Curates*. If the work does show that Ranulph was at home with the lore of constellations, the properties of things, the psychology of dreams, and some of the typical sources of the popular habits and ideals of his age, it shows these as part of the whole cloth of his pastoral efforts, of his endeavor to bring the tenets of the great canon lawyers and theologians into the purview of the ordinary parish priest, into the ambit of the ordinary laity, who needed instruction in a faith that was no longer wholly simple, no longer able to be blindly accepted.

V

The *Ars componendi sermones*

Unlike the *Speculum* (where the chapter's initial letters read seriatim *Cestrensis monachus Ranulphus compilavit hoc speculum anno Domini MCCC quadragesimo*,[102] the *Ars componendi sermones* is not assigned a definite date. Because critical opinion, however, seems agreed that Ranulph hit upon the acrostic scheme not much earlier than 1340, if at all earlier, and because the holograph copy of the *Polychronicon* is similarly dated, it is quite possible that the *Ars*, whose chapter initials spell

---

[100] See the chapter "De articulis fidei" in Balliol College MS 77, fol. 3ᵛ-4ʳ. Ranulph mentions several ways of dividing up the fourteen articles and then assigns the first three to Peter!

[101] This chapter has been treated thoroughly and entertainingly in G. R. Owst's "Sortilegium in English Homiletic Literature of the Fifteenth Century," in *Studies Presented to Sir Hilary Jenkinson*, pp. 272-303. More recent studies of the *Speculum*'s chapters "De ludificationibus demonum" and "De gradibus peccatorum" by Eugene Crook and Margaret Jennings are "The Devil and Ranulph Higden," *Manuscripta*, 22 (1978), 131-140 and "Grading Sin: A Medieval English Benedictine in the *Cura animarum*, *The American Benedictine Review*, 31 (1980), 335-345.

[102] G. R. Owst, *The* Destructorium Viciorum *of Alexander Carpenter: A Fifteenth Century Sequel to Literature and Pulpit in Medieval England* (London, 1952), p. 2, note 1, where the acrostic scheme is discussed. Extant manuscripts of the *Speculum curatorum* are BL Harl. 1004, Balliol 77, Cambridge Univ. Lib. Mm.1.20, Durham B.iv.36, and Univ. of Illinois 251/H53s. As mentioned above, Ranulph may have gotten the idea of an acrostic from Basevorn's *Forma Praedicandi*, where the initial letters spell out "Domino Willelmo abbati Basingwerk Robertus de Basevorn." The Illinois MS differs significantly from those in the British libraries; see Eugene Crook, "A New Version of Ranulph Higden's *Speculum Curatorum*," *Manuscripta*, 21 (1977), 41-49.

Ars Ranulphi Cestrensis, was written after 1340. Several factors help to set its composition at about this time: acknowledgment of the desirable aspects of pastoral functioning even for English Black Monks at the chapters of 1336, 1343, and 1346; emphasis on university influence in the monasteries, which only began in earnest after the reforms of 1336 and which probably took a few years to penetrate to Chester; conditions in Ranulph's own monastery, which may well have encouraged him in more religious pursuits than the compilation of a universal history; increase in the number of priests instituted to ordination through the monastery, a task for which some of the brethren must have felt a responsibility; finally, the exemption of monastic advowsons from episcopal control and the probable monkish *cura* practiced in these places which were beyond the bishop's jurisdiction.[103] It is reasonable to assume, moreover, that Ranulph, having produced a long and detailed manual for the use of the parish priest in the instruction of his flock, would also feel obliged to help that same parson organize the content of his sermons into an intelligible and forceful whole. If this were so, Higden would be following in the footsteps of such manualists as Alain of Lille, Robert Grosseteste, Thomas Chobham (Thomas of Salisbury), John of Wales, Aestanus of Asti, John of Erfurt, Bartholomew of Pisa, Nicolas of Ausimo, Henry of Langenstein, and Jean Gerson, who wrote *artes praedicandi* in addition to their penitential and doctrinal works.[104] That Ranulph's genius for organization and compilation should have come into play in this fashion would certainly be congruent with his previous efforts in the *Polychronicon* and the *Speculum*.

Higden's *Ars* follows the general outline for the genre: theme, protheme, introduction of the theme, division, dilation. Through a preface and twenty concise chapters, it charts an almost foolproof course towards successful preaching in the thematic mode. Adherence to its precepts should result in furthering the divine plan, in encouraging the church militant, and in exciting heartfelt devotion.[105] Having negated sermonizing that is either strident or infelicitous, the *Ars componendi sermones* maintains that true preaching will be founded on the disciplined and practical use of scripture—as is, indeed, the treatise itself. The preface's demand that a parson possess rectitude of intention, holiness of life, and aptitude for delivery is developed in Chapters II, III, and IV, where excellence in motive and example and maturity in style and

---

[103] The rather complicated pattern of monastic *cura animarum*/preaching in the latter Middle Ages is surveyed in Margaret Jennings, "Monks and the *Artes Praedicandi* in the Time of Ranulph Higden," *Revue Bénédictine*, 87 (1975), 119-128.

[104] Useful commentary on these *summae* and their authors is provided in Michaud-Quantin, pp. 16, 54, 60, 77, 81, and *passim* on the *Templum Domini* of Robert Grosseteste.

[105] ". . . ad divini cultus ampliacionem, ad ecclesie militantis illustracionem, ad humani affectus erga deum inflamacionem"; see below, p. 5.

presentation are emphasized. The preface's further development of sermon requisites like thematic congruence, propriety in division, and
overall spiritual utility forms the backdrop for most of the remaining
chapters: five are devoted to theme, five to division and its concomi-
tants, and four to sermon enlargement and audience appeal. Easily outlined for the preacher's convenience, the twenty-one sections detail the
major points to be stressed and the major pitfalls to be avoided in sermon construction. Logical progression is paramount, and though non-
linear argumentation and the more subtle forms of linguistic analysis are
explained the preacher is counseled that these are not useful for ordinary
people.[106] Aside from the advice which is peculiar to its use of Latin
language, areas common to sermon manuals in any age—rhetorical
effectiveness, exemplary storytelling, scriptural accuracy, analytic
lucidity—are treated in Higden's text. Of course, the delightful medieval
bias of both Ranulph and his sources is evident intermittently in the
monk's acceptance of an allegorical signification for biblical names, in
his scriptural exposition which allows for historical, tropological, allegorical and/or anagogical approaches, and in his care to distinguish the Parisian preaching patterns from those in use in Oxford.[107] Again, following
his progenitors in the preaching manual tradition, Ranulph's effort to
incorporate elements of Aristotelian philosophy is especially noticeable;
he presents four causes as they relate to preaching, he contends that
argumentative sermons should employ induction, syllogism, and enthymeme, and he is concerned with universals and particulars, genera and
species, substance and accidents.[108] But tantamount to all of these and
chief among the text's obvious virtues is its clarity. By subscribing to its
directions, even the indifferent preacher would be able to create a sem-
blance of the perfect "tree of preaching" which was the ideal of the
thematic mode.[109]

As in the *Polychronicon* and the *Speculum*, Higden compiled his art of
preaching from the many treatises on the subject available to him and
depended heavily in several sections on Robert of Basevorn's *Forma
Praedicandi*. This fact has, unfortunately, caused the frequent dismissal
of the Higden text as merely an abridgement of Basevorn.[110] Such

---

[106] "Sed talis, scilicet tres ita correspondencie circularitatis, non est multum utilis ad populum." See below, pp. 57. Cf. Chapter 18, *De sermonis dilatacione*, in its entirety.

[107] The allegorical signification of biblical names is treated in Chapter 20, *De regulis dilata-
cionum*; the four senses of scriptural interpretation in Chapter 14, *De thematis introduccione*; and the Paris/Oxford distinctions in Chapter 12, *De oracionis premissione et gracie
imploracione*.

[108] See below, Chapter 18: *De membrorum subdivisione, passim*.

[109] Otto Dieter, "*Arbor Picta*: The Medieval Tree of Preaching," *Quarterly Journal of
Speech*, 51 (1965), 123-44.

[110] So affirm bibliographical annotations in Charland, in Harry Caplan's *Mediaeval Artes
Praedicandi: A Handlist*, and in Murphy's *Rhetoric in the Middle Ages*. James J. Murphy's
"Rhetoric in Fourteenth-Century Oxford," *Medium Aevum*, 34 (1965), p. 14, also minim-
izes Higden's contribution.

scholarly relegation to obscurity is unwarranted because Higden, in his usage of Basevorn and other sources, exhibits some of the best traits of medieval originality: through variations in placement and emphasis he shapes his borrowings and imitations into what is essentially a new entity. In addition, Ranulph seems to have had a stronger sense than Basevorn of overall compositional unity; he avoids his model's long digressions on other types of sermon construction and, perhaps for diplomatic reasons, on canonical principles which touch the preaching apostolate.[111] In the Preface he outlines his own tripartite structure for considering the person of the preacher and a few lines later he encompasses the whole thematic sermon construction in another threefold scheme. He picks up Basevorn's treatment of the Aristotelian four causes as they appear in preaching, but by placing them later in his preface and by changing their content he gives them an entirely different emphasis: they become an elaboration of the formal definition of preaching which has preceded them rather than a bold and bald statement of casual principles apparently divorced from the exploration of the whole sermon-making process. Higden also manages in a short space to give a very full treatment of most of the facets of thematic sermon construction and to outline for the preachers to whom he addressed himself the desirable qualities to be cultivated and faults to be avoided in the performance of this work. Perhaps the most convincing proof of Higden's ability is a comparative analysis of the Preface of the *Ars componendi sermones* with the Prologue and Chapter One of Basevorn's *Forma praedicandi*:

Higden: *Preface*	Basevorn: *Prologue*
Treatise is founded on scriptural and practical principles	Exposition of educations: bad logic=bad reasoning bad form=bad preaching
Three things are required in the person preaching: rectitude of intention holiness of association aptitude for presentation	Lengthy discussion of the need for this treatise "Bold" presentation of the four causes of preaching: Final: God
Three things required in the sermon: congruence of theme propriety of division utility in development	Efficient: God and the preacher Material: the form of preaching Final: orderly procedure

---

[111] The anomalous situation of the monk/preacher might be reflected here, or this may simply be testimony to the more pragmatic nature of Higden's composition: thematic preaching was his concern, not an explication of the ecclesiastical standing of the preacher.

in fifty chapters

True preaching is thematic
and provides motivation
and example. Though public
persuasion, it should not
use scholastic methodology

Chapter one

Preaching is the persuasion
of the multitude within
a moderate length of
time, to worthy conduct

True preaching excludes
both the insignificant
and the excessive

Preaching excludes:
  determining questions
  political oratory

Four causes as related
to preaching:
  Final: three goals
  Material: *verba casta*
  Efficient: "Deus originaliter
  et ipse predicans
  ministraliter"
  Formal: the definition of
  preaching advanced above[112]

Proper reasoning is essential
to preaching

Suitable time spans for
effective preaching

Higden's organizational ability is immediately obvious here in outline and is even more so in the complete tests where Basevorn's verbosity and poor telescoping are very visible. Periodically, it must be admitted, Basevorn appears to be more sure of his material than Ranulph, but these moments of superiority are surprisingly few.[113] Since a manual of this type benefits more from tightness of structure than from lengthy illustration, Higden's ability to select from among exemplary possibilities is a strong point in his favor. Also, he seems to know where to end; while Basevorn's rambles along into some ten minor ways of ornamenting a sermon and into sixteen other types of sermon construction, "quorum subtilitates ex praedictis intelligi possunt," Higden details the rules for dilation and finishes with a short disquisition on verbal coloration, at which point he brings his text to a close.[114] He had set out to provide instruction for the unsophisticated, a task in which wordiness or excessive minuteness would vitiate his efforts.

---

[112] For Higden's text, see below, pp. 4-7; Basevorn's is in Charland, pp. 233 ff. A useful outline of the whole of Basevorn's treatise is available in Murphy's *Rhetoric in the Middle Ages*, pp. 344-55.

[113] Basevorn is more logical than Higden in his approach to the "Introduction of a theme." Maintaining that this introduction can be formed by authority, by argument, or by both methods together, he then organizes his procedural comments under these major headings. Higden, by dispensing with the umbrella categories, is more difficult to follow. Basevorn is also quite precise in detailing the respective strengths of the Parisian and Oxonian schools of preaching, which Ranulph merely mentions. Basevorn's schema is in Charland, pp. 268ff; Higden's is below, Chapter XIV: *De thematis introduccione*.

[114] For the Basevorn text, see Charland, pp. 310-22.

A careful analysis of the contents of Higden's *Ars* reveals obvious borrowings from the Franciscan *Ars concionandi*, the *Forma praedicandi* of John of Wales, the *Distinctiones* of Nicolas Byard, an extended treatment of Richard of Thetford's commentary on dilation, and Thomas Waleys' *De modo componendi sermones* as well as from Basevorn.[115] Echoes of numerous other treatises are also discernible, especially in the chapters *De dicendi circumspeccione* and *De membrorum subdivisione*. Perhaps the best illustration of Higden's ability to select from among possible sources occurs in the section dealing with introducing the scriptural text or theme. Although John of Wales had made provision for this activity, he had emphasized the need for keeping it "parvus" and had mentioned only three methods of procedure: through the canons, through the saints, or through common proverbs.[116] An anonymous writer of slightly later vintage concludes that five methods of introducing a theme can be employed: "per manuduccionem, per similem in natura, per sacram scripturam, per scripturam sanctorum, per auctoritatem philosophorum et poeticorum."[117] Robert of Basevorn incorporates these methods into his discussion of the problem but organizes them more logically under the headings of introduction by authority, by argument, or by both.[118] An authority can be original to the preacher, can be excerpted from a philosopher or a poet, or can come from one of the *auctores*, provided that this excludes scripture and the apocrypha. Introduction by argument provides for such processes as induction, example in art, nature, and history, syllogism, and enthymeme. Basevorn commends the Parisians at great length because they confirm all arguments with biblical citations. For introductions to themes of two or more significant words, any or all of these methods can be employed; for those of just one word, e.g. *intellige*, Basevorn recommends that an authority be first introduced and that three correspondences to the feast and theme be immediately drawn from it. Ranulph Higden charts a middle course in stating that the introduction is able to be made "multis modis."[119] He allows the use of scriptual interpretation as the first of these modes following, no doubt, the lead of some of the John of Wales' texts, but by leaving his initial definition somewhat vague (*per*

---

[115] John of Wales, *Ars Praedicandi* (?Ulm, 1480); the *Ars Concionandi* is found in *Bonaventurae Opera Omnia*, Vol. IX, ed. Guaracchi (Ad Claras Aquas, 1901), pp. 8-21; both Waleys and Basevorn are found in Charland, ibid. Other citations will be provided *in situ*.

[116] "Vel accipiendo auctoritatem canonis, vel alicuius sancti, vel aliquod conmune proverbium." John of Wales, *Ars Praedicandi* (?Ulm, 1480), fol. xx.

[117] "through an introduction, through similitudes in nature, by means of sacred scripture, through the writings of the saints, and on the authority of philosophers and poets," in BL MS Additional 24361, fols. 52ʳ-53ʳ.

[118] Basevorn also devotes a separate chapter (#32) to themes of one word; cf. Charland, p. 351.

[119] See below, pp. 35.

scripturam), Ranulph is able to incorporate here the writings of the saints, poets, and philosophers. Under his second heading, *argumentum*, he discusses inductive reasoning, the syllogism, and the enthymeme—also praising the Parisian emphasis on authority—and proceeds to organize the section on "example" into the categories *per exemplarem manuduccionem* and *per simile in natura*, tacking his reflections about art and history onto the latter. Then, except for an aside on the vagaries of Guy d'Evreux and on proverbial introductions, he follows Basevorn fairly closely in detailing how introductions can stem from a theme on one word. In his selection from and rearrangement of available material and, perhaps above all, in his condensing what is often a long and difficult area in the preacher's rhetoric, Higden proves himself a worthy distiller of mid-fourteenth century thought.

If the composition of the *Ars componendi sermones* is placed in the latter part of Higden's life—probably in the years between 1340 and 1350—this is done with the knowledge that none of the surviving manuscripts can be placed within thirty years of these dates. Indeed, the one thought to be earliest does have many good readings but in no way is it completely authoritative or accurate, and each recension deserves consideration in a disputed passage. Of the five extant copies, scholars deem Bodley 316 to be the closest to Higden's lifetime;[120] yet since the others are generally assigned to the early part of the fifteenth century, all do not differ more than fifty years in date of transcription. They have many other differences, however, and any extended consideration of their contents makes it plain that no one of the five is a copy of any of the others, nor does it seem possible that they can be immediately traced to a common archetype. Some of their more obvious features ought, nevertheless, to occupy us here.[121]

VI

Manuscripts

Oxford, Bodleian Library, *Bodley 316*

Written in Latin on parchment and reputedly dates from 1388. It is an English manuscript, fifteen inches long and ten and five-eights inches wide, containing throughout in double columns of

---

[120] E. Maunde Thompson, in his edition of the *Chronicon Sancti Albani*, Rolls Series, #64 (London, 1874), pp. xviff, concludes that this manuscript and Harley 3634 were originally one volume and were written, in the same script, about 1388.

[121] I have supplemented various MSS descriptions with personal observations of their characteristics.

approximately fifty-five lines per column, it boasts two minia-
tures,[122] several illuminated borders, decorated initials, and a
pleasing compositional balance. The first few leaves are worm-
eaten.

Ranulph's *Ars* begins with the pre-prefatory material on fol. 176^r
and ends on fol. 183^r. It is decorated with red and blue ink initials
and contains indiscriminate paragraph marks in the same colors. It
exhibits as pleasing an arrangement as the rest of the manuscripts
and is written in the same hand, a clear Gothic book hand.

The manuscript begins with a *Prologue* and a *Tabula Cestrensis*, an
alphabetical list of subjects treated in it, which extends to fol. 7^v.
From fol. 8^r to fol. 150^r is contained Higden's *Polychronicon*, the
text of which ends abruptly with A.D. 1342 near the end of book
VII, chapter 44. It is followed immediately by a text "De parli-
amento facto Londonie, quod Bonum a pluribus vocabatur, 1376"
which also finishes abruptly at the end of fol. 151^v. From fol. 152^r
to 175^v is contained a Latin chronicle of England from 1382-88; it
is also unfinished. Higden's *Ars* is the last text contained in the
manuscript. A note on the page facing the alphabetical index (that
is, fol. 1^v) reads: "Liber ex dono M. Thomas Hughes" and probably refers to the Thomas Hughes of Wadham College, Oxford,
and St. Mary's Hall who received an M.A. in 1639. The
manuscript does not appear in the Bodleian lists until about 1655.

It will be referred to in this edition as B3.

Oxford, Bodleian Library, *Bodley 5*

Written in Latin on parchment and dates from about 1400.[123] It is
an English manuscript, measures some six inches in length and
three and seven-eights inches in width, and contains 121 numbered
leaves plus twenty-two others. It has small capital letters decorated
in red and blue ink and is at present imperfect and injured by
damp and worms.

Two texts of Ranulph's *Ars* are contained in this manuscript the
first extends from fol. 1^r to the last section of fol. 27^r; it begins
"me sunt Deus vota tua" being without title, author's name, and
initial part of the preface. The second *Ars*, also untitled, begins
with "Circa sermones" and extends to "quicquid pertinet" of the
pre-preface on fol. 84; after a blank hiatus, it picks up with "Hoc

---

[122] The manuscript is described in Falconer Madan and H. H. E. Craster, *A Summary Catalogue of Western Manuscripts in the Bodleian Library* at Oxford, Vol. II, part 1 (Oxford,
1932), pp. 527-28.

[123] Madan and Craster, p. 82.

de thematis" on fol. 85^r and ends on fol. 102^r.

After fol. 86^{ar} (which contains part of the chapter "De intencionis rectitudine" in a seventeenth-century hand) are six blank leaves followed by fol. 87^{ar} and ^{v} which is separated from fol. 88^r to fol. 102^r. Both copies of the *Ars* in this manuscript are decorated with red and blue ink initials and paragraph marks, and are written in approximately thirty lines, in Gothic book hand written with great freedom and a minimal regard for traditional letter forms—an ordinary working hand.

Between the first and second copies of Ranulph's *Ars*, that is, from the bottom of fol. 27^r to fol. 84^v, is contained the *Liber de methodo et arte concionandi* by Thomas Waleys, O.P. (Charland prints a copy of this text on pp. 325-403 of his *Artes Praedicandi.*) After the second copy of Higden's treatise, from fol. 102^v to fol. 108^r, is an anonymous tract, *Circa scienciam composicionis sermonum*, which ends abruptly at "ex quodlibet illorum argumentorum."

Little is known about the provenance of this manuscript. It is marked "anno Domini 1633—ex dono Ri" and appears to have belonged to a Fellow of Corpus Christi College, Oxford.

The first entry of Higden's *Ars* in this manuscript will be referred to as B1; the second as B2.

London, British Library, *Harley* 866

Written in Latin on parchment in small folio size and dating from early in the fifteenth century.[124] It is most probably an English manuscript, measures eleven and one-eighth inches in length and seven and one-eighth inches in width, and contains 49 folios. The manuscript appears to be a compilation from several sources and is comprised of a variety of treatises in different hands.

Ranulph's *Ars* begins on fol. 8^r and extends to fol. 17^r. The red chalk pagination (see below) runs 127-145, representing this text's position in a differently bound book. The pagination appears on rectos only. The text gives the prefatory material, the preface and table of contents (to fol. 8^v [or p. 128]) in double columns and the rest in approximately 59-60 long lines. Red and blue ink initials and paragraph marks decorate the tract which is principally written in a formal minuscule book hand. Two other hands are also discernible: the corrector's, which is quite similar to the transcriber's and which seems to be written in the same type of ink; the marginal

---

[124] See the *Catalogue of the Harleian Manuscripts in the British Museum*, Vol. I (London, 1808), p. 463.

notator's, which is written in a lighter color ink and is more akin to a formal square literary hand.

The manuscript begins with a series of tracts on various subjects: *De rhetorica, De gustus deceptione, De olfactus deceptione, Sophisticaciones de visu, De ars metrica, De cautelis algorismi, De musica.* These texts extend from fol. 1ʳ to fol. 7ᵛ. Higden's *Ars* comes directly after the disquisition on music and is followed by an incomplete copy of Alain of Lille's *De Planctu Naturae* (fol. 17ᵛ to fol. 32ᵛ) and a fragment of the *Libri Chiromantici* consisting of a part of fol. 49ʳ only.[125]

The manuscript belonged to Robert Talbot (1505?-1558), fellow of New College, Oxford, and prebend of Norwich; his autograph inscription occurs on the first leaf of the text. It was later in the collection, or at least in the hands, of Matthew Parker (1504-1575), Archbishop of Canterbury, whose characteristic red chalk pagination numbers 127-145 on fols. 1-17. It then passed to Edward Stillingfleet (1635-1699), Bishop of Worcester; his manuscripts were acquired in 1707 by Robert Harley (1661-1724), 1st Earl of Oxford. After the death of Edward Harley (1689-1741), 2nd Earl of Oxford, his widow sold for a nominal sum the manuscript portion of the Harley library to the nation.[126]

It is the copy of this edition.

Oxford, Bodleian Library, Auctarium F. 3.5

Written in Latin and English on parchment and comprised of seven manuscripts written in the fifteenth century in England.[127] It measures ten and seven-eighths inches in length in width, and contains 223 numbered leaves plus one unnumbered leaf. Except for the last treatise, it is written throughout in double columns and was bound in white sheepskin about A.D. 1600 over older sewing and boards.

---

[125] The fragment of the *Libri Chiromantici* consists of part of one leaf only, but has been bound in sideways at the end of the MS, so that the foot of the leaf forms a stub between fols. 35 and 36; this stub (formerly unfoliated) has now been numbered fol. 35*, and the text from the *Libri Chiromantici* therefore appears on fol. 49 and fol. 35* verso.

[126] For a general outline, see Seymour De Ricci, *English Collectors of Books and Manuscripts (1530-1930) and their Marks of Ownership* (Cambridge, 1930; repr. Bloomington, Indiana, 1960), passim; for specific references to the owners of Harley 866, see Cyril Ernest Wright, *Fontes Harleiani: a Study of the Sources of the Harleian Collection of Manuscripts preserved in the Department of Manuscripts in the British Museum* (London, 1972), s.v.

[127] Madan and Craster, p. 492. It is very difficult to date the hand of this manuscript, but Richard Hunt of the Bodleian assured me that it is an early fifteenth-century script.

Ranulph's *Ars* extends from fol. 9ʳ to fol. 25ʳ. It begins "Prefacio ad artem predicandi" and continues immediately with a list of twenty chapters which precede the preface. There is no decorative use of red and blue ink in the text and its handwriting differs markedly from the neat semi-cursive of the tract which is placed before it in the manuscript, although it is similar to (but larger than) the script in which the tract immediately following is written. The *Ars* is transcribed in an early fifteenth-century hand of the type generally described as "English Charter."

The Higden text is the second entry in this manuscript. The first is a fragment of a series of theological distinctions and extends from fol. 1ʳ to fol. 8ᵛ. Immediately following the *Ars componendi sermones* is a treatise *De XII utilitatibus tribulacionis* (fol. 26ʳ-34ᵛ). Other components of the manuscript are the *Mythology* of Fabius Planciades Fulgentius (fol. 35ʳ-78ᵛ), the *Opposiciones Petri Blesensis contra Iudeos* (fol. 80ʳ-106ᵛ), the *Summa collacionum* of John of Wales (seven-part series of theological distinctions extending from fol. 108ʳ to fol. 196ᵛ), and Chaucer's version of the first book of Boethius' *De consolacione* (fols. 198ʳ-220ᵛ)—here modified and to some extent accompanied by a commentary.

A note on the flyleaf of the manuscript reads: "Thomas premissione domino hereford Thomas episcopus" and most probably indicates at least one of the places where the members of this compiled text reposed. The manuscript was acquired by the Bodleian Library not later than 1602.

It will be referred to in this edition as A.

Even the most cursory glance at these manuscript descriptions reveals that three of them contain all or part of a kind of pre-preface, that one is defective in its initial section and, therefore, lacks the pertinent area, and that another commences in a quite different manner. The manuscript tradition, then, seems strongly in favor of the extended first section despite the fact that such evidence conflicts with Higden's observable practice in other works. Although the *Ars kalendarii* does not employ an acrostic scheme, it does have a kind of preface and regular chapter numeration beginning with *capitulum secundum*. The *Speculum curatorum*, however, numbers the preface "chapter one," and employs the acrostic pattern starting with the first letter of this preface. Since the *Ars componendi sermones* is similar to the *Speculum* in date and in religious orientation and since the authentication of the pre-prefatory matter would not accord with the acrostic scheme, the Auctarium manuscript probably preserves Higden's original format in its listing of the chapters and in its immediate progression to the preface. Nevertheless, this manuscript has such a large number of syntactically impossible readings and whole sections which appear to be more like commentaries or glosses rather than actual text that its evidence is ultimately invalidated and the pre-preface must remain as at least within the spirit, if not the letter, of Higden's composition.[128]

In addition, Auctarium's antecedents are obviously different from those of the Bodley and Harleian manuscripts. While it is possible that the two MS Bodley 5 treatises were copied from the same, or almost the same, model (since they exhibit a goodly number of identical mistakes), there are enough differences in the transcription to indicate that they were not copied from each other.[129] They may indeed have both been the work of one scribe whose feeling for Latin abbreviations did not greatly improve with exercise, or whose copy text was simply very difficult to decipher. On the other hand, Bodley 316, reputedly the earliest surviving transcript, appears to be a bad copy of a good model. There seems to be little doubt that this scribe's ability to handle Latin abbreviations was extremely poor and he often resolves his difficulties by leaving words unfinished or by simply skipping the confusing parts of a sentence.[130] Harley 866 is, conversely, almost as certainly a good copy of a bad model. Far superior to the Bodley 5 manuscripts in Latinity, word order, and superior completeness, it often exhibits a surprising resemblance to Bodley 316 and periodically to Auctarium F. 3.5. It may perhaps be conjectured that the corrector of Harley compared his copy with the latter two (or even with their models) before he made his final decisions as to the progress of the text. From the editor's viewpoint, then, MS Harley 866 is the best surviving version of Ranulph's *Ars*.

Consequently, the text of this edition follows Harley MS 866. I have chosen to present a modified diplomatic version and this decision, conjoined with the various scribal peculiarities which I will indicate passim, has made certain restrictions in the *apparatus criticus* both valid and necessary. Therefore, although the copy text spelling and inflection (unusual as it may seem in some instances), its significant paleographic elements and the textual variants found in the other four manuscripts have been preserved, simple orthographic changes (for example, *ortodoxi* and *orthodoxi*) are not specially noted, nor are insignificant inversions in word order (like *magnum gaudium* and *gaudium magnum*) which exist in one or two texts but not in others. A concise system of editorial

---

[128] The Auctarium manuscript, for example, specifies "beate marie" as "domini matris," adds opposite "modus" to those contained in the other manuscripts with regard to the reception of God's word, and deletes a scriptural reference which does not further the points being discussed on pp. 11.

[129] For instance, the variants *impetracione* and *et predicacione* might well be misunderstandings of a Latin abbreviation but could hardly be derived one from the other (see p. 6). Likewise, *inter regna et regna* and *inter duo regna* are unlikely to be copied from each other (p. 38).

[130] Bodley 316's transcriber reads "nec cunctos morum equalitas" for "nec punctos per morum qualitas," (p. 13) ignores an unusual word like "truffas" (p. 27), cites "inalumie" for "ingluvie" (p. 67) among many errors.

symbols identifies additions (<>), deletions ([ ]), emendations (*), and other notable features (superscript number) of the copy text and refers the reader to the variants or to the commentary for further information. Since all editors of medieval manuscripts are well aware of the vagaries in punctuation to be found in them, I have chosen to make no allusion to the numerous pause and paragraph marks which abound in each text. Punctuation, then, is modern throughout, although capitalization has been kept to a minimum—upper case being used only at the beginning of a sentence and for personal names; all book names, even when they refer to a single person, appear in lower case. Expansion of Latin abbreviations, an omnipresent necessity in the *Ars*, has been accomplished silently: in addition, I have opted for the version which seemed most in accord with the scribe's usual practice when the abbreviation sign was sufficiently unclear as to permit variety (for example, in the expansion of *aⁱd* as *aliquid* or *aliud*).

The treatment of biblical material and the citation of other common medieval sources should also be mentioned. In the former, when the quotation appears verbatim in the Latin Vulgate, that section of the text is italicized and the book, chapter, and verse given immediately afterward in parenthesis. Acting on the premise that verification of the biblical sources at Higden's disposal is probably impossible, I have made no attempt to change specific identifications contained in Harley 866, even where they do not correspond with modern scriptural numbering. When the quotation is only an approximation or a paraphrase of the Vulgate, no section of it is italicized, although, with a cf., the citation is provided in parenthesis after the last biblically-related word. If any additional explanation is necessary, the reader is referred to the commentary. Similar practices are observable in the identification of other sources. Ranulph's propensity for restatement militates against italicizing, however, and consequently, wherever the text has provided an opportunity, the borrowed matter is indicated in parenthesis immediately after its citation. In all other cases where a note has seemed expedient or desirable, the appropriate number has been affixed superscript and the pertinent explanation will be found in the commentary. The Analysis of the Text, containing a detailed outline of the *Ars componendi sermones* and its major sources, appears after the edition proper.

APPENDIX

SCHEMA OF PASTORALIA

Leonard Boyle's schema of pastoralia, taken from his
"A Survey of the Writings Attributed to William of
Pagula" (diss., Oxford, 1956), presents the various
classifications current.

PASTORALIA for priests
  I. For their own enlightenment
    A. Of a general kind
        1. 'official'
            a. episcopal constitutions
            b. manuals for diocese
                i. 'ad hoc'
                    α. with *synodalia*
                    β. otherwise
                ii. adopted or recommended
        2. 'private'
            a. treatises
                i. theological
                    α. dogmatic
                    β. moral
                ii. theologico-canonical
            b. distinciones
                i. biblical
                ii. theological
                iii. canonical
                iv. mixture of secular and theological knowledge
    B. Dealing with particular subjects
        1. 'official'
            a. 'ad hoc' for diocese, etc.
            b. adopted or recommended
        2. 'private'
            a. theological or canonico-theological
                i. on confession
                    α. in general
                    β. in particular
                        (1) interrogation
                        (2) imposition of penances

                (3) excommunications
            ii. on virtues and vices
            iii. on theological virtues
            iv. on articles of faith
            v. on Sacraments in general
            vi. on Eucharist, Matrimony, etc.
        b. for special purposes
            i. 'artes praedicandi'
            ii. collections of sermons
                α. in full
                β. *themata*
            iii. collections of *exempla*
            iv. rubrics of Mass
            v. Kalendars
            vi. *Computus*, etc.
    II. In respect of the laity
        A. Official programmes of instruction
        B. Private
            1. for adults
            2. for children

PASTORALIA for laity (Latin or vernacular)
    I. Of a general character
    II. Of a particular character
        A. dogmatic
        B. moral
            1. sacramental
                a. preparation for confession
                b. examination of conscience
            2. virtues, vices, etc.

ARS

COMPONENDI

SERMONES

De arte predicandi secundum Ranulphum cestrensis[a]

Circa sermones artificialiter faciendos sunt quedam generalia consideranda, videlicet: thematis assumpcio, eiusdem introduccio, principalis divisio et principalis divisionis prosecucio seu subdivisio, membrorum subdivisionis prolacio, et ipsorum dilatacio.

Quantum ad thematis assumpcionem est sciendum quod debet esse oracio perfecta et non dependens; debet esse proprium vel ad propriandum[b] congruum; debet, inquam, oracio esse perfecta saltem quantum ad[c] intellectum etsi non semper quantum ad vocem et sensum. Si tamen utroque modo sit perfecta,[d] tanto melius.

Voco autem[e] oracionem perfectam quantum ad vocem et sensum, quando in ipsa est debita ordinacio nominis[f] ad verbum, casus ad personam, adiectivi ad substanciam; ita quod quicquid pertinet ad perfeccionem oracionis presto sit ex auditu eius, cuius est ista:[g] *verbum caro factum est* (Ioan. 1:14), et consimiles. Oracionem vero perfectam quantum ad intellectum dico illam[h] in qua aliquid sufficienter intelligitur[i] quod sufficienter perficit intellectum cuius est ista:[j] *surge et ambula* (Matt. 9:5). Hec oracio est perfecta quantum ad intellectum quia inportat in se naturam perfeccionis inclusam mediante qua sufficienter perficit intellectum. Debet ergo thema *oracio esse perfecta et hoc quantum ad vocem et intellectum vel saltem quantum ad intellectum. Ex hoc quodammodo patet quod non debet esse dependens, ita quod sua perfeccio totaliter dependeat[k] ab aliquo quod est extra se; verbi gracia, ut si dicitur[l] tantum *ascendente Iesu in naviculam* (Matt. 8:23), hec oracio utroque modo est inperfecta et dependens quia habet perfici per aliquid extra se positum et quantum ad vocem et quantum ad intellectum. Et ideo nec hec nec aliqua sibi consimilis[m] est pro themate assumenda. Debet eciam thema esse proprium vel ad propriandum[n] congruum et voco illud thema proprium quod ad litteram dicitur de materia illa vel de illo sancto de quo intendit quis[o] predicare, ut siquis intendat[p] predicare de penitencia assumat idem:[q] *penitenciam agite* (Matt.

___

[a] title: De arte predicandi secundum Ranulphum cestrensis *om. B3* Tractatus de arte predicandi *A*   [b] apropriandum *B3*   [c] ad *om. B3*   [d] perfecta et non dependens t. *B3*
[e] v. aute o. *B3*   [f] o. vocis a. *B3*   [g] e. illa v. *B3*   [h] d. istam i. *B3*   [i] subintelligitur *B3*
[j] e. illa s. *B3*   [k] dependat *B3*   [l] dicatur *B3*   [m] n. alia consimiles e. *B3*
[n] appropriandum *B3*   [o] i. aliquis p. *B3*   [p] intendit *B3*   [q] a. illud p. *B3*

___

*oracio esse perfecta : oracionem esse perfectam *H*

4:17). Si de sancto, vel[r] de sancto Iohanne baptista, assumat idem:[s] *fuit homo missus a deo* (Ioan. 1:6), idem autem[t] ad litteram dicitur de eo et ideo sibi est[u] thema proprium. Thema autem ad appropriandum congruum voco illud quod in se continet[v] de materia ista[w] de qua re predicatur ut siquis alicui sancto velit[x] aliquid thema appropriare quod facere videtur ad propositum; verbi gracia, convenienter potest homo beate Andree pro Christi amore in cruce suspenso appropriare illud ad galathas 4: *confixus sum cruce* (Gal. 2:19). Hoc de thematis assumpcione.

Sequitur[y] de eius introduccione que debet fieri per conveniens exemplum vel concordans proverbium, vel aliquod dictum autenticum, vel aliquod in se manifestum, ita quod[z] semper sit brevis et incentiva devocionis et sequitur. Tercio de principalis thematis divisione et cetera.[1][aa]

I
Prefacio ad hanc artem[a]

Ad preeminentem[b] huius artis laudem asserunt[c] plurimi ortodoxi quod inter omnia utriusque testamenti holocaustomata, illud sacrificium deo acceptissimum fore[d] comprobatur quia[e] homo primo et principaliter se ipsum[f] deo offerat[g] per affectuosam devocionem,[2] iuxta illud psalmi: *in me sunt deus*[h] *vota tua*[i]

---

[r] s. ut d. *B3*   [s] a. illud f. *B3*   [t] i. aute *B3*   [u] i. si t. *B3*   [v] c. aliquid d. *B3*
[w] m. illa d. *B3*   [x] velt *B3*   [y] Siquitur *B2*   [z] quod *om. B3*
[aa] et sequitur. . .et cetera *om. B3*
[a] title: Incipit Prefacio ad hanc artem predicandi vel prohemium *A*   [b] preminentem *B3*
[c] asterunt *A*   [d] fore *om. A*   [e] quo h. *B3 A*   [f] i. fore d. *A*   [g] offert *A*   [h] deus *om. A*
[i] tua *om. B2*

---

[1] MS. *A* which probably preserves the original ordering of Higden's text begins with a title which is immediately followed by a Table of Contents, substantially the same as that found in the other manuscripts except that it includes the chapter *De thematis divisione*. MS. *B3*, where the pre-prefatory matter survives in its entirety, and MS. *B2*, where only a small segment remains, have different arrangements for the placement of the Table of Contents: in *B2*, the chapter listing follows the preface, as it does in *H* and *B1*; in *B3*, it precedes the pre-preface. All chapter headings have been collated regardless of their placement in the various MSS.

[2] The sentiment is biblical and shows relationships to Dan. 3:38 ("neque holocaustum, neque sacrificium...") and to Ps. 50:18: "sacrificium Deo spiritus contribulatus..." The abbreviations for the Bible's books which appear in parenthesis in the text are self-explanatory, except for the use of Eccl. to designate the book of Ecclesiastes and that of Eccli. to indicate Ecclesiasticus.

(Ps. 55:12). Secundario[j] et consequenter quoniam proximum suum pro posse deo adquirat[k] per fructuosam predicacionem secundum[l] illud apocalypsis ultimo: *qui audit, dicat: veni* (Apoc. 22:17),[m] et ecclesiastici 12: *unicuique mandavit* deus *de proximo suo* (Eccli. 17:12). Proinde ad erudicionem simplicium qui artem predicandi hactenus non noverunt, hanc artis stillulam ex variis auctorum composicionibus[n] collectam[o] ipsis simplicibus censui propinandam,[p] in qua utcumque tanguntur[q] que[r] circa[s] predicatorem et eius sermonem sunt potissime attendenda.[t]

In ipso namque predicante[u] requiruntur tria, scilicet:[v] intencionis rectitudo,[w] conversacionis sanctitudo, et prolacionis[x] aptitudo. In sermone vero requiruntur tria, scilicet:[y] thematis congruitas, divisionis proprietas, et prosecucionis[z] utilitas. Sed priusquam[aa] de hiis disseratur,[3] notandum est in primis quod secundum[ab] quosdam[ac] predicacio est,[ad] invocato dei auxilio, thema proponere,[ae] propositum dividere, divisum subdividere, auctoritates confirmantes[af] cum racionibus et exemplis adducere, et adductas[ag] explanare ad divini cultus ampliacionem, ad ecclesie militantis[ah] illustracionem, ad humani affectus erga deum inflamacionem;[ai] vel secundum alios, predicacio est publica persuasio debitis loco et tempore pluribus facta ad salutem[aj] promerendam,[ak] in qua descripcione excluditur[al] sermo legencium et disputancium in scolis, cum[am] magis pertineat ad veritatis inquisicionem quam ad predicacionem. Item excluditur[an] exhortacio[ao] paucis[ap] facta quamobrem inproprie dicitur[aq] Christus[ar] predicasse mulieri samaritane, Iohannis 15[as] (Ioan. 4:1-42). Item excluditur clamosa[at] *animacio exhortancium[au]

---

[j] t. et cetera secundo e. *A*   [k] adquirit *A*   [l] p. iuxta i. *A*   [m] 22:7 *A*
[n] confeccionibus *B3* : canalibus *A*   [o] recollectam in i. *B1*
[p] propinandam *B1* : propinand *B2*   [q] coguntur *B2* : tangitur *B3*   [r] que *om. B1 B2 B3*
[s] circa *om. B1* c. ipsum p. *A*   [t] attenda *B2* : observanda *A*   [u] predicacione *A*
[v] t. sed *B3*   [w] r. et c. *B3*   [x] probacionis *B2*   [y] tria scilicet *om. B3*   [z] persecucionis *A*
[aa] priusquam *om. B1*   [ab] secundum *om. B1 B2*   [ac] q. quod quosdam *B2*
[ad] est *om. B3*   [ae] t. proponem p. *B2*   [af] auctoritate conformantes *B1*
[ag] adducere adductas *A* : adducas *B2*   [ah] militantes *B1*   [ai] infamacionem *B1*
[aj] s. anime p. *A*   [ak] promerenda *B1*   [al] d. describitur s. *B1 B2 B3*
[am] c. huisusmodi m. *B3*   [an] excluditur sermo. . .Item excluditur *om. A*
[ao] exordacio *B1*   [ap] e. fautis f. *B3*   [aq] dicitur *om. B1*   [ar] Christum *B1*   [as] 11 *A*
[at] e. hic exclamosa a. *A*   [au] exhortaneum *B3*

---

*animacio : animosa *H*

---

[3] Marginal notations are sparse in all five manuscripts; where they do occur, as here in *H*, their function is merely indicational: "tria in predicacione requiruntur; tria in sermone requiruntur." Since they do occur infrequently, I have chosen to ignore them in the *apparatus criticus*.

in bellis et litigiosa disceptacio postulancium in causis. [av]

In hac autem arte [aw] sicut [ax] eciam [ay] in aliis scienciis, quattuor cause sunt reperte, [az] scilicet: [ba] finalis, materialis, efficiens, et formalis. Causa finalis [bb] predicacionis debet esse ipsius [bc] predicatoris [bd] excitacio, [be] ipsius [bf] auditoris [bg] edificacio, et [bh] creatoris [bi] honoracio. Causa materialis est quod sermo habeat verba casta in [bj] annunciando [bk] virtutes, vicia, [bl] penas, et gaudia. Causa efficiens duplex est quia ipse deus originaliter [bm] et ipse predicans ministraliter. [bn] Causa formalis relucet [bo] in superiori [bp] descripcione et [bq] cetera [br] ipsius predicatoris. [bs]

De intencionis rectitudine   2 [bt]
De conversacionis sanctitudine [bu]   3
De prolacionis aptitudine   4
De dicendi circumspeccione 5 [bv]
De thematis congruitate   6 [bw]
Quod thema congruat [bx] materie proponende 7 [by]
Quod thema sit de textu biblie   8 [bz]
Quod thema [ca] sufficienter dividatur 9 [cb]
Quod concordancias admittat thema   10 [cc]
Quod de eo [cd] prothema elici valeat 11 [ce]
De oracionis premissione et gracie impetracione [cf] 12 [cg]
De auditorum alleccione   13 [ch]
De thematis introduccione   14 [ci]
<De thematis divisione> [cj] 15 [ck]
De clavibus divisionis   *16 [cl]
De sermonis dilatacione [cm] *17 [cn]
De membrorum subdivisione [co] *18 [cp]

[av] Item excluditur. . .in causis *om B1*   [aw] a. sancti s. *B1*   [ax] a. sciendum e. *B3*
[ay] eciam *om. B1* s. et i. *A*   [az] repertis *B1*   [ba] scilicet *om. B1*   [bb] f. ipsius p. *B3 A*
[bc] e. ipsum p. *B2*   [bd] precatoris *B1*   [be] exitacio *A*   [bf] ipsius *om. B1 B3 A*; ipsis *B2*
[bg] auditorum *B3*   [bh] et *om. B3 A*   [bi] c. excitacio h. *B2*   [bj] in *om. B3*
[bk] aniverciando *B2*   [bl] virtutes et vicia *A*   [bm] originatur *B1*   [bn] p. instrumenter *A*
[bo] reluce *B1*   [bp] superiore *B1*   [bq] et *om. B1 B3 A*   [br] cetera *om. B1 B3 A*
[bs] ipsius predicatoris *om. B1 B2 B3*; i. predicacionis *A*; cetera Capitulo *B2*   [bt] 2 *om. B1*
[bu] sanctitate *A*   [bv] 5 *om. A*   [bw] 6 *om. A*   [bx] congruat *om. B1*   [by] 7 *om. A*
[bz] 8 *om. A*   [ca] thema *om. B1*; Q. sit s. *B1*   [cb] 9 *om. A*   [cc] 10 *om. A*   [cd] Q deo p. *B3*
[ce] 11 *om. A*   [cf] g. et predicacione *B1* in peccacione *B3*   [cg] 12 *om. A*   [ch] 13 *om. A*
[ci] 14 *om. A*   [cj] De thematis divisione *om. B1 B2 B3*   [ck] 15 *om. B1 B2 B3 A*
[cl] 15 *B1 B2 B3*; 16 *om. A*   [cm] dilacione *B2*   [cn] 16 *B1 B2 B3*; 17 *om. A*
[co] subdisione *B3*   [cp] 17 *B1 B2 B3*; 18 *om. A*

*16 : 15 *H*
*17 : 16 *H*
*18 : 17 *H*

De *dilatacione [cq] per auctoritates   *19 [cr]
Regule circa dilataciones [cs] *20 [ct]
De coloracione membrorum *21⁴ [cu]

II
< De intencionis rectitudine > [a]

Rectitudo intencionis [b] requiritur [c] scilicet [d] ut propter [e] finem [f] debitum predicet quod tunc fit [g] quando predicat ad dei glorificacionem, ad proximi edificacionem, [h] et ad veritatis insinuacionem; non [i] ad favoris [j] aucupacionem sicut faciunt adulatores, non ad lucri temporalis venacionem [k] sicut faciunt [l] publici [m] questores, nec [n] ad sui ostentacionem sicut faciunt olei venditores de quibus [o] in psalmo dicitur: [p] *deus *dissipabit [q] ossa eorum qui [r] hominibus placent* (Ps. 52:6), id est, placere intendunt; [s] et Paulus [t] ad *galatas [u] dicit: [v] *si hominibus placerem,* [w] id est, [x] placere intenderem, [y] *Christi servus non essem* (Gal. 1:10). Non enim cum oportunum [z] sit [aa] debet ipsa veritas conticeri, nec amore, nec timore, nec odio, nec favore, prece vel

---

[cq] dilacione *B2*   [cr] 18 *B1 B2 B3;* 19 *om. A*   [cs] dilacionis *B1*
[ct] 19 *B1 B2 B3* 20 *om. A*   [cu] 20 *B1 B3* 19 *B2* 21 *om. A*
[a] title: De intencionis rectitudine *om. B3*   [b] i. communis r. *B1*   [c] reperitur *B3*
[d] r. in predicante ut scilicet *B1* r. in predicacione ut scilicet *B3*
[e] r. in ipso predicante ut scilicet ad f. *A*   [f] finem *om. B3*   [g] t. sit q. *B3*
[h] e. ad sui excitacionem e. *A*   [i] n. autem a. *A*   [j] favorem *B3*   [k] venatur *B1*
[l] faciant *B1*   [m] f. populi q. *B3*   [n] q. non a. *B3 A*   [o] v. sicut dicitur i. *A*
[p] dicitur *om. A*   [q] dissipavit *A*   [r] e. quibus h. *B1*   [s] intendent *B1*   [t] Paulus *om. A*
[u] a. corinthios d. *B1 B3*   [v] a. romanos dicitur *A*   [w] h. placere su i. *B3*   [x] id est *om. A*
[y] placere intenderem *om. A* intendere *B1*   [z] oportinum *B1*   [aa] o. fuerit d. *B3 A*

---

*dilatacione : dilacione *H*
*19 : 18 *H*
*20 : 19 *H*
*21 :10 *H*
*dissipabit : dissipat *H*
*galatas : corinthios *H*

---

⁴In *B2* the "cione membrorum" of chapter twenty-one's title is added in a seventeenth-century hand. The opening section of chapter two, from "Rectitudo intencionis" to "XI questio 3" is to be found in the same hand on folio 86ᵃʳ of the *B2* text. It is blurred for the most part and I have made no attempt at collation. About this point, *B2* lacks leaves 1-2 of gathering 21. It does not, therefore, appear again in the text or apparatus until the middle of the chapter *De auditorum alleccione*: "magis deberent corda vestra."

precio, exemplo^{ab} Michee prophete^{ac} tertio regum ultimo, qui cum hortaretur^{ad} ut regi placencia^{ae} nunciaret,^{af} respondit: *vivit dominus; quia* quecumque^{ag} *dixerit*^{ah} *michi dominus, hec loquar* (III Reg. 22:13-14). Unde dicit Chrysostomus, non solum ille proditor^{ai} est veritatis qui palam mentitur, sed qui non libere pronunciat veritatem quam libere pronunciari oportet, XI, questio iii, "nolite"; Extra "quod metus^{aj} causa," capitulo "sacris."⁵^{ak} Et in hac quidem veritate exprimenda non semper requiritur dicendi^{al} subtilitas set quandoque^{am} plus edificat^{an} simplex ruditas;^{ao} unde Paulus ad corinthios 2 ait:^{ap} *sermo meus et* doc-trina *mea non in persuasibilibus*^{aq} *humane sapiencie verbis sed in ostencione spiritus* (I Cor. 2:4).

Item in hac parte^{ar} declinanda^{as} est fabulosa vanitas aut puerilis scurilitas tamquam impertinens^{at} ad salutem^{au} pocius^{av} aurem quam animam demulcens, de quo propheta ait: caupones vestri miscent aquam vino,^{aw} ⁶ de quo habetur 8 Distinccione,^{ax} *Cum multa*,⁷ nisi forsan^{ay} eo modo quo^{az} docet Augustinus, de doctrina christiana libro 2, versus finem dicens quod filii Israelis abstu-lerunt preciosa de Egipto ut ea postmodum meliori usui coap-tarent (*De doctrina christiana*, II, 151), sicut fecit Ieronymus invehendo^{ba} contra Iovinianum dicta philosophorum et gentilium poetarum (*Contra Iovinianum*, Liber I, caps. 1-49 passim).

---

^{ab}exemplum *B1*   ^{ac}Michelis prophetam *B3*   ^{ad}c. portaretur u. *B3*   ^{ae}r. apparet n. *A*
^{af}nunciarem *B3*   ^{ag}quocumque *B3*   ^{ah}dixit *A*   ^{ai}s. predicator e. *B1*   ^{aj}motus *B3*
^{ak}capitulo sacris *om. A* c. sanguis *B3*   ^{al}dicendis *B1*   ^{am}s. quando p. *B1*
^{an}edificat *om. B1*   ^{ao}rusticitas *A*   ^{ap}ait *om. A*   ^{aq}persuasionibus *B1 aA*
^{ar}h. arte d. *A*   ^{as}declinandam *B1* : declinam f. *B3*   ^{at}s. non pertinens a. *A*
^{au}saltem *B3*   ^{av}poci *B1* p. ad a. *A*   ^{aw}a. viro d. *A*   ^{ax}genese VI de quo c. *A*
^{ay}m. forsari e. *B1* m. alia nisi forte e. *A*   ^{az}q. intelligit vel quo d. *A*   ^{ba}I. hendo I. *B1*

---

⁵Thomas Waleys, in his *De modo componendi sermones* (Charland, p. 337), identifies a similar citation as coming from Chrysostom's *Super Matthaeum*. Probably incorrectly at-tributed to Chrysostom, this text is found more frequently in medieval libraries than any of his authentic works; see R. M. Wilson, "The Contents of the Medieval Library," in *The English Library Before 1700*, ed. Francis Wormald and C. E. Wright (London, 1958), p. 89. The citation appears in the *Decretum Gratiani*, Causa XI, q. 3, c. 86 in the *Corpus Iuris Canonici*, ed. A. Friedberg, Vol. I (Leipzig, 1879), col. 667. The "Extra" refers to the De-cretals of Gregory IX, in which "Quod metus causa," is an alternate title for "De his, quae vi metusve causa fiunt"; there cap. "sacris" can be found (1.40.5). See Friedberg, Vol. II, col. 220. I am grateful to Stephanie Tibbetts of the Institute for Medieval Canon Law for locating this reference.

⁶Probably related to Isaias 1:22: "Vinum tuum mixtum est aqua."

⁷Gratian's *Decretum* D. 86c. 5.

III
De conversacionis sanctitudine[a]

Sanctitudo conversacionis requiritur in ipso[b] predicante,[c] nam in psalmo legitur quia[d] peccatori *dixit deus: quare*[e] *tu enarras iusticias meas*[f] et cetera (Ps. 49:16). Et[g] Gregorius in omelia[h] dicit: cuius vita despicitur, restat ut eius[i] contempnatur predicacio, XL Distinccione, *Nullus* (*Homiliarum in evangelia*, Liber I, hom. xii).[8] Idcirco Paulus castigabat corpus suum *ne forte aliis* predicando,[j] *ipse reprobus* efficeretur (I Cor. 9:27). Quando vero[k] predicantis vita est[l] sancta, sermo erit efficax et virtuosus, sicut patuit[m] in beato Stephano, actuum 2,[n] cui non poterant[o] iudei *resistere (Act. 6:7). Et in 4[p] libro historie[q] ecclesiastice legitur quod gens hebreorum conversa sint[r] ad fidem per quamdam mulierem christianam captivam (Socrates-Scholasticus, *Historia ecclesiastica*, Liber I. cap. xx). Nam secundum Gregorium in[s] moralibus:[t] loquendi auctoritas perditur[u] quando vox[v] operibus non iuvatur[w] (*Moralium liber XIX in caput XXVIII beati Iob*, cap. vii). Idem patet[x] secundo libro pastoralis,[y] capitulo 7,[z] ubi dicitur quod predicator instar galli plus debet actibus[aa] quam vocibus resonare (*Regulae pastoralis*[ab] *liber*, III, cap. xl); nam secundum philosophum, quarto ethicorum: dum acciones et voces dissonant,[ac] impediunt verum (Aristotelis, *Ethica Nicomachea*, IV, cap. 1127a-1127b).

---

[a] title: sanctitate *A* [b] i. Christo p. *A* [c] n. idem p. *B3* [d] l. quod p. *B3 A*
[e] d. quia t. *B1* quare *om. B3* [f] mea *B1* [g] Ergo G. *B3* [h] omeliis *B3* [i] eius *om.*
[j] predicans *A* [k] Q. enim p. *A* [l] e. dicta s. *B3* [m] patet *A* [n] a. septimo c. *A*
[o] potuerunt *A* [p] i. decimo l. *A* [q] phistorie *B1* [r] c. fuit a. *B3* sint *om. A*
[s] in *om. A* [t] m. 19 *A* [u] partitur *B1* [v] q. rex o. *B1* v. ab o. *A* [w] concordat *A*
[x] Istud s. *A* [y] pastorum *B3* : pastoralium *A* [z] primo *B3* : tercio *A* [aa] actubus *A*
[ab] p. 10 *A* [ac] dissonent *B1*

---

*resistere : resistem *H*

---

[8] Gregory's words are also cited in the *Decretum Gratiani*, Causa III, q. 7, c. 2 in Freidberg, ibid., col. 526.

IV
De prolacionis aptitudine [a]

Requiritur [b] vero [c] tertio [d] in predicante prolacionis aptitudo ut [e] videlicet: predicet alte, prompte, et mature.[9] Alte quidem [f] ut ab omnibus audiatur; prompte ut sermo bene sciatur antequam proferatur; [g] mature [h] ut libencius capiatur. Que quidem [i] maturitas [j] consistit in duobus, scilicet: [k] in convenienti [l] corporis motu et in modesto oris affatu, [m] de quibus loquitur Valerius [n] Maximus, octavo libro de gestis *memorabilibus, [o] ponens exemplum de Hortensi philosopho de quo incertum [p] erat an plures concurrerunt [q] ad eius decorum gestum spectandum an [r] ad verbum eiusdem audiendum (*Factorum ac dictorum memorabilium liber*, VII, cap. x: "De Quinto Hortensio").

Nam cum predicator vicem gerat oratoris, qualitas sui gestus et [s] pronunciacionis multum imprimit [t] in [u] mentem auditoris. Sic ergo temperetur [v] gestus in eo ut sicut variatur materia [w] de qua predicatur; sic [x] varietur [y] gestus predicatoris et [z] pronunciandi modus de quo tractat Hugo, de institucione noviciorum, [aa] dicens: sic loquens solo ore loquatur [ab] non nimis brachia aut manus ostendendo [ac] sicut faciunt [ad] placitatores, [ae] non capud aut [af] visus exagitando, [ag] nec [ah] oculos velud [ai] ypocrita invertendo.[10] [aj] De qua re loquitur Augustinus, de doctrina christiana (IV, 104): grandia,

---

[a] title: prolacione *B3* aptitudine *om. B1*   [b] Sequitur v. *B1*   [c] vero *om. A*
[d] tercio *om. B1 B3*   [e] a. quod v. *B3*   [f] A. quid u. *A*   [g] perferatur *A*
[h] mature *om. B1*   [i] Q. quid m. *A*   [k] scilicet *om. B1 B3 A*   [l] convonienti *A*
[m] affectu *B1*   [n] Valerianus *B1*   [o] memoralibus *B3 A*   [p] Iohanne de quo iunctum e. *A*
[q] concurrerent *A*   [r] an *om. B3*   [s] et *om. A*   [t] imprimunt *B3*   [u] in *om. B1*
[v] S. igitur comperetur g. *A*   [w] v. modo d. *A*   [x] sic *om. A*   [y] variatur g. *B1 B3*
[z] et *om. B1*   [aa] novicorum *B1 B3*   [ab] loquitur *B1* : loquatur *om. A*
[ac] n. manus aut brachia extendendo s. *B3 A*   [ad] facint *B3*   [ae] placitores *B1 A*
[af] aut *om. B3*   [ag] c. ut ursus e. *A*   [ah] non o. *A*   [ai] velud *om. B3*   [aj] vertendo *B3*

---

*memorabilibus : memoralibus *H*

---

[9] "Maturitas" here implies the third meaning given in du Cange, *Glossarium Mediae et Infimae Latinitatis* (Paris, 1840), Vol. IV, p. 327: "modestia, gravitas."

[10] This is a distillation of some major points in Hugh of St. Victor's twelfth chapter: "De disciplina in gestu servanda" whose substance includes the following: "Gestus hominis in omni actu esse debet gratiosus sine mollicie, quietus sine dissolutione, gravis sine tarditate, alacer sine inquietudine, maturus sine protervia et sine turbulentia severus." (*De institutione novitiorum*, *PL* 176:948)

inquit, granditer sunt dicenda,[ak] ut verbi gracia, quando predicatur[al] contra vicia loquatur acriter[am] et cum detestacione,[an] psalmo *iniquitatem odio habui* et cetera (Ps. 118:163);[ao] unde Seneca,[ap] epistola 184:[aq] volo contra vicia aliquid aspere[ar] dici, contra pericula animose, contra fortunam superbe,[as] contra ambicionem contumeliose,[at] et[au] contra luxuriam obiurgatorie[av] (*Epistolae* 100:10); hec ille. Item quando[aw] predicatur de virtutibus sit[ax] sermo moderacior[ay] quasi[az] obsecrando ad amplexum[ba] virtutum, ad romanos XI:[bb] *vos*[bc] *obsecro ut exhibeatis corpora vestra hostiam vivam* (Rom. 12:1). Quando autem predicatur[bd] de penis sit sermo et gestus[be] terribilior, exemplo Iohannis[bf] baptiste qui dixit luce 3:[bg] *genimina viperarum quis*[bh] *ostendit vobis fugere* (Luc. 3:7). Quando[bi] autem predicatur de premiis sit[bj] sermo et gestus elevacior et devocior,[bk] ad colossenses tertio: *que sursum sunt sapite* (Col. 3:2). Huic autem prolacionis aptitudini incumbit debita dicendi[bl] oportunitas secundum illud ecclesiaste 8:[bm] *omni*[bn] *negocio est tempus et oportunitas*[bo] (Eccl. 8:6). Non enim debet predicator scmpcr aut ubiquc[bp] loqui sct tcmporibus ct locis oportunis;[bq] nam si celum[br] semper plueret,[bs] terra non[bt] germinaret.[11] [bu] Unde Beda[bv] super lucam <dicit>:[bw] non[bx] omne tempus est[by] habile doctrine[bz] (*Expositio actuum apostolorum et retractatio*, XIV, vii).

[ak] s. docenda u. *B1* : s. danda u. *B3*   [al] predicator *A*   [am] l. agiliter e. *B1*
[an] d. peccati unde p. *A*   [ao] h. et abhominatur sum u. *A*   [ap] S. in e. *A*   [aq] 104 *A*
[ar] a. percipere d. *B1*   [as] superbie *B1* : super *B3* : sub superbe *A*   [at] contumeliore *B1*
[au] et *om. B3 A*   [av] obiurgatore *B3*   [aw] I. cum p. *B3 A*   [ax] v. sufficit s. A
[ay] moderacionem *B1* : moderacom *B3*   [az] m. quia o. *A*   [ba] implexum *B3*   [bb] r. 12 *A*
[bc] vos *om. B3*   [bd] a. disseratur d. *A*   [be] p. sic gestus ac sermo fit t. *A*
[bf] Iohanne *B1 B3*   [bg] t. capitulo g. *A*   [bh] v. qui *B3*   [bi] et cetera Quando *A*
[bj] sit *om. B3*   [bk] elevacionem et devocionem *B3*   [bl] d. dandi *B3*   [bm] 8 *om. B3*
[bn] cum n. *B3*   [bo] secundum illud. . .et oportunitas *om. A*   [bp] s. et ubi l. *B3*
[bq] oportunus *B3*   [br] si casu s. *B1 B3* celum *om. A*   [bs] plurumque *B3* p. de celo t. *A*
[bt] numquam g. *A*   [bu] non autem minaret *B3*   [bv] Beata *B1*   [bw] dicit *om. B1*
[bx] n. enim o. *A*   [by] e. ab h. *B1*   [bz] d. quare et cetera *A*

---

[11] Biblical overtones from Gen. 7, II Reg. 23:4 and Amos 4:7 can be discerned in this proverbial statement.

V
De dicendi circumspeccione

Apta dicendi[a] circumspeccio in hac parte requiritur[b] ut secundum quantitatem[c] auditorum formetur sermo predicatoris[d] sicut docet Gregorius super ezechielem, libro[e] primo,[f] omelia 41[g] (*Homiliarum in Ezechielem*, Liber I,[h] hom. xi) et moralibus 24,[12][i] sic dicens:[j] "consideret doctor quid loquatur, cui loquatur,[k] qualiter loquatur, et quantum dicatur," ubi quattuor tanguntur ad hanc artem necessaria: sentencia dicendorum, ibi "quid loquatur"; qualitas auditorum, ibi "cui dicatur"; modus dicendi, ibi "qualiter dicatur"; mensura perorandi, ibi "quantum dicatur." Quoad[l] primum istorum quod est materia dicendorum, consideret quid dicatur,[m] quod quidem in quattuor[n] consistit,[o] videlicet:[p] in[q] viciis detestandis,[r] in virtutibus commendandis,[s] in[t] penis comminandis, et[u] in premiis exhortandis. Ad que[v] annuncianda tendit tota[w] sacra scriptura, secundum illud[x] timothei 3: *omnis scriptura divinitus inspirata*[y] *utilis est ad docendum, ad arguendum, ad*[z] *corrigendum,*[aa] *et ad erudiendum*[ab] (II Tim. 3:16). Ad docendum quidem[ac] gloriam appetentes, ad[ad] romanos 5:[ae] *quecumque*[af] *scripta sunt ad nostram doctrinam scripta sunt* (Rom. 15:4). Item ad arguendum crimina committentes, ecclesiaste 20:[ag] *verba sapiencium*[ah] *quasi stimuli* (Eccl. 12:11). Item ad corrigendum penam[ai] non caventes, ieremie 23: *Numquid non verba mea quasi ignis ardens et quasi malleus conterens petras* (Ier. 23:29). Item ad erudiendum virtutem necgligentes, unde dicit *danielis[aj]

---

[a] A. dandi c. *B3*   [b] c. requiritur in hac arte u. *A*   [c] qualitatem *A*   [d] predicacionis *A*
[e] libro *om. A*   [f] primo *om. A*   [g] 47 *B3*   [h] XI *A*   [i] 14 *A*
[j] summa d. *B3* : scilicet materia d. *A*   [k] q. dicatur q. *A*   [l] d. Vero p. *B3*
[m] predicatur *A*   [n] quattuor predicabilibus c. *B3 A*   [o] consistat *B1*   [p] c. scilicet *A*
[q] in *om. A*   [r] vicii attestandis *B3*   [s] commendandum *B3*   [t] c. en *A*   [u] et *om. A*
[v] que quattuor *B1 B3 A*   [w] t. thoma s. *A*   [x] i. apostoli ad t. *A*
[y] divinitur inspireta *B3*   [z] a. et. c *B1*   [aa] colligendum *B3*
[ab] ad docendum. . .ad erudiendum *om. A*   [ac] d. quid *A*   [ad] ad *om. B3*
[ae] 5 *B1 B3* 3 *A*   [af] quocumque *B3*   [ag] 02 *B3* 24 *A*   [ah] sapientum *B3*
[ai] penas *A* penis *B1*   [aj] danieli *B1 B3 A*

---

*daniel : samuel *H*

---

[12] The *Moralium Liber XXIV in caput XXXIV beati Job* (*PL* 76:316) seems responsible only for the "dicatur" in the following citation; however, it is Gregory's *Liber Pastoralis*, Pars III (*PL* 77:49 ff.) which actually discusses the text quoted initially in this chapter.

12: *qui ad iusticiam erudiunt plurimos quasi stelle in perpetuas eternitates* (Dan. 12:3).

Circa secundum quod est qualitas auditorum,[ak] consideret predicator[al] cui loquatur,[am] quia aliter loquendum est[an] de[ao] diversis personis, aliter[ap] uni et eidem persone diversis viciis[aq] laboranti[ar] sive in diversis *statubus existenti;[as] et ponit Gregorius exemplum moralibus 14[13] de medico vulnus considerante[at] priusquam *emplastrum[au] *apponat, et eciam de agricola qualitatem[av] terre considerante antequam seminet. Propterea dictum est[aw] iob 38: *dedit gallo intelligenciam*[ax] (Iob 38:36), ubi dicit <Gregorius> moralibus 30: gallo intelligencia tribuitur quando predicatori[ay] virtus discrecionis ministratur, ut[az] videlicet: noverit quid, quando,[ba] et quibus[bb] instruat[bc] (*Moralium liber XXX in caput XXXVIII beati Iob*, cap. iii). Non enim una eademque cunctis[bd] exhortacio congruit quia nec cunctos[be] morum equalitas[bf] *constringit sicut dicit[bg] pastoralis[bh] libro tertio: nam lenis sibulus equos vix[bi] mitigat qui catulos instigat (*Pastoralis liber*, pars tertia, prologus); et ut dicit Gregorius in fine pastoralis (cap. xxxvi): quamvis sit laboriosum unumquemque[bj] de propriis instruere, magis tamen[bk] laboriosum est diversos auditores diversis passionibus laborantes eodem tempore eadem voce admonere, quatinus sic superbis predicetur humilitas ut tamen timidis[bl] non augeatur pusillanimitas; sed inter hec[bm]

[ak] a. et cetera c. *A*   [al] peccator c. *A*   [am] loquitur *B1*   [an] loquendum est *om. B1*
[ao] de *om. B1 B3 A*   [ap] diversis personis aliter *om. B1* d. personaliter u. *B3*
[aq] moribus l. *B3*   [ar] laboratim *B1*   [as] sive in diversis statubus existenti *om. B1 B3*
[at] consideranti *A*   [au] p. ei plaustrum a.*B1* : p. vulium imponat emplaustrum e. *A*
[av] qualitatim *B3* : qualitate *A*   [aw] P. dictamen i. *B1* e. ad i. *A*   [ax] intelligenciam *B1*
[ax] tribuimur *B3*   [ay] predicari *B1* : predicatur *A*   [az] m. utique v. *B3*
[ba] quid cuilibet quando *A*   [bb] et quibus *om. A*   [bc] ministrat *A*
[bd] e. puctus *B3* : e. civitas *A*   [be] n. punctos per m. *B3* : n. civitas par m. *A*
[bf] m. qualitas *B3*   [bg] dicitur *B3 A*   [bh] pastorum *B1 B3*   [bi] vix *om. B3 A*
[bj] unumquodque *B3 A*   [bk] m. cum *A*
[bl] h. dum non timidi n. *B3* : h. dum cum tumidis n. *A*   [bm] hec *om. A*

---

*statubus : statibus *H*
*emplastrum : emplaustrum *H*
*apponat : apponit *H*
*constringit : congruit *H*

---

[13] I have expanded ⸬ as "moralibus" knowing that these accounts are not to be found in book 14 of the *Moralium in Job*. There are, however, in the *Homiliarum in Ezechielem*, Liber I, hom. xi, references to both a doctor and a farmer which might have influenced Ranulph's text (*PL* 76:913-14).

difficilimum est uni et eidem homini contrariis viciis servienti predicare[bn] ubi curandum est ut sic non[bo] tegatur[bp] unum ut[bq] augeatur reliquum; quin eciam[br] illi vicio solercius[bs] subveniatur[bt] quod periculosius premit quamvis et illud restringi non[bu] possit[bv] sine[bw] incremento levioris.[bx]

Circa tertium quod[by] est modus[bz] dicendi, videat predicator qualiter loquatur ut videlicet: non sit ita[ca] succinctus et brevis in dicendo ut defectivus[cb] reperiatur; non sit ita diffusus ut tedio habeatur; non sit ita obscurus ut non intelligatur; non <sit> ita invectivus[cc] ut odibilis censeatur; non sit ita ostentativus[cd] ut[ce] superbia seducatur;[cf] non sit ita[cg] meticulosus[ch] ut sermo eius parvipendatur.

Circa quartum[ci] quod est mensura perorandi, videat predicator quantum dicatur quia sapiencioribus[cj] profunda, simplicioribus plana sunt dicenda. De primo dicitur[ck] ad[cl] corinthios 2: *sapienciam loquimur inter perfectos* (I Cor. 2:6); de secundo habetur[cm] ad corinthios 4: *lac vobis potum[cn] dedi non[co] escam* (I Cor. 3:2), exemplo Christi qui in plano et in[cp] campestribus docuit turbas, in monte[cq] vero discipulos erudivit. Unde dixit[cr] in luca: *vobis datum est nosce misterium regni[cs] dei* (Luc. 8:10), set[ct] rudibus et infirmis dixit Iohanni 16: *multa habeo vobis dicere sed non potestis portare modo* (Ioan. 16:12). Et Gregorius in pastoralis libro secundo in fine: curet predicator ne auditoris animum ultra vires trahat ne dum plusquam valet[cu] tenditur[cv] et[cw] mentis corda rumpatur[cx] (*Pastoralis liber*, pars tertia, cap. xxxix). Hinc est quod Moyses coram populo[cy] faciem suam velavit[cz] quia indocte plebi legis archana non revelavit[da] (cf. Ex. 34:33-34); idcirco dicitur iob 16:[db] *qui ligat[dc] aquam in nubibus*[dd] et scienciam doctrine in predicantibus[de] et non in undacione sciencie set moderata distillacione[df] foveantur[dg] (cf. Iob 26:8).

[bn] s. purificare *B3*   [bo] non *om. A*   [bp] tergatur *A*   [bq] ut non a. *A*   [br] qui eciam *A*
[bs] v. celerius *A*   [bt] subveniatur *om. A*   [bu] quod periculosius. . . restringi non *om. A*
[bv] subpossit *A*   [bw] sine *om. B1*   [bx] livoris *A*   [by] quod *om. B1*   [bz] medus *B3*
[ca] s. ista *A*   [cb] defectus *B3* : defectius *A*   [cc] sit ita. . .ita invectivus *om. A*
[cd] ostencius *B1*   [ce] ut odibilis. . . ostentativus ut *om. A*   [cf] superbia seducatur *om. A*
[cg] sit illa m.   [ch] menticulosis *B1* i. non sit illa noticulosus u. *B3*   [ci] quartum *om. B1*
[cj] sapientibus *B3 A*   [ck] d. infra a. *A*   [cl] d. primo a c. *B3*
[cm] s. ad hoc a. *B3* h. infra a. *A*   [cn] v. positum d. *B3*   [co] n. est qui e. *A*
[cp] in *om. B1 B3 A*   [cq] i. mente v. *B3*   [cr] dicitur *A*   [cs] n. ministerium regem d. *B1*
[ct] set *om. B1*   [cu] p. videlicet t. *B1*   [cv] tendatur *A*   [cw] et *om. A*   [cx] rumpantur *A*
[cy] c. templo f. *B3*   [cz] velat *A*   [da] revelat *B3 A*   [db] 20 *A*   [dc] legat *B1*   [dd] nulibus *A*
[de] predicacionibus *B3 A* u. homo i. *A*   [df] moderacionis stillacione *A*
[dg] foveatur *B3* f. auditores *A*

VI
De thematis congruitate

Nunc de illis que concernunt ipsum sermonem, est notandum quod ad thematis congruitatem[a] requiritur quod ipsum thema non sit obscurum[b] sed plenum impartet intellectum; secundo ut congruat rei[c] de qua est loquendum; tertio[d] ut sit de textu biblie non viciato;[e] quarto ut non in plura[f] quam in tria[g] dividatur; quinto ut concordancias reales et vocales admittat;[h] sexto[i] ut de ipso themate antethema sive prothema, quod idem est, elici valeat.

Circa primum istorum est notandum[j] quod thematum aliud est perfectum, aliud est[k] imperfectum,[l] aliud[m] commune, aliud proprium, aliud accomodatum,[n] aliud abusivum. Thema perfectum est ubi[o] cum construccione congrua appositum et suppositum expressum est ut ibi *Christus pro nobis mortuus est* (Rom. 5:9). Inperfectum est ubi oportet aliquid supplere ut si dicatur *pro omnibus mortuus est* (II Cor. 5:15) subauditur[p] "Christus."[q] Item si[r] de aliqua[s] virgine diceretur[t] *virgo filia Syon*[u] (IV Reg. 9:21), <sentencia> suspensiva foret et inperfecta eo quod verbum ibi[v] deficiat. Commune[w] thema est quod sumi potest in omni festo[x] quale est illud:[y] *servite domino in timore* (Ps. 2:11) et illud:[z] *iustum deduxit* dominus *per vias rectas*[aa] (Sap. 10:10). Proprium thema est quod competit[ab] rei[ac] de qua fit sermo sicut[ad] patebit[ae] inferius capitulo proximo. Thema accomodatum[af] est quod dicitur de uno ad litteram et alteri[ag] accomodatur per[ah] misticam significacionem[ai] ut[aj] illud[ak] regum[al] 28:[am] *expoliavit se Ionathas tunica* sua[an] (I Reg. 18:4); ad litteram dicitur de Ionatha, filio Saul, sed allegorice[ao] potest dici de sancto Bartholomeo. Thema abusivum[ap] est quando illud quod[aq] ad litteram dicitur[ar] de aliquo[as] reprobo applicatur alicui sancto ut est illud[at] regum[au]

---

[a] congruitaitem *B1*   [b] obstractum *A*   [c] u. arguat rem d. *A*   [d] secundo u. *A*
[e] non viciato *om. A* vuciato *B3*   [f] i. perlura q. *B3*   [g] t. membra d. *A*   [h] adnitat *B3*
[i] secundo u. *B1*   [j] e. advertendum q. *A*   [k] perfectum aliud est *om. B1*
[l] aliud imperfectum *B3*   [m] e. prosaicum perfectum aliud est c. *A*
[n] p. ad a. ad observandum *B1*   [o] e. esse c. *B3*   [p] subaiditur *B3*   [q] Christus *om. B3*
[r] si *om. A*   [s] alia *A*   [t] diceretur *om. A*   [u] sein *B3*   [v] ubi *B1*   [w] Omne t. *A*
[x] o. tempore et in omni festo q. *A*   [y] istud *B3 A*   [z] istud *B3 A*
[aa] r. convenit sancto P. *A*   [ab] q. convenit r. *A*   [ac] r. de d. *B1*   [ad] s. ut p. *A*
[ae] patet *B3* patebit *om. A*   [af] accomodum *B1*   [ag] aliter *B1 B3*   [ah] a. ad m. *B3*
[ai] significacione *B1*   [aj] ut *om. A*   [ak] illud *om. B3 A* quod dicitur r. *B3 A*
[al] romanorum *B1*   [am] 19 *A*   [an] sua *om. B3*   [ao] allegorico *B1*   [ap] abustuum *B1*
[aq] q. quod dicitur a. *A*   [ar] dicitur *om. B1 A*   [as] de capitulo r. *A*   [at] istud *B3*
[au] romanorum *B1*

18: *vidi Absolon pendere in quercu* (II Reg. 18:10); si exponatur de Christo vel de sancto Andrea,[av] presertim[aw] cum sacra scriptura sit satis fecunda unde thema[ax] congrua[ay] possunt sumi.

VII
Quod thema congruat materie proponende[a]

Ut plenius[b] habeatur thematis congruencia hoc prenotandum est quod cum tres sunt[c] sermonum[d] species penes materiam differentes,[e] scilicet: sermo dominicalis,[f] sermo festivalis, et sermo ad diversos status[g] hominum sive ad diversa negocia rerum[h] ut in[i] visitacionibus[j] et elecionibus,[k] et[l] in sinodis, in processionibus. Unde[m] qui debet[n] predicare de[o] tempore[p] in adventu[q] domini[r] accipiat tale:[s] *veniet*[t] *desideratus* (Aggaei 2:8); in natali domini: *apparuit gracia* (Tit. 2:11), vel *lux orta est* (Matt. 4:16); in quadragesima:[u] *penitenciam agite* (Matt. 4:17); in pascha:[v] *surrexit dominus vere* (Luc. 24:34), et sic de reliquis. Sic[w] qui de aliquo sancto debeat predicare, videat quid in illo sancto sit magis[x] famosum et commendabile, et[y] iuxta[z] hoc statuat sibi thema; verbi gracia, beatus Andreas quia diu pependit, predicans, in cruce[aa] sibi potest[ab] appropriari[ac] illud ad galatas 4: *confixus sum cruci* (Gal. 2:19). Similiter[ad] beatus Nicholaus[ae] quia specialiter emicuit in operibus misericordie competere sibi potest[af] illud iob:[ag] *ab infancia crevit*[ah] *mecum* misericordia[ai] (Iob 31:18), et de[aj] Martino illud:[ak] *nudum*[al] *operit vestimento*[am] (Ezech. 18:7, 16). Similiter in[an] aliis negociis fiat ut in elecionibus: *eligite meliorum* (IV Reg. 10:3);[ao] in sinodis: *mundamini qui fertis*[ap] *vasa domini* (Is. 52:11); in visitacionibus:[aq] *visitat pastor gregem suum,* ezechielis 33[ar] (Ezech. 34:12); in

---

[av] de ato A. *B3*   [aw] preferam *B1*   [ax] themata *B3 A*   [ay] congruat *B1* : congrue *A*
[a] t. sit de materia proponenda vel congruitate et cetera *B3* m. proponendum *B1*
[b] U. prebemus h. *B3*   [c] q. tantum tres sunt s. *B3* sint *B1 A*   [d] sermonis *B3*
[e] m. indifferentes *B3*   [f] s. dominicus s. *A*   [g] stas *B3*   [h] n. rer u. *B3*
[i] ut patet in *B3 A*   [j] i. festivacione i. *A* v. in e. *B1 B3 A*   [k] leccionibus *B1*
[l] et *om. B1 B3 A*   [m] U. et q. *B1*   [n] q. habet p. *A*   [o] id est t. *B3*   [p] t. capiet i. *A*
[q] adventum *B1*   [r] domini *om. A*   [s] accipiat tale *om. B3 A*   [t] veniat *B3*
[u] sexagesima *B1*   [v] i. paschali tempore *A*   [w] Sed q. *B1 B3 A*   [x] s. maius f. *B3*
[y] f. sit commendabilem et *B3*   [z] commendabile iuxta *A*   [aa] c. competere s. *B3 A*
[ab] potuit *B3* potest *om. A*   [ac] appropriari *om. B3 A*   [ad] Aliter b. *B1*
[ae] S. Gregorius q. *B3*   [ae] enituit *B1*   [ae] c. ergo p. *B3* illud ad. . .competere sibi *om. A*
[af] poterit *A*   [ag] job 31 *A*   [ah] cremit *A*   [ai] miseracio *A*   [aj] beato M. *A*   [ak] illud *om. A*
[al] M. idem mundum o. *B3* nudutur *A*   [am] vestitus *A*   [an] S. et in *A*
[ao] m. regem regum secundo capitulo i. *A*   [ap] fortis *B1*   [aq] visitacione *A*
[ar] s. ostendit ezechielis 33 *B1* 33 capitulo *A*

processionibus et pro pace:[as] *rogate que*[at] *ad pacem sunt* (Ps. 121:6); contra pestem: *domine,*[au] *salva nos, perimus*[av] (Matt. 8:25); in funeracionibus: *amicus noster dormit*[aw] (Ioan. 11:11).

VIII
Quod thema sit de biblia[a]

Licitum est immo[b] <et>[c] necessarium ad omnem materiam thema de biblia sumere dummodo non sit aliunde nec preferatur[d] corupte, ut[e] si in festo trinitatis dicatur: tres[f] vidit et unum[g] adoravit, vicium est quia non est textus biblie.[14][h] Item si in festo annunciacionis dominice vel in aliqua visitacione[i] proponatur: *descendi in ortum* mecum,[j] quia vera littera est: *descendi in ortum* meum[k] (cf. Cant. 6:10).[15] Item si de aliquo sancto diceretur:[l] *vestigia dei*[m] *secutus est pes meus*[n] (Iob 23:11), vicium foret[o] quia vera littera est[p] *vestigia eius.* Non enim licet hiis diebus sumere litteram unius translacionis pro altera,[q] ut si modo diceretur:[r] *dicite in*[s] nacionibus *quia dominus regnavit a ligno,* non admitteretur, quia vulgata littera est: *dicite in gentibus quia dominus regnavit* (Ps. 95:9). De quo mirandum est[t] cur prior littera non accepetur,[u] cum de eius veritate pateat per litteram beati[v] Ambrosii:[w] *Impleta*[x] *sunt que*[y] *concinit David fideli carmine, dicendo*[z] *nacionibus, regnavit a ligno deus.*[16]

[as] et pro pace *om. A*   [at] r. quo a. *B1*   [au] domino *B1*   [av] peramus *B1*   [aw] docuit *B1*
[a] de textu biblie *A*   [b] immo *om. A*   [c] i. et n. *B3 A*   [d] proferatur *B3 A*   [e] ut *om. B3*
[f] tres *om. B1*   [g] et onum a. *B3*   [h] bublie *A*   [i] visitacionis *B1*   [j] meum *B3 A*
[k] quia vera. . .ortum meum *om. A*   [l] decoretur *A*   [m] v. domini s. *B3*   [n] p. eius *A*
[o] fore *B1*   [p] vicium foret. . . littera est *om. A*   [q] p. alia ut *A*   [r] diceretur *om. B3*
[s] in *om. A*   [t] est *om. B1*   [u] accipitur non accipit c. *B1*   [v] l. illius A. *B3*
[w] l. illius ympni Ambrosiani scilicet I. *A*   [x] Implata *B3*   [y] s. quo c. *B1*
[z] dicendo *om. B1*

---

[14] Gen. 18:2 reads: "Cumque elevasset oculos, apparuerunt ei tres viri stantes prope eum; quod cum vidisset, cucurrit in occursum eorum de ostio tabernaculi, et adoravit in terram." Thomas Waleys (Charland, p. 342) explains the citation: "enim illud continetur in quodam responsorio Dominicae in quinquagesima, quod responsorium transsumptum est de Genesi, capitulo 18."

[15] The verse in Cant. 6:10 reads: "Descendi in hortum nucum, ut viderem poma." Ranulph's text is probably an incorrect parallel of the texts of Cant. 5:1 ("Veni in hortum meum") or Eccli. 24:42 ("Rigabo hortum meum").

[16] "Impleta sunt. . .ligno deus" is the third verse of the hymn *Vexilla regis prodeunt* which was used at First Vespers on Passion Sunday. It was attributed to Ambrose during the medieval period but was actually written by Venantius Fortunatus about 610. See F. J. E. Raby, ed., *The Oxford Book of Medieval Latin Verse* (Oxford, 1959), p. 75.

Verumptamen[aa] due cause assignantur quare[ab] themata ignote translacionis[ac] non acceptantur,[ad] quarum[ae] prima est[af] quia proponens talia ignota[ag] videtur[ah] laudem appetere quasi[ai] ipse pre[aj] ceteris[ak] sciat ignota. Secunda causa est quia si hoc[al] permitteretur possent[am] heretici[an] fingere sibi themata, et[ao] imponere alicui translacioni[ap] et sic[aq] errorem inducere.[17] Idcirco videtur quod ipse Christus usus[ar] sit[as] illo themate quod preco suus Iohannes preassumpserat,[at] scilicet: *penitenciam agite.*

Quandoque[au] tamen licitum[av] est aliquas[aw] secundarias dicciones pretermittere[ax] in themate utpote coniuncciones et adverbia, ut si dicamus:[ay] *abiciamus opera tenebrarum* (Rom. 13:12), ibi pretermittitur[az] "ergo," nec viciatur[ba] thema. Item cum vera[bb] littera sit: *nunc* autem *proprior[bc] est nostra salus* (Rom. 13:11), potest dici: *nunc proprior est nostra salus;*[bd] et cum vera[be] littera sit:[bf] *et*[bg] *in via peccatorum non stetit* (Ps. 1:1), illa copula[bh] "et"[bi] poterit dimitti ut per hoc complecior[bj] sit sentencia. Set in[bk] medio thematis talis copula non posset bene dimitti, utpote cum vera littera sit: *sana me domine et sanabor* (Jer. 17:14), non bene posset dici[bl] de[bm] Magdalena: *sana me domine,*[bn] *sanabor.*[18] Set et alie coniuncciones que faciunt proposiciones[bo] ypotheticas ex[bp] quibus dependet complementum[bq] sentencie,[br] non possent bene dimitti neque in principio neque in fine; sed interieccio precedens poterit dimitti dummodo sentencia maneat completa. Unde in[bs] exhortacione ad bellum potest dici:[bt] *consolabor super*

[aa] Virtutum d. *B1*   [ab] quarum *A*   [ac] t. vere n. *B1*   [ad] admittantur *A*   [ae] q. et p. *B3*
[af] est hec *A*   [ag] t. signa v. *B1*   [ah] videntur *A*   [ai] quod i. *A*   [aj] p. pre c. *B1*
[ak] certis *B3*   [al] si homo p. *A*   [am] possunt *A*   [an] hertici *B1*   [ao] t. eciam i. *B3*
[ap] translacionem *B1* : translacione *A*   [aq] sic *om. A*   [ar] visus *B1 B3*   [as] sit *om. B3*
[at] presumpserat *B3* : assumpserat *A*   [au] Quando *B3*   [av] l. licitum e. *B3*
[aw] aliquas *om. B3*   [ax] premittere *B1*   [ay] ut si dicamus *om. B1*   [az] permittitur *B1*
[ba] viceatur *B1*   [bb] c. verba l. *B1*   [bc] nunc autem proprior *om. A* prior *B1*
[bd] potest dici. . .nostra salus *om. B1*   [be] c. verba l. *B1*   [bf] est nostra. . .littera sit *om. A*
[bg] et *om. B3*   [bh] ista copula *A*   [bi] i. vera et *B1*   [bj] compleor *B1*   [bk] in *om. B1*
[bl] dici *om. B1*   [bm] de beata maria m. *A*   [bn] d. et s. *B3 A*   [bo] propositos *B3*
[bp] h. lex q. *B1*   [bq] complementam *B3*   [br] omne n. *B1*   [bs] U. et in *A*
[bt] posset dici *om. B1*

---

[17] Concern about heretical adaptations was common throughout the Middle Ages and there was a new upsurge in the century prior to the rise of the sermon manual. For a listing and description of the many heresies of the twelfth and thirteenth centuries, see the *New Catholic Encyclopedia*, Vol. VI (New York, 1967), pp. 1064-65.

[18] This change, of course, turns the cause-effect relationship of the original quotation into one of volition and is therefore false to the biblical sense of "et sanabor."

hostibus meis [bu] (Is. 1:24), cum tamen vera littera sit: *heu, conso-labor* et [bv] cetera. [bw]

Cetere vero partes sentenciose [bx] non possunt bene dimitti si per *omissionem [by] sentencia mutaretur; [bz] verbi gracia, si in [ca] die pentecostes [cb] sumatur hoc [cc] thema: *venit spiritus sapiencie*, non valeret, quia vera littera est: *venit in me spiritus sapiencie* (Sap. 7:7); tamen [cd] bene valeret si sic <"sapiencie"> [ce] omitteretur dicendo, [cf] *venit in me spiritus*. Similiter non licet mutare verbum [cg] unius temporis [ch] in aliud tempus, ut cum littera [ci] sit: *ascendet pandens iter* [cj] *ante eos* (Mich. 2:13), non bene diceretur [ck] in ascensione: [cl] ascendit *pandens iter ante eos*. [cm] Et non solum variatur quandoque littera biblie [cn] per diccionis omissionem [co] set eciam quandoque pervertitur, ut si [cp] pro *quomodo si* [cq] *dixero vobis* (Ioan. 3:12), dicitur [cr] simpliciter: *si vobis dixero* [cs] *celestia, credetis*. Nam [ct] Christus dixit hec [cu] interogative et [cv] negative quasi [cw] diceret [cx] "non credetis." Unde si [cy] traheretur [cz] ad sensum [da] oppositum, perversio [db] est. [dc] Eadem perversio est quando [dd] aliquid aptatur alicui cum quo [de] non convenit, ut si dicatur in die pasche: surrexit Triphon, [df] eo quod triphon [dg] fuit [dh] pessimus.[19] Item si [di] una significacio transferatur in [dj] aliam in eadem diccione, ut si <in> [dk] die [dl] palmarum [dm] diceretur: *cognovi domine quia* [dn] *equitas* (Ps. 118:75), et exponeretur de equita-cione Christi in asino. Item si [do] de sancto Edmundo [dp] rege [dq]

[bu] m. et *B3*   [bv] s. super et *B3*   [bw] cum tamen. . .et cetera *om. A*
[bx] setenciose *B3* luminose *A*   [by] emissionem *B3*   [bz] muteretur *B1*   [ca] in *om. B3*
[cb] pentecoste *B1 B3*   [cc] hoc *om. A*   [cd] sed *om. B1 A* s. si cum b. *B3*
[ce] "sapiencie" *om. B1 B3 A*   [cf] o. diccio v. *B3 A*   [cg] m. vera u. *A*   [ch] t. eciam ad *B1*
[ci] l. scilicet biblie s. *B3* l. biblie s. *B1 A*   [cj] item *B3*   [ck] didiceretur *B*   [cl] a. Christi *A*
[cm] iter ante eos *om. B3 A*   [cn] bublie *A*   [co] commiscionem *B3* emissionem *A*
[cp] p. quem si *B3*   [cq] q. ut si diceret si *B1*   [cr] dicitur *om. B1 B3 A*
[cs] simpliciter si vobis dixero *om. B1 A*   [ct] Non C. *B1*   [cu] hoc *A*
[cv] et in sensu n. *B3 A*   [cw] quod *A*   [cx] diceret *om. A*   [cy] c. Quod igitur hoc t. *B3 A*
[cz] trahatur *B3 A*   [da] ad suum o. *B3*   [db] peversus *B3*   [dc] est *om. B3*   [dd] q. ad a. *A*
[de] quo *om. B1*   [df] thiphon *A*   [dg] eo quod triphon *om. B1*   [dh] fuerat *A*
[di] Idem dicit si *A*   [dj] t. ad a. *B3 A*   [dk] in *om. B1*   [dl] si de p. *B1*   [dm] plasmatis *B3*
[dn] d. qui e. *B3*   [do] Idem dic si *B3* : Idem dicitur si *A* : I. si die *B1*
[dp] sancti Edmundi *B1*   [dq] rege *om. A*

---

*omissionem : amissionem *H*

---

[19] The text of I Mac. 13:14 reads: "Ut cognovit Tryphon quia surrexit Simon. . ." Higden was probably copying from Basevorn without reference to the biblical source.

sumeretur[dr] *peccatores*[ds] *intenderunt*[dt] *arcum* (Ps. 10:13), et in processu adduceretur auctoritas ab[du] **intenderunt**[20] sub alia significacione qualia sunt:[dv] *intende voci mee* (Ps. 140:1), aut illud: *deus*[dw] *in adiutorium meum intende* (Ps. 69:1). Similiter fit[dx] perversio quando sumitur pars clausule precedentis[dy] incompleta una cum clausula subsequente,[dz] ut si ad penitentes dicatur:[ea] *conpungimini,*[eb] *sacrificate sacrificium iusticie* (Ps. 4:5).

Verumptamen aliqua truncacio[ec] et aliqua[ed] disconveniencia[ee] et aliqua significacionis translacio est licita, dummodo non sit excessiva et nimia; ut[ef] dominica prima[eg] quadragesime dicatur: *graciam*[eh] *dei recipiatis* (II Cor. 6:1), tollerabiliter truncatur quamvis sic sumatur affirmative quod[ei] apostolus dixit[ej] negative. Nam littera apostoli est: *ne in vacuum*[ek] *graciam dei recipiatis*[el] et cetera,[em] ubi duo dicuntur quod[en] scilicet: <"graciam>[eo] recipiunt,"[ep] et "ne in[eq] vacuum recipiant." Similiter si[er] in die[es] pasche[et] diceretur: *surrexit*[eu] *homo et apperuit*[ev] *hostium* (Jud. 19:27), quod ad litteram in libro iudicum dicitur de[ew] levita qui dimisit uxorem suam; inter quem et[ex] Christum, magna est[ey] disconveniencia quantum ad litteram.[ez] Item potest aliquando fieri translacio a[fa] litterali significacione ad moralem, ut si de aliquo martire[fb] diceretur: *percussit petram et fluxerunt aque* (Ps. 77:20), in litterali[fc] sensu[fd] fuit ibi percussio boni hominis; in morali fuit[fe] ibi[ff] percussio mali hominis.

[dr] diceretur p. *A*   [ds] p. enim i. *B3*   [dt] intendunt *B1*   [du] ad *B3 A*   [dv] q. habet
[dw] ad id d. *B3 A*   [dx] sit *B1* patet *B3*   [dy] c. precans i. *B3*   [dz] sequente *A*   [ea] dicitur *A*
[eb] conungimini *B3*   [ec] collacio *B1* : tolleracio *B3*   [ed] aliqua *om. A*
[ee] disconniencia *B3*   [ef] et anima ut *B1* ut si in d. *A*   [eg] prima *om. A*
[eh] d. coram d. *B3*   [ei] s. appetive quia a. *B3*   [ej] dicit *B2 B3 A*   [ek] vacium *B1*
[el] dei recipiatis *om. B3*   [em] et cetera *om. A*   [en] d. quia s. *B1*   [eo] graciam *om. B1*
[ep] recipiant *B1 B3*   [eq] recipient et quod non in *A*   [er] S. sed *B1* si *om. A*   [es] die *om. A*
[et] pasche om. *B3* : pasch *A*   [eu] surrexit *om. A*   [ev] aperit *B1*   [ew] de *om. B1*
[ex] qui dimisit. . .quem et *om. B3* i. aquam et *A*   [ey] erant *A*
[ez] Christum magna. . .ad litteram *om. B3*   [fa] t. in l. *B3*   [fb] marture *B3*   [fc] non l. *B3*
[fd] sensum *A*   [fe] m. sit i. *B1*   [ff] m. vel p. *B3* ibi *om. B3 A*

---

[20] Ranulph employs a method of highlighting certain words in his text which was in common use in scholastic tracts of the later medieval period. In the manuscript *intenderunt* is preceded by "ly"—a kind of pointer. Since its sole function is to signal the word following it, I have not transcribed it but have indicated its presence by rendering the appropriate term in boldface.

IX
Quod thema sufficienter dividatur

Potissime considerandum est quod[a] thema tale [thema] sumatur quod sufficiat divisionibus faciendis:[b] quod[c] satis claret[d] ubi thema continet tria vocabula sentenciosa, sicut ibi *rex tuus*[e] *venit*[f] (Matt. 21:5). Possunt tamen[g] cadere[h] alia vocabula[i] super que divisio non possit[j] nec debeat cadere[k] quales sunt preposiciones,[l] coniuncciones,[m] et hoc verbum "est" quando predicat[n] tertium adiacens et quando "est" *generatur[o] in aliquo[p] verbo, ut si[q] thema esset *iustus*[r] *de angustia liberatus est* (Prov. 11:8), nulla divisio caderet super **est**[s] nec super **de**. Set quando hoc verbum[t] "est"[u] est[v] secundum adiacens et exprimit actum suum proprium substantivum[w] ut[x] ibi, "qui est misit me[21] ad vos"[y] et ibi, *tu autem idem ipse*[z] *es*[aa] (Ps. 101:28), tunc potest divisio cadere super **est**,[ab] ut notetur in eo ydemptitas sive stabilitas[ac] sive uniformitas singularis.[ad]

Quantumcumque[ae] ergo dicciones, dummodo possunt[af] dividi in duo vel in tria membra, sufficit ad propositum; verbi gracia, posito[ag] quod in natale[ah] domini vel[ai] in *annunciacione[aj] esset[ak] thema: *misit deus filium suum factum*[al] *ex muliere, factum sub*

---

[a] e. ut t. *A*   [b] faciendis *om. B3*   [c] q. scilicet dividatur s. *A*   [d] clare *A*   [e] r. tibi p. *A*
[f] venit *om. A*   [g] tamen *om. A*   [h] c. in themate *A*   [i] vocabilia *B1*   [j] posset *B3*
[k] c. in themate q. *A*   [l] proposiciones *B1*   [m] coniuncciones *om. B1*
[n] quando predicat *om. B3* e. quod p. *A*   [o] generaliter *B1 A*   [p] alio *B3 A*
[q] v. et si *B1*   [r] iustus esset *B3*   [s] super EST *om. B3*
[t] S. hoc et verbum est quando predicat *A*   [u] est *om. B3 A*   [v] est *om. A*
[w] sustentium *B3* : substantium *om. A*   [x] s. vel i. *B3*   [y] ad vos *om. A*
[z] ipse *om. B1 B3 A*   [aa] est *B1*   [ab] ES *A*   [ac] y. seu s. *B3 A* sive stabilitas *om. B1*
[ad] singularum *B1*   [ae] igitur *B3 A*   [af] plures *om. B1* sunt d. *B1 B3 A*   [ag] posito *om. B3*
[ah] natali *B1 B3 A*   [ai] d. sive in *B3 A*   [aj] ascencione *B1 B3*   [ak] dominica e. *A*
[al] s. natus *B3*

---

*generatur : generaliter *H*
*annunciacione : ascensione *H*

---

[21] The phrase "qui misit me" occurs frequently in the New Testament; for example, in John 9:4, 12:44, 12:45, 12:49, 13:40, 14:24 and so forth. There is probably some confusion there with the text of John 19:11 ("qui me tradidit tibi") or with some of those that exemplify other forms of the verb "mittere"—perhaps even with John 16:7 "mittam eum ad vos" which follows shortly after one of the illustrations of "qui misit me."

lege, ut eos qui[am] et cetera (Gal. 4:4-5); 17[an] sunt hic dicciones ubi tamen totum potest[ao] dividi in tria, ut[ap] dicatur sic:[aq] hic dicuntur tria nam prenotatur in[ar] medico[as] utilitas[at] inpensa copiose, cum[au] dicitur: *misit*[av] *filium suum*; secundo quomodo medicatur humilitas ostensa virtuose, quia *factum[aw] ex[ax] *muliere, factum*[ay] *sub lege*; tertio[az] quomodo dirivatur utilitas inpensa[ba] fructuose, ibi *eos*[bb] *qui sub lege erant redimeret.* Hic partes dividentes correspondent partibus[bc] divisis, verbi gracia, in **deus** relucet subtilitas, in[bd] **misit**[be] inpensa, in **filium** copiose,[bf] et sic[bg] in aliis membris. Unde nichil deficeret hic etsi hec[bh] tria[bi] tribus auctoritatibus[bj] vel saltem unica auctoritate confirmari possent[bk] in qua vocaliter essent[bl] illa tria vocabula: "deus," "mittere," et[bm] "filius," et sententialiter quod tanta altitudo communicaretur[bn] vobis[bo] ac quia[bp] difficile est reperire tales auctoritates, ideo ut communiter non accipiuntur themata tot diccionum in uno membro.

Contingit quoque aliquando[bq] quod thema contineat duas[br] dicciones[bs] sed cum[bt] tribus convertibiles, ita[bu] quod divisio fiat in tria;[bv] verbi gracia, sit thema de sancto Nicholao:[bw] *crevit puer*[bx] (Gen. 21:8), potest dici sic:[by] hic commendatur Nicholaus a condicione puritatis quia "puer"; a proveccione[bz] dignitatis quia "crevit"; et in utroque a[ca] remuneracione felicitatis quia "puer crevit." Et tunc requiritur quod tertium membrum[cb] habeat aliquam auctoritatem[cc] correspondentem et continentem illa[cd] duo "crevit" <et>[ce] "puer"[cf] cum sentencia eciam[cg] divisionis.[ch]

Usus autem modernus non accipit[ci] prolixa[cj] themata nec in plura dividit quam[ck] in tria, ni forte vulgariter loquendo ad

---

am q. sub lege erant redimeret *B3 A*   an 16 *A*   ao potest *om. B3*   ap ut si d. *A*
aq sic *om. A*   ar p. humilitas in *A*   as modico *B3*   at m. sublimitas *A*   au dum d. *A*
av m. deus f. *A*   ax f. sub m. *A*   ay factum *om. A*   az secundo *A*   ba u. intensa *A*
ba i. ut e.   *B1 B3* i. ut illos q. *A*   bc partibus *om. A* p. revili *B1*
bd in primo membro lucet in *B3* in primo membro in *A*   be MISIT *om. A*
bf cepciose *B1*   bg sic *om. A*   bh hic si hec *B1 B3 A*   bi tria membra possent t. *A*
bj a. confirmari v. *A*   bk confirmari possent *om. A*   bl saltem essent *A*   bm et *om. A*
bn quod tanta altitudo communicaretur *om. B1 B3*   bo vobis *om. B1 B3*
bp v. atque d. *A*   bq aliquando *om. B3*   br tercias d. *A*   bs dicciones *om. B3*
bt s. tamen t. *B3* : s. in t. *A*   bu ista q. *A*   bv f. per tercia membra v. *A*   bw Nichus *B1*
bx c. puer a *A*   by sic *om. A*   bz provencione *B3*   ca a *om. A*
cb q. trium membrorum h. *B1*   cc qualitatem c. *A*
cd c. autem in continentem alia d. *B1* c. vocaliter ista d. *A*   ce et *om. B1 A*
cf p. et c. *A*   cg eciam *om. A*   ch diccionis *B3*   ci accipit *om. B1*
cj prolixas *B3* : proluxa *A*   ck quamquam *B3*

---

*factum : natum *H*

populum sumeretur compendiosum thema de evangelio et in prosequendo ^{cl} exponeretur ^{cm} evangelium ^{cn} per particulas ^{co} sine aliqua subdivisione. ^{cp} Quem quidem ^{cq} modum ^{cr} observat ^{cs} frater Iacobus Ianuensis in ^{ct} collacionibus ^{cu} suis dominicalibus ^{cv} quadragesimalibus,[22] et est iste ^{cw} modus utilis pro plebe. Est iterum ^{cx} alius modus consimilis ^{cy} huic ut si sit thema de apostolis: *duodecim sunt hore* (Ioan. 11:9),[23] statim poterit sic ^{cz} destendi: prima hora diei ^{da} poterit dici ^{db} "Petrus" ^{dc} quibusdam de causis et sic de reliquis. Item poterit thema copula ^{dd} dividi in duo equalia, ut ibi: *abiciamus opera tenebrarum et induamur arma lucis* (Rom. 13:12), ubi notantur duo ad ^{de} que apostolus nos invitat, que ^{df} sunt peccatorum abieccio et virtutum induccio. Et poterit thema esse de una diccione si tamen fuerit explicita implicans ^{dg} plura, ^{dh} presertim si fuerit diccio exhortativa ^{di} quales sunt: "intellige," ^{dj} "considera," "*ite," "predicate," "ambulate." ^{dk} Secus ante foret si diccio non plenum expleret intellectum, ut in ^{dl} purificacione sic ^{dm} sumeretur thema, "lumen."[24] ^{dn}

---

^{cl} et in prosequendo *om. B1*   ^{cm} exponetur *A*   ^{cn} evangelioum *B1*   ^{co} particula *B1*
^{cp} subdiccione *B1*   ^{cq} Q. quid subdivisionis m. *A*   ^{cr} m. sepe o. *A*
^{cs} observandum *B1*   ^{ct} in *om. A*   ^{cu} sermonibus *A*   ^{cv} d. et q. *A*   ^{cw} ist *B3*
^{cx} Item est a. *A*   ^{cy} compendiosus *A*   ^{cz} sic *om. B3*   ^{da} h. die p. *B3*   ^{db} p. diei *B1 B3*
^{dc} Petrus *om. A*   ^{dd} t. continua *B1 B3* : t. copulativum *A*   ^{de} vocantur et ad *B1*
^{df} i. quo s. *B3*   ^{dg} implicans *om. B1*   ^{dh} plene *B1 B3*   ^{di} exhortaria *A*   ^{dj} i. respice *A*
^{dk} a. et huiusmodi *A*   ^{dl} ut si in *B1 B3 A*   ^{dm} sic *om. A* p. beate marie s. *A*
^{dn} l. et c cetera *B3*

---

*ite : item *H*

---

[22] See the *Sermones de sanctis per anni circulum fratris Jacobi de Voragine ordinis predicatorum quondam archiepiscopi Januensis* (Pavia, 1499). The first sermon in this collection (on St. Andrew) fits Ranulph's description: "Tria sunt necessaria cuilibet vero perfecto . . . bonam vitam . . . finalem perseverantiam . . . ab eo nunquam declinet per aliquam culpam." See Thomas Kaeppeli, O.P., *Scriptores Ordinis Praedicatorem Medii Aevi* (Rome, 1970-), #2155.

[23] Using the apostles as tags for a particular twelve-part unit was not uncommon in the Middle Ages and was often employed for articles of the Creed. See James D. Gordon, "The Articles of the Creed and the Apostles," *Speculum*, 40 (1965), 634-40.

[24] The many New Testament references for "lumen" illustrate Ranulph's point; for example, Matt. 6:24, 26, 29; Luke 2:32, 8:16, 11:33, 35, 22:56; John 8:12, 12:35 among others.

X
Quod thema concordancias admittat

Hoc requiritur in themate quod dicciones sentenciosas et pregnantes admittant[a] auctoritates[b] ad quas[c] concordancie auctoritates[d] vocales et reales[e] faciliter[f] adduci possunt.[g] Alioquin fatuus erit predicator qui se[h] nimis artat ad[i] dicciones nimis steriles, ex quo[25] sacra scriptura satis est fecunda ad talia recipienda.[j] Et quamvis antiqui hoc non observaverunt,[k] observetur tamen concordancia vocalis[l] in membris principalibus[m] quamvis in lateralibus;[n] hoc[o] non observetur,[p] verbi gracia, in isto themate unius diccionis, "ambulate"; posset sic dici: triplex est[q] via, scilicet: plana, recta,[r] lucida. De[s] via recta que[t] est mandatorum dei dicitur in mattheo:[u] *rectas facite vias vestras semitas dei* (Matt. 2:3). Certe hec est via que[v] dicitur in[w] ysaia:[x] *ambulate in ea, nec declinabitis ad dexteram neque[y] ad sinistram* (Is. 30:21). Quod hic[z] dicitur de via[aa] non est vocalis concordancia ad "**ambulate**" sed tamen concluditur divisio per unam auctoritatem in qua ponitur[ab] "ambulate"[ac] quod quidem[ad] debet sufficere.[ae] Quod si predicetur in anglico, posset hoc verbum "ire"[af] adduci pro[ag] "ambulare," ex quo est ei convertibile;[ah] verbi gracia, si sic diceretur: ambulandum est primo in via domini libenter propter certam[ai] et iustam remuneracionem matthei 20: *ite et vos in vineam meam et quod iustum fuerit dabo vobis* (Matt. 20:4). Nec[aj] est hoc[ak] viciosum in lingua materna[al] nisi forte[am] litterati adessent qui *intelligerent scripturas et[an] notarent[ao] vocalem disconvenienciam, et[ap] sic forte[aq]

[a] p. contineat *A*   [b] auctoritates *om. A*   [c] a. et communis c. *B1 B3*
[d] auctoritates *om. A*   [e] r. ita quod f. *B1 B3*   [f] facile *A*   [g] est *B1*   [h] q. omni n. *A*
[i] ad ad d. *B1*   [i] s. nimis e. *A*   [j] reperienda *A*   [k] observirent *B3*   [l] v. tam *B1 B3*
[m] in membris literalibus *A*   [n] litteralibus *B3*   [o] hoc *om. B1*   [p] non observetur *om. B1*
[q] est *om. B1*   [r] r. et l. *A*   [s] De *om. A*   [t] que *om. A*   [u] matthaeo 30 *A*
[v] v. sicut d. *B1 B3 A*   [w] in *om. B3 A*   [x] y. 30 *A*   [y] nec *A*
[z] Q. si hic *B1* Quia hii d. *B3*   [aa] via *om. B3*   [ab] ponatur *B1*   [ac] ambulare *A*
[ad] q. quid d. *B3*   [ae] sufficeret *B1*   [af] ire *om. B1 B3*   [ag] per a. *B3*   [ah] c. ut v. *A*
[ai] rectam et *B3*   [aj] Nec *om. B1*   [ak] hoc *om. A*   [al] materna *om. B3*   [am] f. forte l. *B3*
[an] intelligentes scripturam n. *A*   [ao] invocerent *B1*   [ap] et *om. A*   [aq] s. facile s. *B1 B3 A*

*intelligerent : intelligunt *H*

[25] "Ex quo" acts as "ex eo quod" syntactically.

subsannarent ipsum predicantem.

XI
De prothematis extraccione[a]

In usu habebant[b] antiqui proposito[c] themate assumere aliquam aliam auctoritatem pro antethemate habentem concordanciam vocalem cum aliqua[d] diccione thematis sicut patet in sermonibus fratris Guydonys;[26] verbi gracia, posito[e] quod thema sit: *videte quomodo caute ambuletis* (Eph. 5:15), statim assumebant[f] aliam auctoritatem in qua esset "videre" vel "ambulare," sic dicendo *quod vidi narrabo tibi* (Iob 15:17). Et tunc istam[g] auctoritatem secundam[h] aptabant[i] ipsi predicatori vel auditori vel ipsi sermoni vel tribus[j] ipsorum aut duobus,[k] cuius consuetudinis non video necessitatem.

Idcirco[l] moderni decencius faciunt extrahendo prothema de ipso themate[m] aptando sicut iam dictum[n] est.[o] Circa quod notandum est quod quattuor modis[p] solet aptari antethema; ut[q] tangantur in ipso condiciones ipsius predicantis que[r] saltem de congruo inesse[s] debent. Et hec sunt [hec] tria: vita sancta,

---

[a] De prothematis extraccione *om. B1* Quod de eo prothem elici valeat *A*
[b] u. hominis a *A*   [c] proposite *B3*   [d] v. aliqua tamen alia d. *A*   [e] proposito *B1 B3 A*
[f] assumebant *A*   [g] t. illam a. *B1 B3 A*   [h] secundam *om. B3*
[i] aptaban *B3* : aptabunt *A*   [j] v. duobus i. *B3*   [k] v. utriusque i. de d. *A*
[l] Iudaico m. *B3*   [m] i. prothemate a *B1*   [n] i. dicimus *A*   [o] est *om. A*   [p] modus *B1*
[q] et t. *B3* aut ut t. *A*   [r] p. quem *B1*   [s] inesso *B1*

---

[26] The "Guydo" mentioned by both Higden and Basevorn is most probably Guy d'Evreux, O.P., whose sermons were recommended by the University of Paris in 1304. According to Pierre Michaud-Quantin's "Guy d'Evreux, O.P., technicien du sermonnaire médiéval," *Archivum Fratrum Praedicatorum*, 20 (1950), 213-33, Guy had completed his "sermonnaire" by approximately 1293. It rapidly rose in reputation and became a kind of *summa* for the use of preachers; in fact, it was often described simply as a *Summa sermonum dominicalium*. This text's 66 sermons follow contemporary sermon-form: the theme, taken from the Bible, is partitioned and given a protheme followed by a *distinctio* which bears a relationship only to the text cited and not to the liturgical celebration. This distinction might also be subdivided. Guy's treatment of the protheme is the segment of his *summa* which most interests the student of preaching manuals and which, incidentally, most upset a manualist like Robert of Basevorn. For Robert, the sermon was all of a piece; for Guy, the two elements (theme and protheme) were two separate entities with only verbal liaison between them. The list of sermon themes and prothemes used at the University of Paris in 1267-68 shows the popularity of the differences between theme and protheme recommended by Guy; see P. Glorieux, "Sermons universitaires parisiens de 1267-68," *Recherches de théologie ancienne et médiévale*, 16 (1949), 40-71. See Kaeppeli, no. 1400.

solida sciencia,[t] congrua loquela, de quibus dicit psalmo:[u] *bonitatem* vite *et disciplinam* formande[v] loquele[w] *et scienciam* sacre[x] scripture, *doce me*[y] (Ps. 118:65-66). Aut eciam ut tangantur condiciones auditorum que sunt sedulitas verbum[z] dei[aa] audiendi, auditum retinendi, et[ab] retentum exequendi,[ac] de[ad] quibus dicitur in[ae] luca:[af] *beati*[ag] *qui*[ah] *audiunt verbum dei et custodiunt illud* (Luc. 9:28). Aut eciam tanguntur[ai] condiciones ipsius sermonis que fundantur in profunditate sacre scripture, secundum illud ecclesiastici:[aj] *ego in altissimis*[ak] habito[al] (Eccli. 24:7). Et tunc implorandum[am] est divinum auxilium propter sermonis altitudinem, propter auditoris et predicatoris[an] necessitatem. Quarto ut solum[ao] fiat divini auxilii imploracio et si placuerit[ap] beate Marie[aq] opiculacio, secundum illud iudith 3:[ar] *ora pro nobis quoniam*[as] *mulier sancta es* (Iud. 8:20).

Si igitur thema[at] sit[au] de aliquo sancto que[av] sit unius diccionis[aw] quale est "intellige," sic poterit antethema elici secundum Gregorium in omelia de pentecoste: nemo docenti homini recte tribuit[ax] quod ex ore docentis intelligit, nisi[ay] assit qui interius doceat lingua exterius, in vanum laborat et cetera[az] (*XL Homiliarum in evangelia*, Liber II, hom. xxx). Ex qua auctoritate patet quod in predicacione fructifica[ba] tria requiruntur, scilicet:[bb] summus doctor—deus[bc]—interius erudiens, verbis doctoris auditor[bd] obediens, et ipsa doctrina[be] utilis[bf] et proficiens,[bg] que tria[bh] evangelium[bi] luce 24,[bj] comprehendit dicens: *apperuit illis sensum ut* intelligant[bk] scripturas (Luc. 24:45). "Apperuit" inquid ecce primum, scilicet, magister intus[bl] erudiens qui scilicet: *aperit et nemo claudit*, apocalypsis secundo (Apoc. 3:7). Clausa est enim scriptura sacra per secretorum misteria[bm] sed aperta[bn] per predicancium ministeria,[bo] quia *declaracio sermonum tuorum*[bp] *dat*[bq] *intellectum*[br] (Ps. 118:130). Secundo[bs] requiritur auditor obediens alioquin[bt] non[bu] intelligeret. Ideo dicitur "ut[bv] intelligerent"

---

[t] sciencia et c. *A*   [u] d. psalmista bonitatem fecisti cum servo tuo b. *A*
[v] formose *B1 B3*   [w] loquele *om. B1 B3*   [x] sacram *B3*   [y] me *om. A*   [z] s. verbi *A*
[aa] dei *om. A*   [ab] et *om. A*   [ac] r. exequendite *B1*   [ad] de *om. B1*   [ae] in *om. A*
[af] luca XI *A*   [ag] beati *om. B3*   [ah] q. bene a. *B3*   [ai] A. et ut tangantur c. *A*
[aj] e. 24 *B3 A*   [ak] altissimo *A*   [al] habito *om. B1*   [am] implendum *B1 B3*
[an] predicantis n. *A*   [ao] solum *om. A*   [ap] p. domini *A*   [aq] matris o. *A*   [ar] 9 *A*
[as] quia m. *A*   [at] thema *om. A*   [au] sit *om. B1 B3 A*   [av] que *om. B1 B3 A*
[aw] u. condiccionis q. *B3* d. thema q. *A*   [ax] t. nisi q. *A*   [ay] n. enim a. *A*
[az] et cetera *om. A*   [ba] fructifera *A*   [bb] scilicet *om. A*   [bc] deus *om. A*
[bd] conditor o. *B3*   [be] et ipsa doctrina *om. B3*   [bf] sit utilis *B3*   [bg] perficiens *B1 B3*
[bh] q. scilicet e. *B1*   [bi] evangelizata *A*   [bj] luce 14 *B1*   [bk] intelligerent *A*
[bl] m. interius *B1 B3*   [bm] ministeria *A*   [bn] m. scilicet aperat p. *B1*   [bo] misteria *B3 A*
[bp] tuorum *om. A*   [bq] da *B1*   [br] i. secundum psalmum 20 *A*   [bs] secundo *om. B1 A*
[bt] aliquem *B3*   [bu] non *om. B1*   [bv] d. nam ut *A*

unde dicitur in [bw] ecclesiastico: [bx] *esto mansuetus ad audiendum* ut intelligas (Eccli. 5:13). Tertio requiritur quod ipsa doctrina sit utilis et proficiens, et ideo condit [by] scripturas non truffas, [bz] de quibus dicitur [ca] ad timotheum: [cb] *omnis scriptura divinitus inspirata utilis est ad docendum* et cetera [cc] (II Tim. 3:16); Glossa: [cd] "ad [ce] docendum"[27] [cf] nescientes [cg] pro primo, ad [ch] arguendum necgligentes pro secundo, ad increpandum [ci] vanis insistentes pro tertio. Set illa tria que dixi, non confido me ex me posse perficere [cj] sed ex [ck] domino deo habere, de quo [cl] *sapiencie [cm] dicit: [cn] *qui confidunt in domino, intelligent veritatem* (Sap. 3:9). [co] Rogemus ergo [cp] more solito *ut deus aperiat [cq] vobis ostium sermonis* sui, [cr] sicut dicitur ad colossenses (Col. 4:3), quatinus sic *psallam [cs] et intelligam* cum psalmista (Ps. 100:1), ad suam et huius [ct] sancti commendacionem, ut [cu] sicut sacra [cv] scriptura dicit: flumina [cw] de nobis immo pocius in vos fluant aque vive, id est, [cx] gracie;[28] et quod [cy] ita sit dicat [cz] quilibet [da] illud psalmi: *da michi intellectum ut sciam testimonia tua* (Ps. 118:125).

Quod [db] si thema sit plurium [dc] diccionum, eliciatur antethema sic: sit thema, *iustus de [dd] angustia liberatus est* (Prov. 11:8). Secundum Gregorium (*Epistolae*, Liber IX, 52), Christus bona et vera docuit et tamen [de] mala pertulit; [df] set semper iste [dg] qui [dh]

[bw] in *om. A*   [bx] e. quinto *A*   [by] p. ideo concludit s. *A*   [bz] truffas *om. B3*   [ca] d. 2 ad *A*
[cb] t. 4 *A*   [cc] et cetera *om. B3 A*   [cd] Glossa *om. B3*   [cf] ad docendum *om. B3 A*
[cg] nescientes *om. A*   [ch] p. ad ad a. *B1*   [ci] ad crepandum v. *B1*   [cj] proficere *A*
[ck] ysaias d. *B1 B3*   [cl] quo *om. B1*   [cm] s. 3 *A*   [cn] dicit *om. A*   [co] Igitur r. *A*
[cp] ergo *om. A*   [cq] apperuit *A*   [cr] sui et s. *B1*   [cs] spallam *A*
[ct] et humanam s. *B1* et habemus s. *B3*
[cu] et ad sancti huius commendacionem ut *A* commendacionis *B1*
[cv] sacra *om. B1 B3 A*   [cw] flamine *B3*   [cx] v. et g. *B1 B3*   [cy] quid *B3*   [cz] dicta *B3*
[da] quibus *B1* quilibet *om. A*   [db] Quod *om. A*   [dc] plurimum *B1*   [dd] de *om. B3*
et cum m. *A*   [df] docuit et tamen mala pertulit *om. B1*   [dg] s. ille q. *B3*
[dh] Set semper iste qui est *om. B1*

---

*sapiencie : ysayas *H*

---

[27] The appearance of the term "Glossa" here points to the kinds of assistance and explication provided by the commentaries on sacred scripture—the most common one being the *Glossa Ordinaria*—which have survived in many forms from the medieval centuries. Ranulph is, however, using his Basevorn source very heavily in this passage; cf. Charland, pp. 256-57.

[28] Reminiscent of Apoc. 21:6 ("Ego sitienti dabo de fonte aquas vitae gratia") and John 4:14 ("sed aqua quam ego dabo ei fiet in eo fons aquae salientis in vitam aeternam").

est *adiutor*[di] *in*[dj] *oportunitatibus* (Ps. 9:10) eum[dk] confortavit. Sic est de Christi imitatoribus, id est, predicatoribus,[dl] quorum triplex condicio exprimitur in hiis verbis que sunt "doctrine serenitas,"[dm] "pressure ferocitas," et[dn] "medele vicinitas." Pro primo dicitur proverbiorum 20: *labia iusti erudiunt*[do] *plurimos* (Prov. 10:21), et illud psalmi:[dp] *corripiet me*[dq] *et*[dr] *increpabit me; oleum autem peccatoris*—id est,[ds] adulacio—*non inpinguet*[dt] <*caput meum*> (Ps. 140:5), id[du] est, non excecet[dv] rationem meam. De secundo,[dw] id est, "pressure ferocitate,"[dx] dicitur[dy] iob:[dz] *lampas*[ea] *contempta apud cogitaciones divitum*[eb] (Iob 12:5). "lampas"[ec] propter lucidam doctrinam,[ed] set "contempta" propter illicitam[ee] contumeliam. Pro hiis duobus dicitur sapientis[ef] 5: *stabunt iusti in magna constancia adversus eos*[eg] et cetera (Sap. 5:1). Set quantumcumque[eh] seviat persecucionum pressura, superhabundat consolacionum,[ei] "medela," quod est tertium pretactum[ej] cui attestatur psalmo:[ek] *clamaverunt iusti et dominus exaudivit eos* (Ps. 33:18). Ergo clament[el] iusti per sinceram[em] doctrinam,[en] quod est primum; et de omnibus tribulacionibus eorum[eo] illatis per[ep] pressuram,[eq] quod est secundum; liberabit eos dominus per assistentem graciam, quod est tercium. Clamemus et nos more solito per oracionem pro ista gracia impetranda, et procul dubio dominus exaudiet,[er] qui teste psalmo[es] exquirentes eum exaudit *et ex omnibus tribulacionibus*[et] et[eu] cetera (Ps. 33:5). Et[ev] hic vide quod in virtute istius[ew] vocabuli "iustus" non includitur doctrine serenitas,[ex] quia aliquis potest esse iustus quamvis non doceat, et econtra[ey] poterit recta docere et non esse[ez] iustus. Set auctoritas correspondens[fa] huic membro non exprimit quod predicatores sustinent angustias, nec[fb] hoc implicat, set alludit secundo membro et[fc] hoc sufficit. Similiter auctoritas adducta pro tertio membro non plus tangit predicatores quam alios, tamen artificialiter

---

[di] auditor *A*   [dj] a. in tribulacionibus in o. *A*   [dk] cum c. *B3*   [dl] predicacionibus *B1*
[dm] d. severitas p. *B3*   [dn] et *om. A*   [do] l. iustidiunt p. *B3*   [dp] psalmiste *A*
[dq] me *om. A*   [dr] me iustus et *A*   [ds] p. et a. *B1 B3*   [dt] inpugnet *B1 B3 A*
[du] i. capit meum id *B3 A*   [dv] exerecet *B1* : excecabit *A*   [dw] s. dicitur *A*
[dx] feroritate *B1*   [dy] dicitur *om. A*   [dz] job 12 *A*   [ea] l. accensa *A*
[eb] apud cogitaciones divitum *om. A*   [ec] lampas *om. B1 B3 A*
[ed] propter lucidam doctrinam *om. B1 B3*   [ee] p. illucidam *A*   [ef] d. capite 5 *B3*
[eg] adversus eos *om. A*   [eh] quamcumque *A*   [ei] consacionum *B1*   [ej] pertactum *B1 B3*
[ek] psalmista *B3 A*   [el] Ergo et clamant i. *B1*   [em] miseram d. *B3*
[en] cinsera doctrina q. *B1*   [eo] eorum *om. A*   [ep] per *om. A*   [eq] illicitis pressuram *A*
[er] exauadiet *B1*   [es] q. iuste teste psalmista e. *A*   [et] t. eorum eripiet eos *A*
[eu] et cetera *om. A*   [ev] Et *om. B1 B3 A*   [ew] v. huius v. *A*   [ex] severitas *A*
[ey] et eciam *B3* : et econverso *A*   [ez] est *A*   [fa] correspondis *B3*   [fb] non hoc *A*
[fc] a. tercium membrum et *A*

coaptatur.

Potest eciam [fd] antethema planius [fe] et levius [ff] elici de ipso themate quando est plurium diccionum et sine aliqua introduccione. Isto [fg] modo sit thema de aliquo [fh] sancto, *acceptus est regi minister intelligens* (Prov. 14:35), [fi] si dicatur [fj] sic: tria debent esse in predicatore, scilicet: [fk] humilitas [fl] eximia quod notatur ibi [fm] "minister" [fn] quia [fo] predicator debet esse humilis in gestu, in ornatu, et [fp] in comitatu; aliter enim [fq] non serviret ei qui venit *ministrare et* [fr] *non ministrari* (Matt. 20:28); contra quod faciunt multi qui [fs] in gestu pompose, [ft] in ornatu curiose, [fu] et [fv] in [fw] comitatu superflue [fx] se habent, [fy] unde tales pocius deberent dici ministri Antechristi quam Christi, [fz] luce 23: [ga] vos autem [gb] non sic [gc] sed *qui maior est vestrum* fiat [gd] sicut *minister* (Matt. 23:11). Secundo debet esse [ge] in predicatore dei familiaritas et complacencia, quod notatur ibi "acceptus est regi"; ad quod requiritur vite mundicia, thobie 12: *acceptus* erat [gf] *deo* (Tob. 12:13). <Tercio debet esse in ipso scripturarum intelligencia nam ibi "intelligens,"> [gg] nam predicare et non intelligere periculum est eversionis et erroris, iob 33: *viri intelligentes loquantur* (Iob 34:34), sed aliter non, proverbiis 5: *si est tibi intellectus* [gh] *responde proximo tuo* (Eccli. 5:14); sed ad timotheum 1 dicitur quod *quidam aberrantes* [gi] *conversi sunt in* [gj] *vaniloquium, non intelligentes neque que* [gk] *loquuntur, neque de quibus affirmant* (I Tim. 1:6-7). Idcirco quia in hiis tribus [gl] sencio me [gm] insufficientem rogo [gn] et cetera.

Aliquando autem [go] antethema non elicitur de ipso themate, nec de aliqua [gp] auctoritate sed introducitur per aliquod vulgare dictum; verbi gracia, qui [gq] igne indiget, digito vel manu vadit illum querere, [gr] sed nos indigemus igne spiritus sancti, ergo et [gs] cetera.[29] Alio modo ut [gt] statim proposito themate sive aliquo adiuncto [gu]

[fd] P. cum a. *A*   [fe] plenius *B1 B3*   [ff] et levius *om. B1*   [fg] Illo m. *B3*   [fh] de aquo s. *B3*
[fi] i. et *A*   [fj] dicitur *A* : dicunt *B1*   [fk] p. si *B1*   [fl] humilitas *om. B3*   [fm] in m. *A*
[fn] minister *om. B1 B3*   [fo] quod B3 *A*   [fp] et *om. A*   [fq] enim *om. A*   [fr] et *om. A*
[fs] quia *A*   [ft] pomposio *A*   [fu] curioso *A*   [fv] et *om. A*   [fw] in *om. B3*   [fx] superfluo *A*
[fy] debent *B3*   [fz] Christi *om. B1*   [ga] 21 *A*   [gb] autem *om. B3*   [gc] sicut *B3*
[gd] v. stat s. *B1*   [ge] esse *om. B1*   [gf] est *B1 B3 A*
[gg] Tercio debet. . .ibi intelligens *om. B1 B3*   [gh] e. ibi intelligens r. *A*   [gi] operantes *A*
[gj] s. ad v. *A*   [gk] que *om. A*   [gl] duobus *B1*   [gm] ne *A*   [gn] rogare *A*   [go] A. enim a. *A*
[gp] a. alia a. *B3*   [gq] q. communiter dicitur qui *A*   [gr] quere *B3*   [gs] s. ideo et *A*
[gt] Alius modus est ut *A*   [gu] s. anglico iniuncto d. *B1*

---

[29] Siegfried Wenzel has identified this proverb from John of Wales' *Ars predicandi*, MS, Bodley 571, fol. 165 va. John seems to be using a French source for his translation.

divinum auxilium invocetur, [gv] ne forte prolixitate prothematis [gw] impediatur utilis prosecucio ipsius [gx] sermonis. Idcirco signanter dicitur in secundo libro machabeorum: *stultum est ante historiam* [gy] *effluere,* et [gz] *ipsa historia succingi,* id est, [ha] succincte procedere (II Mac. 2:33).

XII
De oracionis premissione et gracie imploracione [a]

Consueverunt [b] nonnulli post thema propositum statim premittere [c] oracionem, et hoc quidem bene; nam secundum Platonem in thimeo: [d] et [e] in minimis eciam rebus debet divinum auxilium invocari [f] (*Thimaeo,* 27c). Cum nec [g] minima sine eius influencia fieri [h] possunt, [i] quanto magis in hoc maximo negocio, prout dicit Boecius, de consolacione.[30] Si ista [j] solebant quidem [k] facere ante [l] incepcionem [m] thematis, [n] sicut legitur de beato Francisco, quod statim offerebat pacem suis auditoribus dicens: "pax vobis."[31] In hoc enim [o] secutus est [p] Christum magistrum suum qui docebat [q] in [r] luca: [s] *in quamcumque* [t] *domum intraveritis, dicite "pax huic domui"* et cetera (Luc. 10:5). Similiter in veteri lege [u] dominus docuit filios Israel urbes expungnaturos [v] prius pacem offerre [w] (cf. Deut. 20:10). [x] Sic decet [y] predicatores facere [z] qui intendunt expugnare cubilia peccatorum, sicut suadet Augustinus, [in] [aa] de [ab] doctrina christiana (Liber IV, cap. xv), quod predicator debet prius esse orator quam doctor, [ac] pro se et [ad] aliis, pro [ae] quibus accepit, [af] id est, [ag] didicit.

[gv] invocatur *A*   [gw] p. thematis i. *B3 A*   [gx] ipsis *B1*   [gy] historia *B3 A*
[gz] et in i. *B1 B3 A*   [ha] s. et s. *B3*   [a] et gracie imploracione *om. A*   [b] Posuerunt *B1*
[c] promitere *B1*   [d] themeon *B3*   [e] et *om. A*   [f] divini invori *B1*
[g] nec et *B3* n. unam *A*   [h] fleri *B3* : fiero *A*   [i] possit *A*   [j] Sed illa *B1 B3* : Si istud *A*
[k] q. statim f. *B1 B3 A*   [l] f. sive i. *A*   [m] in concepcione *A*   [n] thematis *om. A*
[o] enim *om. B1 B3 A*   [p] est *om. A*   [q] dicebat *A*   [r] in *om. A*   [s] luca 10 *A*
[t] i. primum d. *A*   [u] legitur testamento d. *A*   [v] expungnatores *B1 A*   [w] offerere *B1*
[x] o. nimirum p. *A*   [y] Sic decet *om. A* dicet *B1*   [z] f. debent q. *A*   [aa] in *om. B1 B3 A*
[ab] A. libro de *A*   [ac] dator *B3*   [ad] et pro a. *B1 B3 A*   [ae] a. a q. *A*   [af] recepit *A* a. et *B1*
[ag] est *om. B3*

---

[30] Probably a reference to Book III, meter ix or to prose ix of the same book.

[31] St. Francis of Assisi's first Rule (1210) incorporates this directive in its seventh section. The Rule of 1223 also advocated conciseness; see Omer Englebert, *Saint Francis of Assisi,* tr. Edward Hutton (London, 1950), pp. 247 ff.

Set moderno tempore magis solitum est primo thema proponere et de illo antethema[ah] elicere, et super illud tam pacem quam graciam invocare, sicut legitur Paulus[ai] fecisse ubi dicit: gracia et pax sit[aj] vobis;[32] verbi[ak] gracia, posito[al] quod thema sit: *fons ascendebat de*[am] *terra* (Gen. 3:6), statim post thema[an] propositum <est>: pax et gracia illius de cuius corde et[ao] latere emanavit fons ad[ap] faciendam pacem mutuo inter deum et hominem—sic[aq] nobiscum—in hoc quod dicit "nobiscum," implicat se cum nobis.[ar]

Si ergo oracio non formetur[as] ante thematis prosecucionem,[at] reputatur presumptuosum ac[au] indoctum. Debet autem[av] oracio[aw] ista[ax] dependere ex precedentibus, sic sit thema: *dirigite*[ay] *viam domini* (Ioan. 1:23). Elicito et prosecuto inde[az] antethemate, incipiatur[ba] oracio super illud "dirigite" sic:[bb] dirigite[bc] ad illum[bd] preces quia sic edocemur[be] ecclesiastici 37: fili,[bf] *in hiis*[bg] *omnibus deprecare*[bh] *altissimum ut dirigat in veritate viam tuam* (Eccli. 37:19); et huius assignatur causa,[bi] ieremie 4:[bj] *non est* nota *via eius nec*[bk] vir[bl] *ut ambulet et dirigat gressus suos* (Ier. 10:23). Iste est modus oxoniensis;[33] [bm] sed modus parysiensis[bn] talis est: videmus experimentaliter[bo] quod si[bp] aliqua[bq] res rubea sulphure[br] fumigetur,[bs] fetet[bt] et perdit[bu] colorem,[bv] que[bw] si iterum fumigetur[bx] thure, recuperat colorem.[34] Moraliter,[by] fumus sulphuris[bz] est peccatum de quo psalmo[ca]

[ah] antethoma *B3*   [ai] Paulum *A*   [aj] sit *om. A*   [ak] verbi *om. A*   [al] vobis ut posito *A*
[am] a. e t. *A*   [an] p. subiungatur p. *A*   [ao] vel l. *A*   [ap] f. gracie ad *A*   [aq] sic *om. B1 B3*
[ar] se et alios *A*   [as] foretur *A*   [at] persecucionem *B1 A*   [au] p. aut i. *B1 B3 A*
[av] autem *om. A*   [aw] oracio *om. B1*   [ax] illa *B1 B3*   [ay] dirigete *B1*   [az] persecuto in a. *A*
[ba] foretur *A*   [bb] sic sic *B1*   [bc] dirigamus *A*   [bd] ad enim p. *A*
[be] edocemus *B3* docemur *A*   [bf] fili *om. A*   [bg] hiis *om. B1 B3*   [bh] deprecars *A*
[bi] causa *om. B1 B3*   [bj] i. 10 *A*   [bk] e. hominis v. *A*   [bl] viri *A*   [bm] m. ex mensus s. *A*
[bn] parisiencium *A*   [bo] experimentum *B1 B3*   [bp] si *om. A*   [bq] aliqua *om. A*
[br] rosa si fungetur sulphure *A*   fungetur *B3* : fumigetur et *B1*
[bt] perfetet *B1* : fetit *B3* rubes fetet *A*   [bu] e. palescit *A*   [bv] colorem *om. A*
[bw] que *om. B1 B3*   [bx] i. fungar t. *A*   [by] moraliter *A*   [bz] sulphurus *B1*   [ca] psalmista *A*

---

[32] This phrase or a similar one forms part of Paul's greeting in his letters to the Romans (1:7), Corinthians (I Cor. 1:3; 11-1:2), Ephesians (1:2), Philippians (1:2), Colossians (1:3), Thessalonians (1:2), and Galatians (1:3), and to Timothy, Titus, and Philemon.

[33] In this, as in other parts of the thematic sermon's construction, the *modus Oxoniensis* is more tightly structured then the Parisian.

[34] The Parisian mode illustrated here seems to make use of a kind of *divisio extra* even in the drawing up of the prayer; that is, a relationship is prepared in view of the principal work in the theme, but that word is not immediately brought into prominence. For a discussion of *divisio extra*, see above.

dicit:[cb] **pluet super peccatores laqueos*[cc] *ignis, sulphur* et cetera[cd]
(Ps. 10:7). Fumus incensi[ce] est oracio cuius vox[cf] sursum ascendit
directe non curve,[cg] unde in[ch] psalmo:[ci] *dirigatur*[cj] *oracio mea*[ck]
sicut[cl] *incensum in conspectu tuo* (Ps. 140:2).

Et potest in principio interpretacio[cm] formari quamvis non
dependeat ab ipso themate, ut si dicatur quamvis[cn] aliquis visum
habeat dummodo[co] ipsum visibile sit presens, tamen absente
lumine non potest[cp] videre.[35] Sic nec anima quamvis sit potens
intelligere, tamen[cq] sine gracia mediante[cr] nichil proficit,[cs] ut
habetur[ct] iohannis 15:[cu] *sine me nichil potestis facere* (Ioan. 15:5).
Ideo in principio rogemus.[cv]

XIII
De auditorum alleccione[a]

Expedit in[b] principio predicatori ut[c] quantum poterit[d] deo
inoffenso[e] auditores reddat[f] benivoles et attentos[g] ad audiendum
et sollicitos ad exequendum,[h] quod quidem fieri potest multis
modis.[36] Uno modo primo[i] proponatur[j] aliquod[k] insolitum et
subtile[l] et curiosum, utpote de aliquo mirabili[m] autentico quod
ad propositum trahi possit et allicere auditores; verbi gracia, si
thema sit: *fons ascendebat de terra* (Gen. 2:6), adduci potest illud
quod[n] narrat Giraldus *Cambrensis[o] in *topographia Hibernie

---

[cb] dicit *om. A*   [cc] laqueos *om. B1*   [cd] cetera *om. A*   [ce] i. et *A*   [cf] v. natura s. *A*
[cg] n. obloquium u. *A*   [ch] in *om. A*   [ci] psalmista *A*   [cj] dirigetur *B1*   [ck] mea *om. A*
[cl] o. in sacro i. *B1*   [cm] p. illa predicacio f. *A* p. imprecaccio f. *B1 B3*
[cn] non dependeat. . .dicatur quamvis *om. A*   [co] h. et i. *A*   [cp] a. luce non poterit v. *A*
[cq] i. et ipsum verum sit intelligibile cum s. *A*   [cr] mediate *B1* : meditante *A*
[cs] possunt *B1* : potest *B3* : prosit *A*   [ct] ut habetur *om. A*   [cu] j. 3 *A*   [cv] rogare et *A*
[a] eleccione *B3* De auditorum alleccione *om. A*   [b] in *om. A* E. ut p. *A*
[c] predicator in q. *A*   [d] possit *A*   [e] deo inoffenso *om. A*   [f] reddunt *B1*   [g] aptos *B1 B3*
[h] et sollicitos ad exequendum *om. A*   [i] primo *om. B3*   [j] m. ut si primo preponatur *A*
[k] aliquid *A*   [l] insolitum subtile *A*   [m] mirabiliantur *B1*   [n] quod *om. A*
[o] Cambensis *B1 B3* Giraldo Cambreum *A*

---

*pluet : pluit *H*
*Cambrensis : Cambensis *H*
*topographia : tripographia *H*

---

[35] Possible references here to John 12:35 ("Ambulate dum lucem habetis") and Ps. 35:10
("In lumine tuo, videbimus lumen").

[36] This is quite similar to the Ciceronian definition of the "exordium"; see Cic., *De inventione*, 1, 20.

de quodam fonte in Cicilia, ad quem fontem^p accessit^q quis rubea veste indutus,^r statim educebatur^s aqua de fonte que tamen ad omnes alias *viros manet^t invicta.^u [37] *Iste fons Christus est^v de quo in ecclesiastico^w dicitur: *fons sapiencie verbum dei in excelsis*^x (Eccli. 1:5), ad quem accedens rubea veste indutus,^y id est^z Christus,^{aa} passo compaciens^{ab} attrahet aquam vivam gracie.[38] Nam Christi sanguine fluente *petre*^{ac} *scisse sunt et terra mota*^{ad} (Matt. 27:51), multo magis deberent corda vestra ad^{ae} clamorem verbi dei^{af} moveri et scindi nisi forsan sint saxis duriora (cf. Ioel 2:13). Ad idem^{ag} eciam^{ah} valet^{ai} quando signatur^{aj} causa alicuius dicti ignoti,^{ak} ut si dicatur^{al} quare oculus non^{am} est alicuius determinati coloris,^{an} quia si sic esset talem colorem^{ao} solummodo reciperet qualis coloris ipse^{ap} oculus esset^{aq} et tot oporteret esse sensus quot colores. Et potest hoc applicari ad peccatores, potissime ad avaros et lubricos,^{ar} qui effectum verbi dei non^{as} recipiunt eo quod determinetur^{at} ad eius oppositum.

Alius modus est^{au} terrere^{av} auditores in principio aliqua narracione^{aw} vel exemplo^{ax} terribili,^{ay} sicut narrat Iacobus de *Vitriaco^{az} quod qui nuncquam^{ba} voluit audire sponte^{bb} verbum dei, quo tantumdem de^{bc} mortuo et ad ecclesiam^{bd} ad

---

^pfontem *om. A*   ^qsi accederit q. *A*   ^rinductus *B1*   ^ss. obtulit a *A*
^to. alios colores manent *A*   ^uinmota *B1 B3 A*   ^vest *om. B1*   ^win esset d. *B1*
^xexcelso *B1*   ^yindictus *B1*   ^zi. et C. *B1* : i. in C. *B3*   ^{aa}Christo *B3 A*
^{ab}p. id est compacies *A*   ^{ac}f. pene s. *B3*   ^{ad}mota est *A*   ^{ae}c. nostra ad *A*
^{af}d. magis m. *A*   ^{ag}illud *B1*   ^{ah}eciam *om. B1 B2 B3 A*   ^{ai}e. videlicet q. *B1 B2 A*
^{aj}assignatur *A*   ^{ak}ignorati *B3*   ^{al}dicitur *B2 A*   ^{am}non *om. B2*   ^{an}coloris *om. B1*
^{ao}colorum *A*   ^{ap}c. ille o. *A*   ^{aq}foret *A*   ^{ar}libricos *B2*   ^{as}d. nihil r. *A*
^{at}determinentur *B3 A*   ^{au}est *om. B1 B2 B3*   ^{av}t. ipsos a. *B1 A*   ^{aw}narracionem *A*
^{ax}vel exemplo *om. B3*   ^{ay}n. terribili vel exemplo s. *A*
^{az}Viciato *B1 B2 B3* V. de quodam q. *A*   ^{ba}nuncquam *om. B2*   ^{bb}sponte *om. B3*
^{bc}q. causa de *B1* q. tandem m. *B3 A*   ^{bd}in ecclesia *A*

---

*viros : vires *H*
*Iste : Ista *H*
*Vitriaco : Viciato *H*

---

[37] The citation is from the chapter entitled "De duobus Britannie scilicet Armorice et Scicilie fontibus admirandis" in *Giraldis Cambrensis in Topographia Hibernie*, ed. John J. O'Meara, *Proceedings of the Royal Irish Academy*, Vol. 52, Section C, no. 4 (Dublin, 1949), p. 139.

[38] Isaias 63:2 and 1:18 underlie this passage.

sepeliendum delato, dum sacerdos inciperet commendacionem mortuorum, ymago crucifixi que[be] stabat inter navem ecclesie et chorum, avulsis clavis manuum suarum, obturavit aures proprias, ne audiret oracionem pro mortuo[bf] factam qui dum viverit[bg] noluit audire verbum dei[bh] crucifixi. Ad idem faciunt alie narraciones continentes quomodo Christus apparens cuidam cepit[bi] in palma sua[bj] sanguinem de latere[bk] suo et proiecit[bl] in[bm] faciem eiusdem[bn] indurati[bo] dicens: "iste sanguis quem modo[bp] induratus[bq] contempnis[br] testificabitur contra te in die iudicii"; et compertum est postmodum quod sanguis ille[bs] sic proiectus[bt] nulla potuit arte deleri,[bu] sed mansit in corpore defuncti[bv] et sepulti.[39] Alius modus[bw] est ostendere quomodo[bx] qui libenter audiunt[by] verbum dei habilitantur[bz] ad multa commoda.

XIV
De thematis introduccione [et cetera][a]

Secundum modum[b] modernorum post oracionem factam[c] resumendum est thema, quod notandum[d] est quantum ad[e] librum de quo sumitur et eciam quantum ad capitulum sicut prius fiebat in principio. Nec[f] requiritur omnino[g] quod[h] plus connotetur quoad capitulum[i] in reliquis locis nisi forte professor[j] in theologia[k] voluerit omnia connotare exquisite,[l] nec decet quod ab aliquo sic conmuni[m] cotetur diminute[n] sicut: "dicit scriptura." Immo liber de[o] quo sumitur auctoritas debet cotari.[p]

[be] qui s. *A*   [bf] mortuis *A*   [bg] venirit *B1* : vixit *A*   [bh] dei *om. A*   [bi] cespit *B3*
[bj] incepit palam suam s. *A*   [bk] latero *B1 B2*   [bl] iecit *B1*   [bm] in illius f. *A*
[bn] eiusdem om. *A*   [bo] indirati *A*   [bp] s. quomodo modo i. *B2*   [bq] indurat *A*
[br] c. stabit *B3*   [bs] s. iste *B1*   [bt] priectus *A*   [bu] delere *A*   [bv] defuncto *B1*
[bv] m. et in corupus sepulti sed in confessis et contritis delebatur *A*   [bw] modis *B1*
[bx] quomo *B3* o. quem diabolus nititur impedire homines ab auditu verbi dei et alius modus est ostendere quod q. *A*   [by] audit *A*   [bz] habilitatur *A*
[a] De modo introducendi thema *A*   [b] modum *om. B3*   [c] o. perfectam r. *B3*
[d] cotadum *B1* : cotandum *B3* : connotandum *A*   [e] e. quam ad *B1*
[f] Nec *om. B1 B2 B3*   [g] omnia *B2 A*   [h] quod *om. B3*   [i] capitula *A*
[j] processor *B3* : professori *A*   [k] t. qui v. *A*   [l] exquisite *om. B1*   [m] conmuni *om. A*
[n] dimitte *B1*   [o] l. saltem de *A*   [p] a. decotari *B3*

---

[39] Sources in which the second exemplum—"The Knight unrepentant at death"—appears are listed in Frederic C. Tubach, *Index Exemplorum*, F F Communications, no. 204 (Helsinki, 1969), 2960. The first is also attributed to Jacques de Vitry, the renowned exempla creator, in *Jacob's Well*, ed. A. Brandeis, EETS, O.S. no. 115 (London, 1900), p. 110.

Immo[q] resumpto themate potest introduccio[r] fieri multis modis utpote per scripturam, per argumentum, per exemplarem manuduccionem,[40] per simile in natura,[s] per[t] vulgare dictum; verbi gracia, de primo[u] sit thema: *nupcie facte[v] sunt in Chana Galilee* (Ioan. 2:1). Sedundum Augustinum verba sacre scripture quadruplicem habent intellectum, scilicet: historialem,[w] tropologicum, allegoricum,[x] et anagogicum;[41] et secundum illud,[y] hec verba ad[z] litteram intelliguntur de nupciis Iohannis evangeliste; secundum allegoriam de[aa] desponsione[ab] Christi et nostre nature in utero virginali; secundum tropologiam, id est, moralem sensum, intelligitur[ac] de unione humane anime ad Christum per[ad] graciam; secundum[ae] anagogiam intelligitur de nupciis anime nostre ad[af] Christum[ag] in paradiso.[ah] Et tunc fiat prosecucio[ai] secundum illum[aj] sensum quem[ak] inter omnes magis acceptaverit,[al] et eodem modo fiat[am] in thematibus que[an] tot sensus important.

Item in[ao] annunciacione dominica, thema sit: *habitabit iuvenis cum virgine* (Is. 62:5), poterit[ap] introduci per scripturam sacram Biblie.[aq] Preceptum erat in lege quod summus sacerdos non acciperet sibi[ar] in coniugem, nec[as] repudiatam nec meretricem, set solummodo[at] virginem de stirpe sua (cf. Lev. 21:13-14), set filio dei dictum est: *tu es sacerdos in eternum[au]* et cetera (Ps. 109:4).

---

[q] Igitur r. *A*   [r] introductam *B2*   [s] n. vel p. *A*   [t] p. aliquid v. *A*   [u] de primo *om. A*
[v] facte facte *B3*   [w] historiciter *A*   [x] allegoricum *om. B1* allegorice *A*   [y] istud *B3*
[z] v. hec l. *A*   [aa] a. intelliguntur de *A*   [ab] sponsacione *A*   [ac] intelligitur *om. A*
[ad] per *om. A*   [ae] secundum *om. B1*   [af] ad *om. B2*
[ag] graciam secundum. . .ad Christum *om. A*   [ah] paradisum *A*   [ai] t. stat proleuicio *B3*
[aj] istum *B2*   [ak] s. quod i. *B1*   [al] q. predicans acceptaverint *A* : acceptaveritur *B2*
[am] fiat *om. B3*   [an] t. qui t. *A*   [ao] I. si in *A*   [ap] v. sic potest i. *A*   [aq] Bilie *B3*
[ar] sibi *om. B1*   [as] nec viduam nec r. *A*   [at] solomodo *B2 B3*
[au] e. secundum ordinem melchisedech deservit e. *A*

---

[40] By 870 A.D., "manuduccio" was used to signify "guidance" or "leading" but in John the Scot's translation of Dionysius' *De divinis nominibus* "manuduccio" meant a kind of "introduction" (e.g., as in the phrase "in theologiam scientiam manuduccio"). See the *Novum Glossarium Mediae Latinitatis* (Copenhagen, 1959), col. 160.

[41] The four levels of biblical exegesis were an immensely popular tool in the Middle Ages. Perhaps the simplest statement of their meaning is contained in the rhyme purportedly from the pen of Augustine of Dacia, ca. 1260: "Littera gesta docet, quid credas allegoria/Moralis quid agas, quo tendas anagogia." Although he does not follow this fourfold scheme, St. Augustine is generally credited with the originating of a multi-level exegetical method; certainly the most important work describing theoretical principles of scriptural interpretation is his *De doctrina christiana*. For detailed commentary, see D. W. Robertson, Jr., *A Preface to Chaucer* (Princeton, 1962), pp. 292ff., James J. Murphy, "Saint Augustine and the Debate about a Christian Rhetoric," *Quarterly Journal of Speech*, 46 (1960), 400-10, "Saint Augustine and Rhabanus Maurus: The Genesis of Medieval Rhetoric," *Western Speech*, 31 (1967), 88-96, and *Rhetoric in the Middle Ages*, pp. 302-303.

Debuit ergo habere virginem. Et quamvis hoc mistice verificetur de Christo et ecclesia, secundum illud[av] apostoli ad corinthios: *despondi vos uni viro virginem castam* et[aw] cetera (II Cor. 11:2), hoc tamen ad litteram fuit verificatum de Christo et Virgine gloriosa, cum qua tamquam cum matre, tamquam cum sponsa et sorore, cepit hodie[ax] habitare, sicut previdit Ysayas dicens: *habitabit[ay] iuvenis cum virgine.

Item[az] introducitur illud thema per scripturam sanctorum[42] sic: nichil apud nos ita discordes consiliat sicud[ba] vinculum matrimoniale. Set quia nostra natura non potuit tollerare divinam offensam quam per peccatum incurrit, necesse[bb] fuit aliquam sponsam[bc] virginem Christo[bd] provideri cuius matrimonio offensa illa tolleretur; et nos ad Christum tamquam ad generum[be] nostrum fiducialius[bf] accedere possemus,[bg] immo ad hominem de genere[bh] nostro[bi] tamquam ad filium sororis nostre, unde dicit Augustinus, quarto confessionum: descendit huc[bj] illa[bk] vitaque tollens[bl] mortem occidit ipsam, intonuitque clamans ut[bm] redeamus[bn] hinc ad eum[bo] in illud[bp] secretum, unde[bq] venit ad nos—hoc est virginalem[br] uterum ubi[bs] nupcit ei natura nostra,[bt] caro mortalis, ne semper[bu] foret[bv] mortalis (*Confessionum*, Libro IV, cap. xii). Ipsa[bw] sponsalia previdit[bx] Ysayas cum dixit: *habitabit[by] iuvenis cum virgine.*

Item introducitur idem[bz] thema[ca] per scripturam philosophicam[cb] seu poeticam, sicut[cc] dicit Seneca in quadam

---

[av] s. idem a. *B2*   [aw] c. exhibere Christo et *A*   [ax] c. hoc die *B1*
[ay] habitabit *om. B1* habitavit *B2 B3 A*   [az] idem *B2*   [ba] c. sic v. *B2*
[bb] i. ecclesie f. *B2*   [bc] speciosam *B1* spinosam *B3*   [bd] v. primo p. *B3*   [be] regem n. *A*
[bf] fiducius *A*   [bg] possemus *om. A*   [bh] genero *B2*   [bi] nostre *B1 B3*   [bj] d. hunc *B2*
[bk] ipsa *B1 B3 A*   [bl] t. et m. *B2*   [bm] c. et r. *B2*   [bn] redeas *A*   [bo] e. ad i. *B1*
[bp] illum *A*   [bq] unde *om. B3*   [br] virginale *B2*   [bs] u. unde n. *B2*
[bt] naturam nostram *B3 A*   [bu] semper *om. A*   [bv] f. spiritus m. *A*   [bw] Ista *A*
[bx] perdit *B3*   [by] habitat *A*   [bz] illud t. *B1 B3*   [ca] thema *om. B1*   [cb] propheticam *A*
[cc] p. ut d. *A*

---

*habitabit : habitavit *H*

---

[42] The phrase "per scripturam sanctorum" seems unspecified, but the "sponsa Christi" concept which follows shortly probably refers to Paul's letter to the Ephesians (5:22ff.). The equation of the Church and "Bride of Christ" had become quite common by the third century; see Eusebius' *Ecclesiastical History*, Book X, chapter 4, ed. H. J. Lawlor (London, 1932), pp. 399-445.

epistola ad Lucillium:[43] miraris[cd] homines ad deum venire aut[ce] deum ad homines. Immo quod[cf] magis est[cg] in[ch] homines venit; set[ci] si in homines venit,[cj] in nullum magis quam in illam[ck] cuius se[cl] filiam[cm] vocat qui dicit: *venit filius hominis querere et salvare quod perierat* (Luc. 19:10). Ipse vero[cn] solus est filius hominis quia filius solius[co] matris; non enim[cp] dicitur[cq] "filius hominum" quia non habuit hominem[cr] patrem sicut[cs] ceteri hominum[ct] habent;[cu] quemadmodum previdit Ysayas dicens: *ecce virgo concipiet* (Is. 7:14). De[cv] qua virgine[cw] posset intelligi illud[cx] poeticum: virgo decora nimis, David de semine[cy] regis et de eius prole.[44] Recitat Augustinus, in quadam omelia de adventu, quosdam versus virgilianos:[cz] [45] "Iam reddit et virgo, *redeunt[da] saturnia regna; iam nova progenies celo dimittitur[db] alto." Nam isto[dc] die mittebatur progenies celi in uterum[dd] virginis et[de] iam impleatur illud Ysaye: *habitabit* et cetera.[df]

Item introduccio potest fieri per argumentum, ita[dg] ut quot[dh] modis contingit[di] argumentum,[dj] tot[dk] modis contingit introduccioncm[dl] ficri,[dm] scilicet: inductive, exemplariter, syllogistice, et[dn] emptimematice. Et primo inductive sic: sit thema *diligentibus deum[do] omnia cooperantur[dp] in bonum* (Rom. 8:28), et dicatur sic: quicquid est in mundo vel est prosperum[dq]   vel

---

[cd] miratis *A*   [ce] venire *om.*   v. ad d. *A*   [cf] I. ad m. *B2*   [cg] est *om.*   [ch] in *om. B2*
[ci] sed *om. A*   [cj] si in homines venit *om. A*   [ck] illum *B3 A*   [cl] se *om. B1*
[cm] filium *B3 A*   [cn] vero *om. B3 A* I. ille s. *B3*   [co] solius *om. A*
[cp] enim *om. B1 B2 B3*   [cq] dei f. *B1*   [cr] hominis *B2*   [cs] s. et c. *A*   [ct] homines *B3 A*
[cu] habent *om. A*   [cv] c. et de *A*   [cw] virgo *B3*   [cx] idem *B2*   [cy] de summe r. *B3*
[cz] v. dicens *B3 A*
[da] et virgo redeunt *om. B2* virgo reddit *B1* : v. reddunt *B3* : v. reddiunt *A*
[db] dinititur *B2* : dimittatur *B3*   [dc] illo *B3*   [dd] u. matris et v. *A*   [de] v. ut i. *B1 B2 B3 A*
[df] iuvenis cum virgine *B3 A*   [dg] ita *om. B3*   [dh] tot m. *A*   [di] modum continet *B3*
[dj] argui *B1* : argumenti *B2 B3*   [dk] quot m. *A*   [dl] introduci sui introduccio f. *A*
[dm] f. quod est i. *B3 A*   [dn] et *om. B3 A*   [do] deum *om. B3*   [dp] comparatur *B3*
[dq] prospum *B1 A*

---

*redeunt : reddit *H*

---

[43] Possibly a reference to Seneca's Epistle XLI, "On the God within us"—particularly to sections 1 and 2.

[44] The scriptural "germ" for this citation—probably part of a hymn—is Gen. 24:16: "puella decora nimis, virgoque pulcherrima. . ."

[45] Undoubtedly Ranulph alludes to the Pseudo-Augustinian "Sermo contra Judaeos, Paganos, et Arianos," *PL* 42:1126. The Virgilian citation is to *Eclogue IV*, lines 6 and 7, a favorite medieval text.

adversum; set[dr] siquis deum diligit, prospera mundi causant in eo timorem presentis vite; adversa vero causant[ds] amorem sequentis[dt] vite; ergo *diligentibus deum omnia cooperantur in bonum*. Item sillogistice sic: omnia que recta[du] racione veniunt[dv] secundum[dw] sentenciam et[dx] appetitum conformem ad bonum suum cooperantur,[dy] set diligentibus deum omnia eveniunt[dz] secundum recte rationis sentenciam et appetitum[ea] conformem; ergo, *diligentibus deum* et[eb] cetera. Item emptimematice[ec] sic: odientibus[ed] deum omnia cooperantur in malum;[ee] ergo, *diligentibus deum*[ef] et cetera.[eg] In isto[eh] modo introducendi, si sit[ei] thema[ej] aliquid[ek] dubium, oportet[el] illud probare, et sic[em] in themate illud[en] concludere. In hiis modis arguendis parisienses introducunt particulas per auctoritates vel per figuram,[eo] sicut dictum est supra: quicquid[ep] in mundo est, prosperum est vel[eq] adversum, in[er] cuius rei figuram[es] dominus divisit[et] totum tempus in diem prosperitatis et in[eu] noctem adversitatis.[46]

Item introducitur thema per exemplarem manduccionem sic:[ev] sit thema ut prius *habitabit iuvenis cum virgine* et dicatur sic: quando[ew] inter duo[ex] regna est ingens[ey] guerra[ez] et periculosa, non possit firmiori modo concordia[fa] stabiliri quam si filius[fb] unius regis filiam alterius[fc] desponsaret;[fd] set modo est ita quod post peccatum primum ingens[fe] guerra[ff] fuit inter regnum celeste et terrenum,[fg] que sedari non potuit donec filius celestis filiam terrenam sibi coniungeret federe maritali.[fh] Hec coniunccio[fi] fuit hodie[fj] celebrata, set diu ante[fk] per prophetam[fl] enunciata

<hr>

[dr] sed *om. A*   [ds] timorem presentis. . .vero causant *om. A* : causant in eo a. *B1*
[dt] a. celestis v. *A*   [du] rectam *A*   [dv] eveniunt *B1 B3* : veniunt *B2* : adveniunt *A*
[dw] s. eius s. *A*   [dx] s. in a. *A* s. e a. *B2*   [dy] operantur *A*   [dz] evenient *A*
[ea] et apponit c. *B1*   [eb] d. onmia et *B3* d. omnia cooperantur in bonum *A*
[ec] entimatice *B1 B2*   [ed] obedientibus *B1*   [ee] in bonum *A*
[ef] d. omnia cooperantur in bonum *B3*   [eg] ergo diligentibus deum et cetera *om. A*
[eh] illo *B3*   [ei] sit *om. A*   [ej] thema *om. B3 A*   [ek] a. sit d. *A*
[el] o. ibide p. *B3* : o. idem p. *A*   [em] s. hic dum t. *A*
[en] t. idem c. *B2* t. ibidem c. *B3* illud *om. A*   [eo] filiam *B1 B2*   [ep] q. est in *A*
[eq] prosperum vel *B1 B2*   [er] a. est in *A*   [es] filiam *B1 B2*   [et] dimisit *B1 B2 B3*
[eu] in *om. A*   [ev] sic si s. *A*   [ew] q. iter d. *B3*   [ex] i. regna et r. *B1*
[ey] erit *A* e. iugis g. *B3 A*   [ez] gurra *B1 B2*   [fa] concordia *om. B1*   [fb] si filius *om. A*
[fc] alteria *A*   [fd] desponsaverit *B3* : desponsari *A*   [fe] iugis *B3 A*   [ff] gurra *B1 B2*
[fg] terreni *B1 B3* : tere *A*   [fh] moritali *B2*
[fi] coniuncia *B3* c. homine f. *B1* : c. hore f. *B3*   [fj] hodie *om. B1 B3*   [fk] ante *om. B2*
[fl] p. pronunciata *B3 A*

<hr>

[46] The sentiment is biblical; night is associated with trouble (cf. Job 27:30) while day is connected with both spiritual and material productivity (II Cor. 6:2).

quando dixerat: *habitabit*[fm] et cetera.

Item introducitur thema[fn] per similem in[fo] natura, sic: animalia[fp] fortissima[fq] elephas[fr] et unicornus sic capiuntur[fs] quod[ft] scilicet elephas in cantum[fu] virginis[fv] mitescit et[fw] unicornus in gremio virginis mansuescit.[47] Sic[fx] filius dei fortissimus ostensis virginis uberibus, de quibus[fy] dicitur in luca: *beatus venter qui te portavit et ubera que succisti* (Luc. 11:27),[fz] emollitus[ga] per cantum[gb] virginis; quando cecinit *ecce ancilla domini* (Luc. 1:38), mitis effectus est. Similiter et iste[gc] unicornus ferocissimus[gd] dei filius,[ge] qui hominem et angelum sibi[gf] resistentem ac[gg] supra quam[gh] debuit[gi] appetentem prostravit,[gj] mitis effectus[48] est quando edificavit, sicut unicornus, sacrificium suum in gremio virginis[gk] *implens illud Ysaye: *habitabit*[gl] et cetera.

[fm] h. iuvenis cum virgine *B3 A*   [fn] thema *om. B3*   [fo] in *om. B3*   [fp] aliam f. *B1*
[fq] f. et e. *A*   [fr] eliphas *B3*   [fs] sic capiuntur *om. B2*   [ft] quia s. *B3*   [fu] cantu *A*
[fv] v. et ostencionem uberis m. *B1* v. et extensionem ubere m. *B3* v. in ostensione verbum m. *A*   [fw] quodscilicet. . .mitescit et *om. B2*   [fx] sic sic F. *B3*   [fy] de quibus *om. A*
[fz] *om. A*   [ga] est mollitus *B3* : emolitum *B2*   [gb] per tactum v. *B1*
[gc] et ille u. *B1 B2 B3 A* ille *B1 B2 B3 A*   [gd] fortissimus *B3*   [ge] d. si f. *A*   [gf] a. sic r. *A*
[gg] r. hac *B3*   [gh] gracia *B1*   [gi] dixit *B3* : docuit *A*   [gj] prostravit *om. B1* p. et m. *A*
[gk] in utero v. *B3*   [gl] h. iuvenis cum virgine *B3 A*

---

*implens : imples *H*

---

[47] The elephant is the subject of long accounts in both Latin and French bestiaries; it was said to possess no desire for sexual intercourse and to gestate only once, producing one offspring. Christ is sometimes called the "wise elephant." Cf. G. C. Druce, "The Elephant in Medieval Legend and Art," *Archaeological Journal*, 76 (1919), 1-73. The virgin's song and its calming effect are treated in the *Gesta Romanorum*, ed. Hermann Oesterley (Berlin, 1872; repr. Hildesheim, 1963), cap. 115, p. 457. . ."quod elephas mundas virgines multum diligeret et earum cantu delectaretur." To the unicorn, also, the medieval church ascribed many characteristics. It was the symbol of chastity and fierceness but because it would inherit the earth, it could be very meek. See Odell Shephard, *The Lore of the Unicorn* (London, 1930), pp. 47 ff. Both elephant and unicorn are treated in Beryl Rowland, *Animals With Human Faces* (Knoxville, 1973), pp. 70-74 and 152-57.

[48] Traditionally, the unicorn could only be tamed by the touch of a virgin or by the sight of her breasts at which point it would become gentle enough to rest its head in her lap; Maria Leach, ed., *The Standard Dictionary of Folklore, Mythology, and Legend*, Vol. II (New York, 1950), p. 1150. Allegorically, all versions of the unicorn story agree in designating Christ as the spiritual unicorn who, descending into a virgin's womb, became incarnate and subject to condemnation and death. The unicorn's horn symbolizes the unity of Christ and the Father; the animal's fierceness, the inability of even heavenly powers to know Christ and of hellish ones to hold him. See Florence McCulloch, *Medieval Latin and French Bestiaries*, University of North Carolina Studies in the Romance Languages and Literatures, no. 32 (Chapel Hill, 1960), pp. 179-83.

Item[gm] introduccio per exemplum in arte sic: sit hoc[gn] thema *diligentibus deum*[go] et cetera. Videmus[gp] in arte quod medicus accedens[gq] ad infirmum[gr] sanandum[gs] primo inducit in eum[gt] spiritum convalescendi ut sic eger, credens omnia que[gu] sumpserit[gv] sibi[gw] valitura, facilius curetur. Set medicus noster deus est,[gx] nos quoque[gy] infirmi;[49] si[gz] ergo nostram in deo proiecerimus affeccionem et confidenciam omnia[ha] nobis valebunt ad medelam[hb] morbi, quod est[hc] peccatum. Et hoc est quod dicit:[hd] *diligentibus deum*[he] et cetera.

Item fit introduccio[hf] per exemplum in historia, sicut narrat[hg] Valerius[hh] Maximus de gestis *memorabilibus,[hi] quod duobus existentibus amicis alterque[hj] pro altero moreretur[hk] in certo[hl] die[hm] posito[hn] iuxta constitucionem tirannidis.[ho] [50] Miratus Dionisius amicicie constanciam in redditu unius[hp] dampnandi supplicium remisit[hq] et in sodalicium[hr] eorum se commisit. Ecce hic[hs] fedus amicicie inducias[ht] mortis impetravit, tirannidem mitigavit, vitam donavit, fidelia[hu] divulgavit. Sic[hv] diligentibus invicem omnia cooperantur in bonum, set multo magis <diligentibus>[hw] deum omnia cooperantur[hx] in bonum.[hy]

Item fit[hz] introduccio per vulgare[ia] proverbium sic:[ib] sit thema *habitabit iuvenis cum virgine*[ic] quia quadrupliciter dicitur quod[id] "iuvenis"[ie] similis similem sibi querit[51] et omne simile suo

---

[gm] I. fit i. *A*   [gn] hoc *om. A*   [go] d. omnia cooperantur in bonum *B3 A*   [gp] videns *A*
[gq] attendens *B1*   [gr] ad firmam s. *B2*   [gs] senendum *B1* : servandum *B3*
[gt] in eum *om. A*   [gu] que *om. B1*   [gv] sumpservit *B3*   [gw] s. fore v. *A*   [gx] est *om. B3*
[gy] q. influi *B3*   [gz] i. in si *A*   [ha] o. in. n.*A*   [hb] medullam *B1*   [hc] est *om. B1 B2 B3 A*
[hd] dicit dicit *B3*   [he] d. apostolus *B1 B3 A*   [hf] i. thematis p. *A*   [hg] gnarrat *B3*
[hh] Valerianus *B1*   [hi] memoralibus *B1 B3 A* : moralibus *B2*
[hj] alter qui p. *B3* : alter p. *A*   [hk] morretur *B3* : moreretur *om. A*   [hl] ut certo *A*
[hm] d. rediret se vadium ponente *A*   [hn] posito *om. B3*
[ho] tirannidum *B1 B2* : tirannidis *om. A*   [hp] r. huius d. *B1*   [hq] s. dimisit *A*
[hr] sodalium *A*   [hs] h. quod f. *A*   [ht] indicias *B3*   [hu] v. in infideles *A*
[hv] dimulgat et sic *A*   [hw] diligentibus *om. B2*   [hx] cooperatur *B3*
[hy] sed multo. . .in bonum *om. B1*   [hz] facit *B3*   [ia] v. verbum s. *A*   [ib] p. non sic *B3*
[ic] v. ut prius quod communiter d. *A*   [id] quod *om. A*   [ie] iuvenis *om. B1 B2 B3 A*

---

*memorabilibus : moralibus *H*

---

[49] Probably an allusion to the story recounted in Matt. 9:12, Mark 2:17, and Luke 5:31 where Jesus remarks: "Non opus valentibus medicus, sed male habentibus" (Matthew) and later, "Non veni vocare iustos sed peccatores ad paenitentiam" (Luke).

[50] Valerius Maximus, *De gestis memorabilibus*, Book IV, chapter vii, "De amicitia."

[51] Cicero, *De amicitia*, XIV, 50. The proverb was common to Homer, Empedocles, Aristotle, Theophrastus, Plutarch, Callimachus, and Quintilian. There is a biblical parallel in Eccli. 13:20: "omnis caro ad similem sibi coniungetur, et omnis homo simili sui sociabitur."

*simili [if] applaudit; [ig] cum magna [ih] sit similitudo inter iuvenem et virginem, signanter hodie [ii] dici poterit: *habitabit.* [ij] Item [ik] ad idem si [il] thema sit [im] *sancti estote quia ego sanctus sum* (Lev. 11:44), vulgariter dicitur qualis dominus, talis familia;[52] quia sicut [in] nos deberemus esse de dei [io] familia, [ip] deceret [iq] nos moribus eius conformari, [ir] ad quod hortamur in [is] hiis verbis: *sancti estote* [it] et cetera.

Isti [iu] predicti modi valerent [iv] ad themata que sunt [iw] duarum diccionum, ut [ix] supra, set in [iy] thematibus unius diccionis non oportet uti omnibus istis modis; in quibus omnibus [iz] abhorrent moderni facere prolixam introduccionem sicut facit frater Guydo in sermonibus suis eo quod sit nugatorium *ante historiam *effluere* [ja] et [jb] ipsa historia succingi* (II Mac. 2:33). Quod si thema sit unius diccionis poterit introduci [jc] per auctoritatem. Ita [jd] quidem [je] quod ex illa auctoritate possint elici tria membra que festo conveniunt et [jf] themati; [jg] verbi gracia, sit [jh] thema "intellige," sic dici poterit sicut dicit [ji] Plato in *thimeo: [jj] deus [jk] optimus est et [jl] ab optimo longe relata [jm] est [jn] invidia.[53] Consequenter, cuncta secundum nature capacitatem voluit [jo] esse *capacia [jp]   bonitatis ut sicut ipse est bonus, ita et alia forent

---

[if] simile *B2* : similiter *B3*   [ig] plaudit *B3*   [ih] c. maxima s. *B1*
[ii] v. significari h. *B3* s. homine *B1*
[ij] p. et cetera *B1* p. habitabit iuvenis cum virgine *B3* p. habitabit iuvenis et cetera *A*
[ik] illud *B1 A*   [il] sic *B1 A*   [im] sit *om. A*   [in] q. ergo n. *B1 B3 A*   [io] dei *om. B3*
[ip] de f. Christi *A*   [iq] doceret *B2* : decoret *B3*   [ir] confirmari *B3*   [is] in *om. A*
[it] e. quia ego sanctus sum *B3 A*   [iu] Isti isti *A*   [iv] valent *A*   [iw] sunt *om. A*
[ix] d. sunt et s. *A*   [iy] s. si in *B1*   [iz] omnibus *om. A*   [ja] efflile *B2*
[jb] et in i. *B1 B3* : et ante i. *A*   [jc] i. pro antethema i. *A*   [jd] a. illa q. *B3*   [je] quid *A*
[jf] conveniant *A* c. in t. *B1 B2 B3*   [jg] themata *B1* t. et v. *B3*   [jh] g ut t. *B1*
[ji] dici *B2 A*   [jj] thimo *B3* : thimotheo *B2 om. A*   [jk] deo *B1*   [jl] et *om. B1*
[jm] relongata *A*   [jn] i. est *A*   [jo] veluit *B1*   [jp] capacitatem *A*

---

*simili : simile *H*
*effluere : efflile *H*
*thimeo : thimotheo *H*
*capacia : capaciam *H*

---

[52] A common proverbial structure in the medieval period, deriving ultimately from the "qualis dominus, talis servus" of Petronius' *Satyricon*, 58. Siegfried Wenzel has identified Higden's version as deriving from the *Ars predicandi* of John of Wales, MS. Bodley 571, fol. 166ra: "sicut dominus sic et familia sua."

[53] Chalcidius translated *Timaeus* 29E thus: "Optimus erat, ab optimo porro invidia longe relegata est." Basevorn's version (Charland, p. 272) is: "Deus optimus est, et ab optimo longe invidia est relegata." Ranulph uses Basevorn with a few changes.

bona; et sicut ipse[jq] foret intelligens, ita et alia forent intelligencia secundum nature sue[jr] capacitatem. Unde et in rerum[js] natura est aliquid omnia intelligens[jt] per essenciam,[ju] que[jv] est solus deus; est[jw] aliquid omnia[jx] intelligens, set[jy] partim per species, partim per[jz] essenciam, et[ka] hoc est angelus.[kb] Cum[kc] ergo non[kd] sint[ke] plures modi[kf] intelligendi, nec plures erunt nature intellectuales, quamvis Aristotelis videatur[kg] fingere[kh] celum animatum.[54] In celo emperio[ki] residet ipse[kj] deus ut imperator, discernens[kk] et imperans in inferiori celo,[kl] et quandoque[km] in aere tanquam in[kn] medio ministrat angelus ut cooperator[ko] in infimo[kp] mundi tamquam suburbio velut alienigena militat homo ut obtemperans. Inter quos[kq] ille[kr] sanctus[ks] semper[kt] plene parebat[ku] imperio quia per[kv] doctrine veritatem conformabatur[kw] intellectui divino, per vite puritatem[kx] equabatur[ky] intellectui angelico, per passionis acerbitatem quodammodo exaltabatur supra intellectum humanum. Ut sic de eo vere intelligi[kz] possit, quod fulgebat doctrine[la] gracia, quod[lb] pollebat vite[lc] mundicia,[ld] quod[le] preiminebat[lf] pugne[lg] victoria.[55] Et sic[lh] in tribus efficaciter adimplevit[li] quod in uno specialiter est impletum: "intellige."

Item alio modo sic: sit thema, "ambulate," necesse[lj] est unumquodque in[lk] via presentis procedere[ll] aut retrocedere,[lm] quia[ln]

[jq] i. est *A*   [jr] sue *om. A*   [js] et infinita n. *B1 B2 B3*   [jt] intelligunt *B1 B2* i. sed p. *A*
[ju] essenciam *om. A*   [jv] sive qui e. *A*   [jw] d. et est *A*   [jx] a. omnino i. *B3*   [jy] s. per p. *A*
[jz] p. se materia et *B1* : p. se in natura et *B3*   [ka] e. a natura *B1*
[kb] anglicum *B3* a. et est aliquid non per species non per essenciam intelligens ut hic
[kc] cum *A* cum *om. B3*   [kd] autem non *B1 B3*   [ke] sic sint *B2* sunt sunt *B3*
[kf] p. mortis i. *B1* : p. motus i. *B2* : p. motis i. *B3*   [kg] A. velit ut vietur f. *A*
[kh] f. aranatorum *B1*   [ki] c. empureo r. *A*   [kj] ipse *om. A*   [kk] decernens *A*
[kl] in librum celum *B1* : in finitum celum *B2* : in infinitum celum 3
[km] quandocumque *B1 B2 B3*   [kn] et tamquam in *A*
[ko] cooperatur *B1 B3* : cooperantur *B2*   [kp] in fimo m. *B2* : in imperio m. *B3*
[kq] I. que *B1 B2 B3*   [kr] illo *B3* iste *A*   [ks] sancto *B3*   [kt] semper *om. A*
[ku] parebat *om. B1*   [kv] per *om. A*   [kw] confluebatur *B1* : confirmabatur *B2 B3*
[kx] paritatem *B1*   [ky] equibatur *B1*   [kz] intellectus *B3*   [la] d. supra *B1* d. sentencia *B3*
[lb] g. quia *A*   [lc] pollebant ut m. *B1*   [ld] mundiciam *B1*   [le] quia *A*   [lf] preminebat *B3*
[lg] patriarchie v. *B1 B3* : pugno *A*   [lh] sic *om. A*   [li] complevit *A*   [lj] necesse *om. B3*
[lk] u. necesse est unumquodque in *B3*   [ll] precedere *B1* p. vite incidere a. *A*
[lm] aut retrocedere *om. B1*   [ln] quod s. *A*

---

[54] Aristotle outlines his thoughts on the circularly-moving heavens in *De Caelo*, I. 5, 272 b 14 and I. 9, 278 b 11-14.

[55] Ranulph is condensing the fuller explanation given by Basevorn (Charland, pp. 272-73). It is difficult to trace this theocracy to any one medieval author, although the triplicate structure reflects the emphases of Pseudo-Dionysius' *Celestial Hierarchy* which was translated into Latin by John the Scot. See A. H. Armstrong, ed., *The Cambridge History of Later Greek and Early Medieval Philosophy* (Cambridge, 1967), pp. 457-72.

secundum Bernardum:[lo] diu hic[lp] stare in eodem gradu bonitatis[lq] est quasi impossibile; set retrocedere est periculosum, procedere vero[lr] fructuosum.[56] *Omnis*, inquit dominus, *locus quem calcaverit pes vester* (Deut. 11:24), <vester> erit, <ergo>[ls] "ambulate."

XV
De thematis divisione[a]

Tenendum est hoc[b] in dividendo quod divisiones formentur iuxta vocabulorum significaciones, ne scilicet idem sit[c] vocabulum dividens et divisum, aut quasi idem[d] et[e] sinonymum[f] aut impertinens aut impugnans;[g] verbi gracia, si[h] thema sit: *acceptus est regi minister intelligens*[i] (Prov. 14:35), hec[j] tria tanguntur de isto sancto, scilicet:[k] intellectualis perfeccio quia "intelligens," ministralis humiliacio quia "minister," et[l] supernalis acceptacio quia "acceptus est." Hic quantum ad[m] omnia membra viciosa est divisio[n] propter nimiam similitudinem horum vocabulorum "intelligens" et "intellectualis," "minister" et "ministralis,"[o] "acceptus" et "acceptacio."[p] Verumptamen si eadem res sub aliis vocabulis[q] diceretur, non foret viciosum; ut verbi gracia,[r] si sic diceretur[s] in hiis verbis: tria tanguntur racionalis perfeccio—"intelligens,"[t] spiritualis submissio—"minister," supernalis gratificacio quia "acceptus."

Item si in hoc[u] themate *habitabit iuvenis cum virgine* dicatur, hec[v] tria notantur:[w] filii dei familiaris habitacio quia[x] "habitabit"; secundo dei coniunccio[y] singularis quia "iuvenis"; et[z] tertio matris condicio puellaris quia[aa] "cum virgine." Hic est triplex[ab]

[lo] Boecium *B1*   [lp] hoc *B1*   [lq] g. veritatis *B1 B3*   [lr] vero *om. A*
[ls] ergo *om. B1 B2 B3* ergo ergo a. *A*   [a] De thematis divisione *om. A*   [b] hic *B3*
[c] s. nec illud sit *B1*   [d] q. illud *B1* : illd *B3*   [e] et *om. B1 B3* et sic s. *A*   [f] synodum *B3*
[g] a. repignans v. *B1* : repugnans *B3 A*   [h] g. sed si *B2* g. si scilicet t. *B3* : g. sic t. *A*
[i] i. et cetera dividatur h. *A*   [j] hic *B2 B3*   [k] scilicet *om. B1 B2 B3 A*
[l] et *om. A* est *om. A*   [m] quemcumque ad *B1* : quamcumque ad *B3*   [n] d. per *A*
[o] ministerialis *A*   [p] et acceptus *B1*   [q] verbis *A*   [r] non foret. . .verbi gracia *om. A*
[s] si sic diceretur *om. A* dicitur *B1 B2 B3*
[t] per intelligens s. *B1* : intelligentis *B2* : intelligencie *A*   [u] hoc *om. A*
[v] hec d. *B1 B3* d. hic t. *B2 B3 A*   [w] n. scilicet f. *A*   [x] qui *B1 B2 B3*   [y] c. sui s. *A*
[z] et *om. A*   [aa] p. qui c. *B2*   [ab] t. et tercio matris condiccio puellaris d. *A*

---

[56] Higden refers to Bernard of Clairvaux's "De gradibus humitatis et superbiae," *Opera*, Vol. II, ed. Jean Leclerq and H. M. Rochais (Rome, 1963), pp. 35-37.

defectus, quia in primo membro ponitur ipsa diccio [ac] que est [ad] membrum [ae] diccionis, [af] scilicet, "habitabit"; in secundo ponitur aliquid quod est inpertinens quia coniunccio in nullo notificat iuvenem; in [ag] tercio ponitur [ah] nomen synonymum [ai] quia "puella" et [aj] "virgo" [ak] conveniunt.

Debet ergo divisio [al] dari per alia vocabula exprimencia tamenque [am] propria vel appropriata illi diccioni que impartat [an] membrum divisionis; verbi gracia, habitare est morari per aliquod magnum tempus in aliquo loco; condicio appropriata iuveni est [ao] pulcritudo vel leticia, quia iuvenis naturaliter est iocundus [ap] sicut senex tristis et iracundus;[57] condicio virginis est mundicia mentis et corporis. Item condicio posita [aq] in divisione debet realiter [ar] relucere in ista [as] auctoritate per quam debet membrum divisionis confirmari, ut [at] verbi gracia, requies vel mora que est condicio [au] habitacionis relucet in [av] hac auctoritate: *habitabit in tabernaculo,* [aw] *requiescet* [ax] et cetera (Ps. 14:1). Similiter condicio iuvenis, que est leticia, [ay] relucet in hac auctoritate: *introibo* [az] *ad altare dei, ad deum qui letificat iuventutem* [ba] *meam* (Ps. 42:4). Condicio virginis, que est [bb] mundicia, relucet in hac auctoritate: *virgo* [bc] *cogitat* [bd] *que dei* [be] *sunt ut sit sancta corpore et spiritu* (I Cor. 7:34). Potest ergo thema sic [bf] dividi: [bg] hic primo delectamur [bh] ex dei venientis [bi] ad [bj] nos morosa requie et iocunda, cum dicitur "habitabit"; unde dicitur in [bk] psalmo: *habitabit in tabernaculo,* [bl] *requiescet in monte sancto tuo.* [bm] Secundo letamur [bn] ex nascentis facie formosa et letabunda, cum dicitur

---

[ac] i. condiccio *A*   [ad] est *om. B1 B2*   [ae] membrorum *B1*   [af] d. que est *A*   [ag] et t. *B3*
[ah] aliquid quod. . .tercio ponitur *om. A*   [ai] synodum *B1 B3*   [aj] et *om. B1 B3*
[ak] v. que idem sunt *B1* v. quasi c. *A*   [al] e. dicit d. *A*   [am] tamen *B1 B3* : tamen a p. *A*
[an] importat *A*   [ao] i. est est p. *B1*   [ap] iocundis *B2*   [aq] positiva *B1*   [ar] realiter *om. A*
[as] illa *B3 A*   [at] ut *om. A*   [au] v. noxa *B1 B2 B3*
[av] h. realiter lucet in *A* : relucet relucet *B1*   [aw] t. tui r. *A*
[ax] requiescit *B1* r. in monte sancto tuo *A*   [ay] que est leticia *om. B1 B2 B3*
[az] introbo *B2*   [ba] iuventure *B2*   [bb] e. in m. *B1*   [bc] virgitat *B2*   [bd] cogitat *om. B2*
[be] q. domini s. *B1 B3 A*   [bf] sic *om. B1*   [bg] d. sicut h. *B1*   [bh] dilatantur *A*
[bi] nominientis *B1* : advenientis *A*   [bj] ad *om. A*   [bk] unde in p. *B1 B2 B3 A*
[bl] t. tuo r. *A*   [bm] tuo *om. A*   [bn] letamus *B2*

---

[57] The irascible and saddening qualities of old age were commonplace attributions long before Cicero chose to refute them in his *De senectute.* However, the medieval tradition which underlies Ranulph's citation seems traceable to Horace's *Art of Poetry,* lines 169-74; see George R. Coffman, "Old Age from Horace to Chaucer: Some Literary Affinities and Adventures of an Idea" *Speculum* 9 (1934), 249-77. The "joyful youth" also became a medieval type but the genesis of this phrase is more easily traceable to Scripture, e.g., Eccli. 11:9.

"iuvenis"; unde dicitur in psalmo: *introibo ad altare*[bo] et cetera. Tercio admiramur[bp] ex parientis specie gloriosa atque munda, quia "cum virgine"; unde ad corinthios: *virgo*[bq] *cogitat que*[br] dei *sunt*[bs] et cetera.

Et[bt] est hic notandum quod[bu] ad habendum concordanciam[bv] sufficit eam[bw] habere non solum in primitivo[bx] set eciam[by] in dirivativo[bz] a principali,[ca] ut **letyficacio** dirivatur a leticia et iuventus a iuvene[cb];[58] quod si[cc] significata vocabulorum[cd] nequeant[ce] congruere[cf] divisioni[cg] faciende, recurrendum est tunc ad eorum consignificata, que[ch] sunt casus, numeri, genera, vel eciam ad[ci] circumstancias[cj] thematis que sunt quis, quid, ubi, quibus auxiliis, cur, quomodo, quando; verbi gracia, sit[ck] thema[cl] in nativitate: *evangelizo vobis gaudium magnum quod erit omni*[cm] *populo quia natus est salvator*[cn] *in civitate David* (Luc. 2:10). Hic consideratur "quis"—quia angelus, "quid"—quia gaudium, "ubi"—quia in civitate david, "quibus"—quia vobis.

Item videndum est quia[co] in dividendo quod non passim[cp] preposceretur[cq] diccio diccioni,[cr] ut prius ponatur[cs] divisio[ct] super secundum vocabulum thematis quam super[cu] primum, nisi[cv] cogat ad[cw] illud ordo[cx] construccionis vel ordo rei geste vel ordo prolacionis.[cy] Exemplum in illo[cz] themate: *acceptus est regi minister intelligens,*[da] ubi talis est ordo: quoad primum quod precedat boni faciendi cognicio succedat conformis conversacio et tandem sequatur[db] ex hiis gratifica[dc] remuneracio. Et sic[dd] hic[de]

[bo] A. dei ad deum qui letificat iuventutem meam et *A*   [bp] miramur *A*
[bq] nichil dicitur v. *B1* dicitur v. *B3 A* v. dicitur c. *B2*   [br] quo *B3* q. domini s. *A*
[bs] s. ut sicut sancta corpore et spiritu *A*   [bt] Et *om. B2*   [bu] quod quod *B1*
[bv] concordia *A*   [bw] s. tam h. *B1* : s. causa h. *B2*   [bx] primativo *A*   [by] eciam *om. B1*
[bz] dirativa *B2*   [ca] p. et L. *B1 B3*   [cb] iuve *B1* : iuvone *B2*   [cc] quia si *B1* : sed si *A*
[cd] vocabulo *B1*   [ce] nequeat *B2*   [cf] congrue *B1 B2 B3*   [cg] divisia *B2*
[ch] ad corum s. *B2*   [ci] g. et ad *A* eciam *om. B1 B2 B3*
[cj] certum statim *B1* : certum statum *B2* : certum status *B3*   [ck] g. si t. *A*
[cl] thema *om. B2*   [cm] e. cum p. *B3*   [cn] est nobis *B1*   [co] quia *om. B1 B3 A*
[cp] possim *B2 A*   [cq] prepefletur *B2* : prepriosturetur *A*   [cr] diccioni *om. B1 B2 B3*
[cs] ponitur *A*   [ct] divisia *B2*   [cu] supra p. *B1 B3*   [cv] ni *B3*   [cw] interogat ad *B1*
[cx] ordo *om. B1*   [cy] probacionis *B1*   [cz] isto *A*   [da] intelligere *B1*   [db] sequitur *B1*
[dc] h. significata r. *A*   [dd] Et secundum h. *A*   [de] hec *B1* : hoc *A*

---

[58] From Cicero's *notatio* (which he lauded "cum ex vi nominis argumentum elicitur" *Topica* 35), the use of etymology as a category of thought was given *auctoritas* for the Middle Ages. Assisted by Ovid (*Fasti*, V-VI), St. Matthew (16:18), Jerome (*Liber de nominibus hebraicis*), Augustine, Cassiodorus (*PL* 70:28 ff), and especially Isidore of Seville, growth in the use of explanatory derivations was rapid. The *Legenda Aurea*, of course, provided reinforcement for etymological thinking. See Ernst Robert Curtius, *European Literature and the Latin Middle Ages* (New York, 1953), pp. 495-500.

primo [df] cadit divisio super **intelligens**; [dg] secundo super **minister**; tercio [dh] super **acceptus est**. Item [di] secundum [dj] quod vite mundicia proxime disponit ad scienciam vel ad graciam sic: iuxta ordinem construccionis primo ponitur divisio, id est, vite innocencia super **minister**; secundo concomitans sciencia super **intelligens**: [dk] tercio gratificans complacencia super **acceptus est**. [dl] Set verum [dn] secundum [do] ordinem prolacionis [dp] sic: potest ordinari divisio secundum Augustinum: [dq] omnia bona opera gracia prevenit, [dr] set ut bona [ds] voluntas velit efficaciter [dt] consequitur et tandem ex utroque, scilicet, [du] gracia et voluntate.[59] Secundum sanctos, [dv] perfeccio [dw] sciencie comitatur [dx] que [dy] ordinem psalmista [dz] tenet dicens: *bonitatem*, scilicet [ea] gracie [eb] prevenientes, *et* [ec] *disciplinam*, [ed] humilitatis [ee] obedientis, *et scienciam*, veritatis perficientis, [ef] *doce me* (Ps. 118:66).

Similiter advertendum [eg] est in dividendo quod cum omne thema proponatur aut narrando, aut describendo, aut cominando, aut despiciendo, [eh] aut promittendo, aut consonando, [ei] aut conquirendo, aut terrendo, aut corripiendo, ita proprietas dicti debet retineri, quod si alicubi allegimus [ej] [allicimur] [ek] non dicatur ibi [el] quod increpamur vel econverso quia [em] hoc [en] foret ridiculosum; verbi gracia, non [eo] proponitur [ep] illud matthei: [eq] *quid hic statis tota die ociosi* (Matt. 20:6). Si [er] dicatur, [es] hic [et] hortamur [eu] ad

---

[df] primo *om. A*   [dg] **intelligere** *B1*   [dh] et t. *A*   [di] Item *om. B1 B2 B3*   [dj] s. hoc q. *A*
[dk] secundo concomitans scientia super **intelligens** *om. A*
[dl] **est** *om. A* [dm] secundum quod. . .**acceptus est** *om. B1 B2 B3*   [dn] verum *om. B1 B3 A*
[do] secundum *om. B2*   [dp] probacionis *B1*   [dq] A. hec o. *B1*   [dr] pervenit *A*
[ds] bona bona v. *A*   [dt] effaciter *A*   [du] u. et g. *A*   [dv] sanctior *B1* : sanctorum *B3*
[dw] perfecte *B1*   [dx] comutatur *B2* concomitatur *A*   [dy] quem *B1 B2 B3 A*
[dz] o. prima *B1* : psalmi *B3*   [ea] b. secundum g. *A*   [eb] graciam *B1*   [ec] et *om. B1*
[ed] indisciplinam *B1*   [ee] humanitatis *B1*   [ef] proficientis *A*
[eg] addendum *B1* : adducendum *B2 B3*   [eh] deficiendo *B1*   [ei] consolando *A*
[ej] allegimus *om. B2 A*   [ek] allicimur *om. B1 B3*   [el] ibi *om. B1 B2 B3*   [em] quod *B1 B3*
[en] nam h. *A* hic *B1*   [eo] non *om. A*   [ep] preponatur *A*   [eq] m. 20 *A*   [er] Set *A*
[es] dicamur *A*   [et] hic *om. B1 A*   [eu] hortatur *B1*

---

[59] Augustine's *De gratia et libero arbitrio*, chapter VII, contains an extended discussion of the operations of God's grace without which one is not able to perform any good work; this is closest to the content of Ranulph's citation. *PL* 44:892-93 illustrates the interaction of grace and good works in a succinct and very clear manner. Augustine's concern with the operations of the will and the effect of grace upon it as a human faculty had been evident as early as 388 when he began the *De libero arbitrio*; his interest, however, was more clearly focused upon this question when he attacked the doctrines of Pelagius. Consequently, Augustine's views on the interrelationship of grace, free will, and the performance of good works can be seen in numerous anti-Pelagian tracts, particularly *De spiritu et littera* (412), *De natura et gratia* (415), *De gratia Christi et peccato originali* (418), and *De correptione et gratia* (426) as well as in *De gratia et libero arbitrio*, which he wrote in 425.

operandum, inproprie dicitur quamvis hoc dici posset.[ev] Idcirco proprie loquendum est[ew] ut principalis sensus thematis explicetur; verbi gracia, hic increpat Christus ociosos et[ex] operarios[ey] negligentes; increpat enim ex[ez] parte nature, dicendo *quid*[fa] *statis*, id est[fb] qui[fc] nati estis ad laborem—iob:[fd] *homo nascitur ad laborem*[fe] (Iob 5:7). Secundo ex parte loci cum dicit[ff] hic[fg] ubi[fh] non est locus quietis set erroris et[fi] vaste solitudinis,[60] michee 2 dicitur:[fj] *surgite quia non habetis hic requiem* (Mich. 2:10). Tercio ex parte temporis cum dicit:[fk] *tota die*, id est, toto[fl] tempore vite que milicia debet esse super terram,[fm] secundum illud iob: *milicia*[fn] *est vita hominis super terram*[fo] (Iob 7:1). Quarto ex parte deordinacionis cum dicitur *ociosi*. Igitur de istis[fp] quattuor Christus signanter[fq] comprehendit[fr] quem illa quattuor movent[fs] non esse[ft] standum hic, scilicet:[fu] nature[fv] indite[fw] proprietas, loci vastitas,[fx] temporis brevitas, racionis perspicacitas, et[fy] hoc in aliis thematibus[fz] est observandum.

Item observandum[ga] est quod omne vocabulum sentencionale in themate exigit divisionem, ita quod duo sentencionalia non tangantur[gb] sub una divisione, ut[gc] verbi gracia, si in illo[gd] themate *domine, salva nos, perimus* (Matt. 8:25) diceretur:[ge] hic apostoli duo faciunt quia implorant benignitatem, quia dicunt "domine,[gf] salva nos,"[gg] et[gh] allegant necessitatem quia[gi] "perimus." Hic "**domine**" cum sit vocabulum[gj] sentenciosum[gk] non cadit sub aliquo membro dividente. Idcirco melius est sic[gl] dividere: hic[gm] primo allegant potenciam[gn] —"domine,"[go] implorant[gp] clemenciam—"salva[gq] nos," assignant indigenciam[gr] —"perimus."[gs]

[ev] possit *A*   [ew] est *om. B2 A*   [ex] et *om. A*   [ey] operari *A*   [ez] i. autem ex *B1 B3 A*
[fa] d. qui s. *B2*   [fb] stat *B3* s. psalmo q. *B1 B2 B3*   [fc] quia n. *B1 B3* : quid n. *A*
[fd] i. 5 *A*   [fe] laborem *om. B1*   [ff] l. tamen dicitur *A*   [fg] hic *om. B1 B2 B3*
[fh] ibi n. *B1 B2 B3*   [fi] s. horrorum et *A*   [fj] dicitur *om. A*   [fk] t. credit *B3*
[fl] d. in t. *B1 B3*   [fm] super terram *om. A*   [fn] i. et milia e. *A*   [fo] super terram *om. A*
[fp] de esti q. *B2*   [fq] C. significanter c. *B1 B3*   [fr] reprehendit *A*   [fs] moverunt *A*
[ft] n. est s. *B1*   [fu] stand *B3* s. sic nec s. *A*   [fv] nature *om. A*   [fw] vite p. *A*
[fx] vestitas *B3*   [fy] prospicacitas *B2 B3 A* p. temporis brevitas et *B1*   [fz] thematis *B1*
[ga] Item observandum *om. A*   [gb] tanguntur *B1 B3* : includatur *A*
[gc] u. diccione ut *B1* ut *om. A*   [gd] in certo t. *A*   [ge] sic d. *A* dicere *B3*
[gf] b. ibi domine *A*   [gg] nos perimus *A*   [gh] et *om. A*   [gi] n. ibi p. *A*   [gj] dicit v. *B1 B3*
[gk] sentencionale *A*   [gl] e. scilicet d. *B3*   [gm] hic *om. A*   [gn] p. ibi d. *A*   [go] domino *B2*
[gp] et i. *B1 B3 A* imploravit *B1* : implorat *A*   [gq] solvos n. *B3* ibi salva *A*
[gr] indigenciam *om. B1 B2 B3*   [gs] ibi p. *A*

[60] Probably a corruption of Deut. 32:10: "In hoc loco horroris et vastae solitudinis."

Set quando thema est unius [gt] diccionis, totalis [gu] divisio potest poni in primo principio [gv] sive in secundo sive in tercio [gw] sive [gx] in [gy] plura [gz];[61] verbi gracia, [ha] sit thema [hb] "confide," hic dici potest: confidendum [hc] est [hd] proper tres rationes sive propter plures raciones. Item si thema sit "respice," sic [he] dici potest: respiciendum [hf] est secundum sex [hg] differencias quia [hh] retro ad nobiles et ignobiles qui decesserunt, ante ad futurum iudicium, a dextris quia ad mundi prospera [hi] quanto [hj] sunt [hk] caduca, a sinistris ad mundi [hl] adversa quanto [hm] sunt consueta, deorsum ad infernum, [hn] sursum ad celum. Item si thema sit "audi," ergo audi [ho] sacram [hp] scripturam disceptantem de presenti miseria, [hq] de infernali pena, de celesti gloria, de quibus habetur ezechieli 2: *et *scripte [hr] erant in eo [hs] lamentaciones carmen et ve* (Ezech. 2:9): "lamentaciones" [ht] —presentis miserie; [hu] "carmen"—glorie; "et ve"—gehenne. Item si thema sit "dilige," ergo dilige [hv] deum in intellectu [hw] sine errore, voce [hx] sine contradiccione, memoria sine oblivione; vel sic: dilige deum per glorificacionem, proximum per subvencionem, [hy] teipsum per castigacionem.[62]

Item si <thema> [hz] sit duarum diccionum poterit dividi in duo quorum utraque pars possit [ia] subdividi [ib] in duo [ic] vel in tria vel in quattuor; verbi gracia, sit thema *ambulate in dileccione* (Eph. 5:2), hic duo facit apostolus quia movet ad profectum [id] ibi "ambulate"; secundo ostendit [ie] iter rectum ibi "in [if] dileccione."

[gt] est 7 d. *B1 B3*   [gu] totalis *om. B1*   [gv] principio *om. A*   [gw] tercia *A*
[gx] sive *om. B1 B3*   [gy] in *om. A*   [gz] ut v. *A*   [ha] vero g. *B1*   [hb] sit thema *om. B1*
[hc] confitendum *B1* : considerandum *A*   [hd] est *om. A*   [he] sic *om. A*
[hf] repenitendum *B3*   [hg] sex *om. B1* s. tres d. *A*   [hh] que r. *B2*
[hi] mundi prospera *om. B2*   [hj] quanta *B1* : quantum *A*   [hk] sint *B2*
[hl] s. ad mundi ad *B2*   [hm] quante *B1* : quantum *A*   [hn] ad misterium s. *B1*
[ho] ergo audi *om. B1 B3*   [hp] sacram *om. B3*   [hq] miseriam *B2 B3*
[hr] scripta *B1 B3 A* : scriptura *B3*   [hs] ea *B1*   [ht] ve mentaciones *B1*   [hu] p. vite et c. *A*
[hv] ergo dilige *om. B1*   [hw] in mente s. *B1 B3*   [hx] voco *A*   [hy] subieccionem *B1 B3*
[hz] si thema *om. B2*   [ia] potest *B1 B2 A*   [ib] *A* dividi *B1*
[ic] quorum utraque. . .in duo *om. B3*   [id] perfectum *B1 B2 B3*
[ie] s. cum dicit *B1* : duo cum dicit *B2 B3*   [if] inter *B3*

---

*scripte : scripta *H*

---

[61] "In plura" is found in all manuscripts and seems to act as a syntactically independent entity signifying "in those beyond the third."

[62] "Confide," "respice," "audi," and "dilige"—all have many scriptural "loci." In MS. B1, the "ad nobiles. . .futurum iudicium" section of the "respice" commentary precedes the "Item si. . .quia retro."

Quoad primum, ambulandum est duobus modis [ig] seu triplici via seu quadriplici racione; [ih] quoad secundum, [ii] ambulandum est [ij] in dileccione quia duas [ik] habet alas [il] elevantes [im] vel quia [in] triplicem boni [io] condiccionem [ip] includit, scilicet, [iq] delectabile, utile, et honestum. Set quando thema [ir] est trium [is] diccionum sentencionalium, [it] divisio congrue fit [iu] in tria et subdivisio cuiuslibet membri [iv] foret [iw] in tria; [ix] si autem in plura dividatur vel subdividatur, honerosum reputatur.

Item notandum est in hac [iy] materia quod thema [iz] potest dividi per verba sic: *ite et vos in vineam* [ja] *meam* [jb] (Matt. 20:4); hic tria [jc] facit: sollicitat, specificat, et [jd] certificat; sollicitat ad actum seu profectum—"ite," [je] specificat obiectum [jf]—"in vineam," [jg] et [jh] certificat premium [ji] cum dicit [jj] "et quod iustum" et [jk] cetera. Et [jl] poterit quis quasi [jm] exponendo dirigere divisionem suam ad [jn] secundariam personam [jo] sic: secundum illud [jp] danielis 4: domine, qui carnem assumpsisti, *magnificatus es*; ibi [jq] quando nos de lacu [jr] eduxisti, [js] *invaluisti*; cum de morte surrexisti, [jt] *magnitudo* [ju] *tua crevit* dum super celos ascendisti; vel sic: *magnificatus es* in incarnacione; *invaluisti* in passione; *magnitudo tua* [jv] *crevit* [jw] in resurrexione. [jx] Item [jy] potest dividi per casualia et primo per rectos casus [jz] ut ibi *ecce* [ka] *rex tuus venit tibi* [kb] *mansuetus* [kc] (Matt. 21:5), tria [kd] nominantur: [ke] propinquitas venientis [kf] —"ecce," [kg] et [kh] sublimitas accedentis [ki] —"rex tuus," [kj] et [kk] utilitas advenientis [kl] quia "venit tibi mansuetus." [km] Item per dativum casum sic: *tu es qui venturus es, an alium expectamus* (Luc. 7:19), hic duo facit quia obsequitur [kn] veritati ibi [ko] "tu es qui venturus es," [kp] consulit [kq] infirmitati [kr] dum dicitur [ks] "an [kt] alium

---

[ig] modis *om. B1 B3*   [ih] q. varracione *A*   [ii] q. primum secundo a. *A*   [ij] est *om. B1 B3*
[ik] q. alias tercias h. *A*   [il] alias *B1 B2*   [im] eleviaces *B1* : elevantur *A*
[in] v. qui t. *B3* quia dileccio t. *B1*   [io] beni *B1*   [ip] commendacionis *A*
[iq] includit scilicet *om. A* i. sed *B1 B3*   [ir] tamen t. *B1*   [is] tercium *B1*
[it] setencionalium *B1* s. dummodo *A*   [iu] sit *B1 B3 A*   [iv] m. et cetera *A B3 A*
[iw] congrue f. *B1 B3* : congrua fieret *A*   [ix] terciam *B1 B2 B3 A*   [iy] hac parte m. *B3*
[iz] theme *B1*   [ja] v. et cetera *B1 B3*   [jb] meam *om. B1 B3*   [jc] h. tercia f. *B1 B3*
[jd] et *om. A*   [je] p. ibi i. *A* p. item s. *B3*   [jf] s. obedienciam *B1 B2 B3*
[jg] ibi in *A* in vineam *om. B2*   [jh] et *om. A*   [ji] p. ita *A*   [jj] dicit *om. A*   [jk] i. fuerit et *A*
[jl] et *om. A*   [jm] porrexit quasi *A*   [jn] s. a s. *A*   [jo] parabolam *A*
[jp] s. idem d. *B2* i. dictis q. *A*   [jq] ibi *om. A*   [jr] qui de lacu nos *A*
[js] eduxisti *om. B1* deduxists *A*   [jt] cum de morte surrexisti *om. A*
[ju] impassionem magnitudo *A*   [jv] dum super. . .magnitudo tua *om. B1 B2 B3 A*
[jw] crevit *om. B1 B2 B3 A*   [jx] in surreccione *B3*   [jy] I. thema p. *B1 B3 A*
[jz] casus *om. A*   [ka] i. cocce r. *B3*   [kb] tibi *om. B1*   [kc] mansuetus *om. A*
[kd] tercio *B1 B2 B3*   [ke] nominantis *B1* : notantur *A*   [kf] veniet *B1*
[kg] ecce *om. B1 B2 B3*   [kh] et *om. A*   [ki] accidentis *B1 B3*   [kj] tuus *om. A*   [kk] et *om. A*
[kl] adventus *A*   [km] mansuetus *om. A*   [kn] subsequitur *B1*   [ko] ibi *om. A*
[kp] qui venturus es *om. A*   [kq] consiluit *A*   [kr] divini d. *B3*   [ks] dum dicitur *om. A*
[kt] ibi an *A*

expectamus." [ku] Similiter in accusativo casu ut ibi *mitto angelum meum*, malachie tercio (Mal. 3:1), hic tria notantur: tercio primo [kv] quod pertinet ad mittentis auctoritatem ibi "mitto"; secundo quod pertinet ad legati sanctitatem—"angelum"; [kw] *tercio [kx] quod pertinet ad officii [ky] dignitatem ibi "qui [kz] preparabit viam." Similiter in ablativo [la] casu: *ecce venio et merces mea [lb] mecum*, apocalypsis tercio (Apoc. 22:12), hic proponitur [lc] mediatoris [ld] adventus sub triplici racione: sub [le] accedendi [lf] propinquitate [lg] ibi "ecce venio," sub largiendi facultate ibi [lh] "merces mea," [li] sub [lj] reddendi [lk] equitate ibi [ll] "reddere unicuique" et cetera, [lm] ut ex propinquitate solicitet [ln] hominem ad properandum, [lo] ex facultate [lp] alliciat ad diligendum, ex equitate terreat [lq] ad precavendum. [lr]

XVI
De clavibus divisionis [a]

Recte [b] nunc [c] ad delucidacionem principalis divisionis addunt quidam secundariam divisionem, [d] que vocatur parcium declaracio sive [e] clavis, eo quod aperit sive [f] elucidat [g] sensus [h] divisionis. Et tunc non oportet ad utramque [i] divisionem [j] adducere auctoritatem; verbi gracia, sit [k] hoc thema: *ecce ascendimus ierosolimam* (Luc. 18:31) sic dividatur: hic [l] predicitur [m] discipulis [n] futurum misterium [o] passionis [p] quantum ad tria, [q] quia quantum ad [r] tempus—"ascendimus," scilicet modo, quantum ad locum quia "ierosolimam," quantum ad effectum—"consummabuntur." Et tunc quoad divisionem [s] clavium resumatur divisio sic: tempus describitur sub racione propinquitatis [t] —"ecce"; [u] locus

---

[ku] hic duo. . .alium expectamus *om. B2*   [kv] primum *B2 B3 A*
[kw] s. ibi angelum *A* a. meam malach *B1*   [kx] tercium *B1 B2 B3 A*   [ky] officium *B1*
[kz] ibi *om. A* i. quia p. *B1*   [la] S. ab a. *B1*   [lb] meas *B2*   [lc] h. ponitur*A*
[ld] mediatorum *B1*   [le] tria racione racione s. *B1*   [lf] accidneti *B1* : accedente *A*
[lg] appropinquitate *A*   [lh] f. in m. *B2* f. ecce m. *A*   [li] meas *B2* mea *om. A*
[lj] tercio sub *A*   [lk] reddenti *B1 B3*   [ll] e. id est r.   [lm] et cetera *om. A*   [ln] solicite *B1*
[lo] preparandum *B1* : preperandum *A*   [lp] f. scilicet *A*   [lq] torrat *B1*
[lr] predicandum *B1* : preliandum *A*   [a] De clavibus divisionis *om. A*   [b] Ecce *B2 A*
[c] nunc *om. A*   [d] s. diccionem q. *B1*   [e] d. qui c. *A*   [f] a. et e. *A*   [g] elucidet *A*
[h] sensum *A*   [i] utram *B3*   [j] diccionem *B1*   [k] g. divisionis h. *B1 B3*   [l] hic *om. B1 B3*
[m] producitur *B3*   [n] discipulus *B1 B2 B3*   [o] ministerium *B1 B3*   [p] passionis *om. B2*
[q] ad primum q. *B1 B2 B3*   [r] q. quem ad *A*   [s] diccionem *B1*   [t] r. congruitatis *B1 B3*
[u] ecce *om. B3*

---

tercio : tercium H

describitur sub racione congruitatis[v] vel communitatis ibi[w] "iero-solimam"; effectus describitur sub[x] racione generalitatis <vel>[y] utilitatis[z] quia "consummabuntur."[aa]

Item per divisionis extra potest thema introduci[ab] et clavis adiungi sic:[63] si[ac] thema sit *sic currite ut comprehendatis*[ad] (I. Cor. 9:24), potest[ae] sic dici: triplex est lex—naturalis, scripta, et[af] evangelica, quarum prima docet[ag] quid faciendum, secunda quid et quodmodo faciendum, tercia quid,[ah] quomodo et[ai] ad quid faciendum. Ideo Paulus evangelice legis predicator docet quid faciendum cum dicit[aj] "currite"; quomodo sit faciendum[ak] —"sic"; ad quid faciendum—"ut comprehendatis." Primum istorum[al] actum specificat, scilicet,[am] "currite"; secundum meritum rectificat[an] —"sic"; et[ao] tertium premium fortificat—"ut[ap] comprehendatis."[aq] Item si thema sit *magister sequar te* (Luc. 9:61), sequendus est ut[ar] pastor[as] quia[at] reficit in labore, ut dominus quia protegit in temptacione,[au] ut medicus quia[av] medetur in dolore. Item si thema sit *propter te*[aw] *mortificamur tota die* (Ps. 42:22), poterit sic dici: penitencia describitur[ax] hic tripliciter:[ay] nam debet esse recta quod notatur ibi "propter te";[az] strenua[ba] quod[bb] notatur ibi "mortificamur"; continua quia "tota die," ut sit[bc] sic recta racione intencionis, strenua[bd] racione accionis, continua[be] racione duracionis. Et tunc subiungenda est auctoritas[bf] ad confirmacionem cuiuslibet membri[bg] seu clavis,[bh] nisi forte omnia membra possent confirmari unica auctoritate,

[v] locus describitur sub racione congruitatis *om. B3*   [w] ibi *om. A*   [x] sub *om. A*
[y] vel *om. B1 B2 B3 A*   [z] utilitas *B1 B2 B3*   [aa] consummabunt *B1*   [ab] induci *A*
[ac] s. sit t. *A*   [ad] c. primum igitur *B1 B3*   [ae] potest *om. B1* actum p. *B3*   [af] et *om. A*
[ag] docet *om. B1*   [ah] ergo quid *B1 B3*   [ai] et *om. B1*   [aj] cum dicit *om. A*
[ak] quomodo sit faciendum *om. A*   [al] P. ideo a. *B1 B3*   [am] specificat ibi c. *A*
[an] certificatur s. *A*   [ao] et *om. A*   [ap] p. sertificat ut *A*
[aq] c. primum istorum actum i. *B2*   [ar] ut *om. B1 B3*   [as] pasto *B1*   [at] p. qui r. *B2*
[au] in tempta *B2*   [av] m. est m. *B1*   [aw] te *om. B1 B3*   [ax] docebitur *B1 B2 B3*
[ay] hic tripliciter *om. B1 B2 B3* triplex *A*   [az] te *om. B1*
[ba] strenua *om. B1* strenia *B3*; quod notatur. . .te strenua *om. A*   [bb] quia n. *B1 A*
[bc] sit *om. B1*   [bd] strenue *B2*   [be] continue *B2*   [bf] auctoritates *B3*   [bg] membri *om. A*
[bh] s. clamas n. *A*

[63] The editors of the Franciscan *Ars concionandi* (*Bonaventurae Opera Omnia*, Vol IX [Ad Claras Aquas—Quaracchi, 1901] pp. 9, 11) make a useful comparison between *divisio intra* and *divisio extra*, as does Boethius' commentary on Cicero's *Topica* (*PL* 44:1054, 1064) where *locus in ipso* and *locus extrinsecus* are discussed. However, the theory of a "clavis" method into which these categories fit is part of the study of medieval rhetoric where "celui qui possède cette clef, et qui sait s'en servir, révèle au jour le contenu integral du texte qu'elle ouvre. . ." Etienne Gilson, *Les Idées et Les Lettres* (Paris 1932), pp. 118-19.

quod [bi] foret [bj] pulcherimum.

Item est alius modus [bk] breviter implicans ipsam divisionem et clavem corespondentem, ut si proponatur illud: *evangelizo vobis gaudium magnum* et cetera (Luc. 2:10). Hic considerandum est [bl] quod [bm] quis evangelizat quia angelus—ecce dignitas; [bn] *secundo [bo] quid evangelizatur quia gaudium [bp] —ecce utilitas; [bq] tercio [br] quibus [bs] evangelizatur quia [bt] omni populo—ecce congruitas. Isto modo solebant antiqui [bu] declarare et dividere per quis, [bv] quid, qualiter; verbi gracia *corripiet me iustus in misericordia* et cetera [bw] (Ps. 140:5), hic notatur de iudice [bx] qualis esse debeat quia "iustus," quid agere quia [by] "corripiet," qualiter quia "in [bz] misericordia." Set modo [ca] subtilius procedunt [cb] dicendo: hic describitur iudex quoad substanciam, quoad actum, [cc] et quoad modum. Quoad substanciam qualiter se [cd] debet exhibere, quoad actum [ce] quem [cf] debet se [cg] exercere, [ch] quoad modum [ci] quem debet tenere.

Potest eciam [cj] declaracio diversimode [ck] secundum sciencias [cl] diversas fieri quia [cm] grammatice, philosphice, logice; verbi [cn] gracia, [co] grammatice per verba, per nomina, [cp] per participia, per adverbia, ut si sit thema *misit verbum suum [cq] et sanavit eos* (Ps. 106:20), [cr] dicatur "verbum" quod erat activum cum [cs] patre in rerum creacione; "misit pater"—ut foret passivum [ct] <in> [cu] incarnacione; "et sanavit [cv] eos"—dum erat neutrum in sanguinis et acque [cw] effusione; "et [cx] eripuit [cy] eos"—dum erat deponens [cz] in patrum [da] extraccione; "de internicionibus" [db] —quibus erat [dc] verbum conmune in iudicii [dd] examinacione. [de] Item sit [df] declaracio per tempora verbi sic: [dg]   utinam saperent [dh]   preterita ac

---

[bi] a. qui f. *B2*   [bj] foret *om. B1*   [bk] est alius modus *om. B2*   [bl] est *om. B1*
[bm] quod *om. A*   [bn] ecce dignitas *om. B1 B2 B3*   [bo] tercio *B2*
[bp] evangelizatur quia gaudium *om. B2*   [bq] ecce utilitas *om. B2*   [br] tercio *om. B2 A*
[bs] quibus *om. B2*   [bt] B2 q. cum *B3*   [bu] s. aut qui *B1*   [bv] quis *om. B1*
[bw] cetera *om. A*   [bx] iudex *B1*   [by] a. qui c. *B3*   [bz] qualiter in *A*   [ca] modus *A*
[cb] proceditur *A*   [cc] accidentem *B1 B2*   [cd] s. qualem se *A*   [ce] accidentem *B1 B2*
[cf] quomodo d. *B1 B2 B3*   [cg] debet se *om. A*
[ch] e. quo accidentem quomodo debet se exercere q. *B1*   [ci] m. quomodo q. *B1*
[cj] P. omni d. *B1* P. et d. *A*   [ck] diversimodum *B3*   [cl] sonas *B1 B3* : summas *B2*
[cm] f. qui g. *B3*   [cn] l. et p. *A*   [co] g. primo g. *A*   [cp] n. et p. *A*   [cq] suum *om. B1*
[cr] e. et d. *A*   [cs] c. iusit p. *B1*   [ct] p. et i. *B1*   [cu] in *om. B2*   [cv] et lavavit e. *B1*
[cw] aquo *B1*   [cx] et *om. B1*   [cy] erruipuit *B3*   [cz] disponens *B3* e. verbum d. *A*
[da] patrium *B1*   [db] interniccibis *B3* i. et e. *B1* i. et sic e. *B2 B3*   [dc] erit *B1 B3*
[dd] in medicti e. *B1*; quibus erat . . .in iudicii *om. A*   [de] examinacione *om. A*
[df] fit *B1 B3*
[dg] v. e quibus est verbum communi in iudicii examinacione item sit declaracio per tempora sic *A*   [dh] saperunt *B3*

---

*secundo : tercio H

intelligerent presencia[di] <ac>[dj] novissima[dk] providerent[dl] quantum ad[dm] futura. Item quantum ad[dn] modum[do] verbi[dp] sic: hoc verbum[dq] fuit[dr] indicativum in nostre nature assumpcione, imperativum in predicacione, optativum in[ds] nostra salvacione et cetera.[dt] Item fit declaracio quantum ad personas sic:[du] sit thema in purificacione in persona virginis loquuntis[dv] ad Symonem[dw] *ostendam*[dx] *tibi omne*[dy] *bonum* (Ex. 33:19), post[dz] cuius divisionem dici potest: hic ostenditur in prima persona communicacionis benignitas—"ostendam";[ea] in secunda persona disposicionis[eb] humilitas—"tibi";[ec] in tercia persona concluditur fruicionis utilitas—"omne bonum." Item quantum ad participium[ed] sic: sit thema de Magdalena Maria: *optimam partem elegit* (Luc. 10:42), Maria fuit participium in statu culpe, partem capiens a nomine dum proprium nomen[ee] amittens peccatrix appellaretur, partem capiens a verbo in principio sue penitencie quando[ef] audivit a verbo *remittuntur tibi peccata tua* (Luc. 7:48), partem ab utroque dum per tres annos[eg] postmodum partim peccata sua deflendo,[eh] partim contemplando[ei] manibus angelicis[ej] elevata fuit.

Item fit[ek] declaracio logice secundum partes[el] tocius[em] diversimode sumpti vel prout sunt partes tocius virtualis vel tocius[en] universalis vel tocius[eo] integralis. Item fit[ep] declaracio philosophice sic: sit thema *relinquo mundum et*[eq] *vado ad patrem* (Ioan. 16:28), in motu tria requiruntur:[er] terminus a[es] quo, et terminus ad quem, <et> fluxus[et] inter terminos. Quantum[eu] ad primum dicit[ev] "relinquo mundum," quantum ad medium dicit "vado," quantum ad terminum[ew] ad quem dicit[ex] "ad patrem."

Item in themate copulative oracionis sic: potest[ey] procedi, *abiciamus opera tenebrarum et induamur arma*[ez] *lucis*, ad[fa] romanos 13 (Rom. 13:12), duo notantur ad[fb] que apostolus nos invitat[fc]

[di] ac intelligerent presencia *om. B1* [dj] ac *om. B2* [dk] novissimo *B2* [dl] provideret *B2* [dm] ac in ad *B1* [dn] I. qualiter ad *B3* I. que ad *A* [do] motum *B1* modum *om. A* [dp] verbum *B2* [dq] verbum *om. A* [dr] fit *B1 B2 B3* [ds] predicacione in n. *B1* [dt] cetera *om. A* [du] p. verbi sic *A* [dv] loquntur *B2* [dw] Simeone *A* [dx] quamdam t. *B1* ostenda *A* [dy] t. esse b. *B1* [dz] b. opus c. *B1 B2 B3* [ea] ostenditur *B1 B2 B3* [eb] p. supposicionis h. *B1* [ec] tibi *om. B1 B2 B3* [ed] participionis *A* [ee] nomen *om. A* [ef] p. quia a. *A* [eg] 30 annos *A* [eh] defluendo *B1 B3* : efflendo *A* [ei] contemplanda *A* [ej] angelorum *B1* [ek] fuit *B1* [el] partem *A* [em] tocius *om. A* [en] tocius *om. A* [eo] universalis vel tocius *om. B1* [ep] fuit *B1* [eq] m. quantum et *B2* [er] r. scilicet t. *A* [es] tres a *B1 B2* : tres ad *B1 B2* [et] quem fluxus *B2 B3* f. medius i. *A* [eu] Quem *B2* [ev] dicitur *A* [ew] ad tercium *B1 B2 A* [ex] ad quem dicit *om. A* [ey] c. tercius prima *B1* : c. sermonis sic *B2* : c. cuiusius sic *B3* : os eius potest p. *A* [ez] induamur arma *om. A* [fa] lucis ad *om. A* [fb] d. id est ad *B1* d. dicuntur *B3* [fc] n. amittat *B1* : mutat *A*

que sunt peccatorum abieccio [fd] et virtutum induccio. [fe] Circa primum duo considerantur: [ff] quare peccata dicuntur "tenebrarum opera" et quare abicienda; [fg] similiter circa secundum duo, quare [fh] virtutes [fi] dicuntur "arma lucis" et qualiter inducenda [fj] sunt. [fk] Ad hanc ergo declaracionem [fl] parcium sive clavium [fm] addenda est statim [fn] confirmacio per auctoritatem, verbi gracia, sit thema *iustus de angustia liberatus est* (Prov. 11:8), dividatur sic: tria tanguntur, facientis [fo] sanctitas [fp] cum dicitur [fq] "iustus," sequentis [fr] malignitas "de [fs] angustia," eruentis benignitas ibi "liberatus est." Et [ft] declaratur [fu] sic cum confirmacione auctoritatis: in sanctitate premittitur conversacio exemplaris [fv] —"iustus"—proverbiorum: [fw] *iustorum semita quasi lux splendens* [fx] *procedit* (Prov. 4:18); in malignitate additur tribulacio singularis [fy] ibi "de angustia"—iob: [fz] *terrebit eum* [ga] *tribulacio et* [gb] *angustia* [gc] *vallabit* [gd] *eum* [ge] (Iob 15:24); in benignitate concluditur [gf] dileccio familaris [gg] quia [gh] "liberatus est"—ad timotheum 2: [gi] *liberavit me deus ab* [gj] *omni opere* (II Tim. 4:18).

XVII
De sermonis dilatacione [a]

Est hic notandum quod dilatacio fit duobus modis: per membrorum subdivisionem [b] et per auctoritatis adducte expositionem; [c] verbi gracia, proposito et diviso hoc themate: [d] *habitabit iuvenis cum virgine* (Is. 62:5), est sciendum [e] <quod> [f] potest dici sic: [g] circa [h] virginem est sciendum [i] quod quedam est detestanda, [j] quedam imitanda, quedam admiranda. Detestanda est illa que deo non dedicatur, [k] set propter vanam gloriam celebratur; de

---

[fd] obieccio *B1*   [fe] induacio *B1 B2 B3*   [ff] c. scilicet *B1 A*   [fg] et quare abicienda *om. A*
[fh] s. scilicet quare *A*; peccata dicuntur. . .secundo quare *om. B1 B2 B3*   [fi] v. domini *B1*
[fj] inducanda *B1*   [fk] sunt *om. A*   [fl] determinacionem p. *B1*   [fm] clavum *B1*
[fn] e. stacio *B3*   [fo] t. pacientis s. *A*   [fp] s. ibi *A*   [fq] dicitur *A*   [fr] i. persequentis m. *A*
[fs] m. ibi de *A*   [ft] Et *om. A*   [fu] delatur *B1* : declaretur *A*
[fv] exemplo conversacionis ibi i. *A* exemplaris *om. B2*   [fw] iustus prout i. *B2* p. 4 i. *A*
[fx] splendorum*A*   [fy] singularum *A*   [fz] i. ?ai tenebit *A*   [ga] t. cum t. *B2*
[gb] tribulacio et *om. A*   [gc] a. et *A*   [gd] illabit *B3*   [ge] eum *om. B2* e. tribulacio *A*
[gf] concluditur *om. B1*   [gg] famularis *B2 A*   f. qua l. *A*   [gi] t. 3 *A*   [gj] me dominus ab *A*
[a] dilacione *B2* De sermonis dilatacione *om. A*
[b] s. est sciendum quod quedam est detestanda quedam imitanda quedam admiranda *B1* subdivisione *B3*
[c] adducte expositionem. . .hoc themate *om. B3* adducte exemplacionem et verbi exposicionem *A*   [d] themate scilicet h. *A*; et per. . .hoc themate *om. B1*
[e] est sciendum *om. A*   [f] quod *om. B2 B3 A*   [g] sic *om. B1 B2 B3*   [h] contra v. *B2*
[i] est istud q. *A*   [j] est distanda *A*   [k] non educatur *B1* : nondedicat *B3*

qua dicitur in[l] scriptura sacra:[m] *virgines eius squalide*[n] (Lam. 1:4), set si ad[o] hoc corroborandum adduceretur exemplum vel manuduccio vel[p] auctoritas, tanto[q] melius foret. Virginitas imitanda est ista[r] que deo dedicatur nam sicut[s] virgines sequuntur[t] parentes suos ad ecclesiam a[u] quibus preservantur sic[v] illi qui deo virginitatem suam donaverunt,[w] ipsum sequuntur[x] a quo[y] custodiuntur; unde in[z] apocalypse[aa] dicitur:[ab] *hii sunt qui cum mulieribus non sunt coinquinati, virgines enim sunt et sequuntur agnum*[ac] (Apoc. 14:4). Tercia virginitas admiranda est illa que[ad] non habet parem,[ae] ut videlicet, ibi sit virginitas ubi et fecunditas quod solum in beata[af] Maria reperitur; unde in[ag] ecclesiastico reperitur:[ah] *mulier a virginitate suscipiet illum* (Eccli. 15:2), et in[ai] luca 1 dicitur:[aj] *missus est angelus Gabriel et cetera*[ak] (Luc. 1:26). Ecce quomodo et[al] illo modo dividendi[am] primum membrum est imperativum,[an] secundum[ao] commendativum,[ap] et tercium precellentivum.

Poterit subdiviso[aq] tamen fieri ita ut[ar] quodlibet membrum sit commendativum et in fine cuiuslibet membri sit inpaccio[as] ad dicti oppositum,[at] quomodo utitur frater Nicholaus in distinccionibus suis[au] qui[av] incipiunt *"abeuncium,"[aw] [64] et beatus Augustinus[ax] in exposicionibus suis ubi dicit *quod[ay] "contra

[l] in *om. A*   [m] tenorum primo *A*   [n] e. sopolide s. *B1*   [o] s. et ad *A*
[p] vel necessario vel *B2*   [q] tante *B1*   [r] illa *B1 B2 B3 A*   [s] sicut *om. B1* sic *B3*
[t] sequentur *B1*   [u] s. adducat q. *B1* s. ad intra q. *B2 B3*   [v] sicut *B1 B2*
[w] devoverunt *B1 A* : deveverunt *B3*   [x] sequntur *A*   [y] q. et c. *A*   [z] u. et in *A*
[aa] apocalypse 14 *A*   [ab] dicitur *om. A*   [ac] a. quocumque ierit *A*   [ad] que *A B1*
[ae] partem *B1*   [af] b. virgine m. *A*   [ag] u. et in e. *A*   [ah] dicitur *A*   [ai] in *om. A*
[aj] dedicat *B3*   [ak] et cetera *om. A*   [al] et *om. A* et in *B1 B3 A*   [am] dicendi *B1*
[an] e. impactum *B3* : e. mutativum *A* imperativum *om. B2*   [ao] secundarius *A*
[ap] nuendativum *B2*   [aq] subsidio *B1*   [ar] ut ad q. *A*   [as] inpaccio *om. A*
[at] ad dictum membrum q. *A*   [au] d. eius *B2*   [av] que *B3 A*
[aw] abeversum *B1* : abeundum *B3*; qui incipiunt abeuncium *om. B2*
[ax] Gregorius *B1 B3 A*   [ay] quo *B2 B3*

*abeuncium : abeversum *H*
*quod : quo *H*

[64] The "distinctions" to which Ranulph refers are probably the *Distinctiones fratis Nicholai de Gorran de ordine predicatorum secundum ordinem alphabeti* which has survived in some 35 or more manuscripts. The treatise begins "Abeuncium per hunc mundum abeunt mali alii bene. Abeunt male tria genera hominum secundum triplicem malam concupiscenciam eos ducentem." The quotation illustrates Ranulph's comment. For fuller discussion see André Wilmart, "Un Répertoire d'exégèse composé en Angleterre vers le début du xiiie siècle," *Memorial Lagrange* (Paris, 1940), pp. 342-43. See also Kaeppeli, no. 3090.

de reprobis dicitur."[65] Et est modus ille perutilis ad populum eo quod fecunde se extendat[az] ad virtutes[ba] comendandas[bb] et vicia[bc] detestanda; verbi gracia, ad virginem spectat habere[bd] tres condiciones bonas que sunt ornamentum[be] decoris;[bf] ieremiae[bg] dicitur, *nunquid oblita est ornamenti sui* (Ier. 2:32), set[bh] contra hoc est illud in biblia:[bi] *virgines eius squalide.* Secundo dicitur[bj] habere munimentum pudoris,[bk] genese:[bl] *virgo pulcherima et*[bm] *incognita viro* (Gen. 24:16), quod est contra filiam *Iepte[bn] que circuiens montes[bo] defloravit[bp] virginitatem suam.[66] Tercio debet[bq] habere condimentum amoris,[br] secundum illud matthei 25: *acceperunt*[bs] *oleum in vasis suis cum lampadibus*[bt] *suis*[bu] (Matt. 25:4), quod est contra fatuas virgines oleo carentes.

Isto[bv] modo poterit secundum membrum et tercium in tria subdividi et in illo[bw] modo triplex[bx] est modus procedendi quia primo poterunt[by] expediri tria membra primi, secundo tria membra secundi,[bz] et tercio tria[ca] membra tercii; vel primo[cb] dicitur[cc] de triplici virginitate, secundo de triplici iuventute, et tercio de triplici habitacione.[67] Et tunc decens[cd] foret si <in>[ce] ultimo membro primi[cf] posset[cg] introduci secundum[ch] principale, et si

---

[az]extendit *A*   [ba]veritates *B1 B2* : veritate *B3*   [bb]comendancias *B1* : et mendandas *B3*
[bc]et ad vicia *A*   [bd]s. hore t. *B3*   [be]ornamentis *B1*   [bf]decorum *A*   [bg]i. 20 *A*
[bh]s. oportet c. *B2*   [bi]hoc eiusdem tenorum primo capitulo v. *A*   [bj]s. debet h. *A*
[bk]pudorem *A*   [bl]g. 24 *A*   [bm]et *om. A*   [bn]repte *B2*   [bo]criminis modo d. *B1*
[bp]deploravit *B1 B3* : deplanxit *A*   [bq]dicitur h. *B1*   [br]c. honoris *A*   [bs]accepit *A*
[bt]lampatibus *B1 B2* : lampidibus *B3*   [bu]suis *om. A*   [bv]Illo *B2 B3*   [bw]isto *A*
[bx]duplex *B1 B3 A*   [by]poterint *B1*   [bz]secundi *om. A*   [ca]tria *om. A*   [cb]prius *A*
[cc]dicatur *B1 B3*   [cd]dices f. *B3*   [ce]f. sed in *A*   [cf]primo *B1*   [cg]possent *A*
[ch]secundo *B2*

Iepte : Repte H

---

[65] Augustine wrote several treatises which qualify as "expositions" and which offer a "contra" to the machinations of the reprobate in numerous places; see especially the *Expositio quarumdam propositionam ex Epistola ad Romanos* and the *Expositio ad Galatas* (*PL* 35 and 36).

[66] The story of the unfortunate arrival of Jepthe's daughter is recounted in Judges 11:29 ff. It was apparently a popular one in the later Middle Ages; Abelard, in the twelfth century, had written a long "Planctus Virginum Israelis super filia Jepthae Galaditae" (in *PL* 178:1819 ff.). Defloravit=deflevit or deploravit.

[67] In his *Liber de exhortatione castitatis* (*PL* 2:915), Tertullian speaks of a "triple virginity," so it may be assumed that this type of explication received an early start within the Christian tradition. Triplicate schematization was common in the medieval period; see, for example, the poetry of Hildebert of Lavardin (*PL* 171:1388 ff.) for illustrations of explication by threes.

in ultimo membro secundi principalis posset introduci tercium principale,[ci] quasi per *quandam[cj] continuacionem[ck] sive convexcionem[cl] mediante[cm] alia auctoritate in qua[cn] primum et secundum membrum reperirentur,[co] et iterum alia auctoritate[cp] in qua[cq] secundum et tercium membrum reperirentur.[cr]

Item alius modus est per correspondenciam[cs] membrorum ad[ct] invicem et[cu] coaptetur[cv] primum primi[cw] ad secundum secundi et ad *tercium tercii;[cx] et iterum[cy] secundum primi ad secundum secundi et ad *secundum[cz] tercii; et iterum[da] tercium[db] primi ad tercium secundi et ad tercium[dc] tercii.[dd] Set talis[de] curiositas[df] correspondencie circularitatis[dg] non est multum[dh] utilis ad populum; quidam adhuc[di] curiose subdividunt utpote dividentes primum membrum in tria, secundum[dj] membrum in duo, et tercium[dk] membrum in[dl] unum, quod manet[dm] indivisum[dn] ut sic sit quasi[do] sermo piramidalis,[dp] id est, habens basum latum[dq] tendens in conmuni.[68] Si autem[dr] sermo habeat duo membra vel tria sine ulteriori divisione vocatur sermo linearis[ds] quia ad[dt]

[ci] et si. . .tercium principale *om. A*   [cj] quodam *B2*   [ck] condicionem s. *B1*
[cl] convencionem *B1 B2* : commixitonem *A*   [cm] m. supra *B1*   [cn] qua *om. A*
[co] repientur *B1* : repirentur *B2* : reperietur *A*   [cp] auctoritas *B1 B3*   [cq] quo *B1*
[cr] reperietur *A*   [cs] carenciam *B3*   [ct] membrorum ad *om. B1* c. verborum ad *A*
[cu] et *om. A*   [cv] coaptare ut coaptetur *A*   [cw] invicem et coaptetur primum primi *om. B1*
[cx] primum tercii *B1 B2 B3*   [cy] et tercium s. *B1*   [cz] ad tercium t. *B1*
[da] et tercium t. *B1* et in casu t.   [db] tercium *om. B2*
[dc] tercium quarti et ad tercium t. *B1*   [dd] et iterum. . .tercium tercii *om. A*
[de] t. scilicet tres ita c. *B3*   [df] curiositas *om. B1*
[dg] circulariter *B1* : circularitas *B2* : circularitatis seu stalaritatis n. *A*   [dh] est intum u. *B2*
[di] quid autem adhuc *A*   [dj] secundum in *A*   [dk] in tria *A*
[dl] membrum *om. A* m. et u. *B2*   [dm] mane *B1*   [dn] divisum *B1 B2 B3 A* in unum d. *A*
[do] q. ut sic sit s. *B1*   [dp] s. principalis *B1*   [dq] basim *A* b. altera t. *B2* : latera *B1 B3 A*
[dr] autem *om. A*   [ds] literalis *A*   [dt] quod ad *A*

---

*quandam : quodam *H*
*tercium : primum *H*
*secundum : tercium *H*

---

[68] The section between notes 67 and 68 is somewhat difficult to understand. Basically, the first part (from "Et tunc" to "reperirentur") advocates the employment of certain mutually acceptable authorities that might act as bridges between the first and second divisions and between the second and third. The section between "Item alius modus" and "tendens in conmuni" describes the result of reciprocal correspondence among three different groups. Higden concludes that circular correspondence is not very useful for the ordinary people. He endeavors, however, to describe pyramidal construction which involves the division of the first member into three parts, the second into two, and the third into just itself so that there might be a wide base with sides tending towards a common point.

modum linee quia^{du} non habet^{dv} nisi unam divisionem,^{dw} et est
ille^{dx} modus clarus et utilis ad populum. Et tunc insistendum est
multum circa exposicionem adductarum^{dy} auctoritatum, eo quod
tunc^{dz} non fit aliqua subdivisio ad dilatandum sermonem. Quod
si subdivisio primi membri sit pregnans, tunc poterit prosecucio
subdivisionis aliorum membrorum dimitti illa^{ea} quod denique^{eb}
ubicumque contigerit^{ec} finis sermonis.[69] In fine eterna premiacio
postuletur.

XVIII
De membrorum subdivisione^a

Notandum est hic circa modum subdividendi quod quot
modis^b contingit dividere, tot^c modis^d contingit^e subdividere.
Fit^f autem divisio sex modis secundum Boicium in libro divisio-
num,[70] quia dividitur^g totum universale in partes subiectivas,
quod est differentie^h etⁱ generis in^j species, ut si beatitudo divi-
deretur in beatitudinem^k rei et spei.^l Est eciam^m divisio tocius
integralis in partes integrantesⁿ ut quod beatitudo^o rei consistit in
dei unione^p et in dei fruicione.[71] Fit eciam^q divisio vocis in

---

^{du} l. non h. *B1 B2 B3 A*   ^{dv} n. hunc n. *B2*   ^{dw} dimensionem *A*   ^{dx} iste *A*
^{dy} est multum circa exposicionem adductarum *om. B1*   ^{dz} q. talis n. *A*
^{ea} d. ita quid q. *A*   ^{eb} denique *om. A*   ^{ec} contigerit *om. A*
^a De membrorum subdivisione *om. A*   ^b modus *B1* : modum *B2*   ^c tot *om. B3*
^d modum *B2*   ^e contingitur *B3*   ^f Sic a. *B1*   ^g quod dividit *A*   ^h e. divisio *A*
ⁱ et *om. A*   ^j g. et s. *B3*   ^k habitudo *B1* : habitudinem *B1*
^l rei *om. B2* r. ut species *B1* et speciei *B2 A* : et spe *B3*   ^m E. autem d. *A*
ⁿ integritatis *A*   ^o habitudo *B1*   ^p d. visione *B1 B3 A*   ^q Sit et d. *B1* F. autem *A*

---

[69] Thomas Penketh, a fifteenth century sermonizer, repeats Ranulph's remarkable description of methods by which subdivisions might be used to give diversity of form to sermons.
He devotes quite a bit of space to the plane or surface sermon and also to the cubical or
solid or corporeal sermon (constructed out of numerous divisions and subdivisions). Having elaborated somewhat on the *Ars componendi sermones*, Penketh (Oxford Univ. MS 36,
fols. 245-6) also deigns to discuss the "circular sermon" (see note 67 above). Higden's
treatment of these sermon diversities is most interesting, for although Basevorn does mention correspondence, circularity, and convolution in sermon patterns, he does not immediately draw up the analogies to pyramid and line which are found in the *Ars componendi
sermones*.

[70] Boethius, *Liber de divisione, PL* 64:877 ff.

[71] The question of the actual content of "heaven" to the blessed was a real one to
fourteenth-century theologians and its implications are reflected here. Apparently, there
was no certain agreement on the part of the Fathers on the "when" of entry into heaven
and some of Augustine's words (especially in *De trinitate* VIII and XIII, 28-31 and in *De
genesi ad litteram*, XII, cap. xxv) appeared to favor delayed entry. In 1241, William of
Auvergne and the faculty of theology at Paris make a clear declaration for immediate entry
and so did Aquinas, but Bernard seems to have adopted an Augustinian position that the
beatific vision in its plenitude was reserved for resurrected saints (*De diligendo deo*, XI,

significaciones, ut si dicatur templum^r domini secundum^s sensum literalem significat templum Salamonis ex lignis^t et lapidibus constitutum;^u secundum allegoriam designat beatam^v Mariam vel ecclesiam militantem; secundum tropologiam denotat^w animam christianam sive conscienciam; secundum anagogiam denotat ecclesiam triumphantem. Quarto modo fit divisio subiecti in accidencia, ut si dicatur secundum morem litterarum nostrarum hominum quidam^x sunt innocentes, quidam penitentes,^y quidam^z perfecti. Quinto^{aa} modo fit divisio accidentis^{ab} in subiecta^{ac} ut sanctorum quidam^{ad} sunt apostoli et^{ae} quidam^{af} angeli. Sexto modo fit divisio accidentis in accidentia,^{ag} ut sanctorum quidam^{ah} sunt martires, quidam^{ai} confessores. Hiis modis poterit addi septimus modus quo dividitur^{aj} totum potentiale in partes^{ak} potentiales, ut si dicatur sanguis Christi est regenerativus^{al} a peccato original, est ablutivus^{am} ab actuali, et^{an} redemptivus^{ao} a pena infernali.[72] Cum ergo volueris subdividere aliquod membrum, considera *sensum^{ap} membri^{aq} et racionem subdividendi et

---

^rt. dei s. *B1*   ^sd. secundum est s. *A*   ^tlinguis *B1*   ^uconstructum *B1 B3 A*
^vd. sanctam m. *A*   ^wt. designat a. *A*   ^xh. quid s. *A*   ^yquid p. *A*   ^zquid p. *B2 A*
^{aa}Coniuncto m. *B2*   ^{ab}accionis *B1 B2 B3*   ^{ac}subiectum *B1 B2 B3*   ^{ad}s. quid s. *A*
^{ae}et *om. A*   ^{af}quid *B2 A* q. sunt a *A*   ^{ag}in subiecta accidentia *A*   ^{ah}s. quid s. *A*
^{ai}q. sunt c. *B3* quid c. *A*   ^{aj}q. dividi *A*   ^{ak}in parte p. *B3*
^{al}regeneratus *B1* : generativus *B3* : regeneracio *A* r. sanguis *A*
^{am}ablatus *B1* ablativus *B2 B3 A*   ^{an}et *om. A*   ^{ao}redemptativus *B1 B2 B3 A*
^{ap}sensus *B1 B2 B3*   ^{aq}secundum membrum *A*

---

*sensum: sensus *H*

29-31). Pope John XXII originally shared the belief held at Paris for in a Bull issued on the death of Louis of Anjou in 1317, he spoke of Louis' having entered into heaven to see his God face to face. However, in a sermon preached on All Soul's Day in 1331, Pope John quoted Bernard's view that the reward of the just before the General Judgement was the "sinus Abrahae" of the Dives-Lazarus parable or more generally a contemplation only of the humanity of Christ. John repeated this argument in sermons preached on the Third Sunday of Advent, 1331, and on Epiphany and Purification in 1332, causing the theologians to take up cudgels against him. John retracted all these statements on his deathbed (Denifle-Chatelain, II, p. 441, no. 984) and in January 1336, Pope Benedict's Constitution "Benedictus Deus" made direct entry into heaven a Church dogma. In addition to commenting on a matter of vital concern to the earlier fourteenth century, Higden may be making a reference to a fellow manualist, Thomas Waleys, who became embroiled in this whole controversy and wound up in prison as a result; see Dorothy Grosser, tr., "Thomas Waleys: *On the Manner of Composing Sermons*," Unpublished M.A. Thesis (Cornell, 1949), pp. iii-v. (I owe these citations to Michael Haren, University College, Dublin.)

[72] Both "templum domini" and "sanguis Christi" have numerous biblical referents. Higden's sentiment here is probably akin to I John 1:7: "sanguis Christi filii eius, emundat nos ab omni peccato."

vide^{ar} si primo poteris subdividere^{as} in partes subiectivas; quodsi non tunc per partes integrales et sic deinceps quousque^{at} reperis^{au} aliquam divisionem proposito tuo congruentem,^{av} ita quidem quod membra subdivisionis non sibi coincidant nec sint^{aw} nimis multiplicia, et quod unum membrorum ex^{ax} alio sequatur si fieri possit,^{ay} et quod membra consonent^{az} in colore; ut verbi gracia, debemus transire per viam penitencie peccata detestanda,^{ba} per viam paciencie adversa tolleranda,^{bb} per viam^{bc} iusticie unicuique quod suum est^{bd} tribuendo. Sed in predicando non est^{be} multum utendum illa divisione que est vocis in significaciones,^{bf} nam illa plus pertinet ad disputantes pro solucione *paralogismorum^{bg} et ad legentes in scolis^{bh} pro solucione contrarietatum^{bi} quam ad predicantes.^{bj} [73]

XIX
<De dilatacione facienda per auctoritates>^a

Sermo poterit dilatari multis modis. Uno modo ponendo^b oracionem pro nomine, sicut fit in^c diffinicionibus,^d descripcionibus,^e interpretacionibus, et aliis quibuslibet notificacionibus; verbi gracia, sit thema *iustum deduxit* dominus[74]

---

^{ar} videre *B3*   ^{as} s. per p. *A*   ^{at} d. qui *B1 B2 B3*
^{au} recipere *B1* : reperire *B3* : repereris *A*   ^{av} congruente *B2 B3*   ^{aw} sunt *B2 B3 A*
^{ax} u. membrum ex *A*   ^{ay} possunt *B1* : posset *B3*   ^{az} concinent *A*   ^{ba} detestando *B1 B3*
^{bb} tollerando *B1 B3 A*   ^{bc} viam *om. B1*   ^{bd} quod suum est *om. B1*
^{be} p. et ideo est *B3*   ^{bf} in sanguines *B1 B3* significaciones *om. B2*
^{bg} prologismorum *B1* : plogismorum *B2* : pro sologismorum *B3* : per logismorum *A*
^{bh} in cholis *B1 B3*   ^{bi} contrietatem *B1*   ^{bj} quam ad predicantes *om. A*
^a De dilatacione facienda per auctoritates *om. A*   ^b penendo *B1*   ^c det d. *B1 B3*
^d d. in d. *B2 A*   ^e in i. *A*

---

*paralogismorum : parlogismorum *H*

---

[73] It would seem that, although he was copying rather directly from John of Wales, the words "vocis significatio" brought to Basevorn's mind (and possibly to Ranulph's) the long and acrimonious debate about universals which broke the scholarly world of the twelfth century into realist and nominalist camps. These sermon theorists apparently harbored a distrust (if not a dislike) for university exercises which threaten the true function of preaching and leave no loophole for their entrance into their *artes*.

[74] Sap. 10:10: "Iustum deduxit per vias rectas." Actually, the addition of "dominus" can be traced to liturgical usage: the common Responsory of the Divine Office for Bishops, Confessors, Doctors, and so forth reads: "Iustum deduxit Dominus per vias rectas."

per vias rectas (Sap. 10:10) vel *iustus ut palma florebit* (Ps. 91:13) et describitur[f] "iustus" sic qui tribuit unicuique quod suum[g] est, utpote quid deo[h] tamquam superiori, quid equali ut sibi, quid[i] inferiori[j] tamquam[k] proximo, et qualiter debeat reddere. Et cum[l] diffinitur aut describitur aliud poterit predicator se transferre ad oppositum illius,[m] quoniam declaracio unius oppositorum[n] valet[o] ad notificacionem[p] alterius oppositi, et sic[q] descripta una virtute[r] poterit descendere[s] ad alias virtutes,[t] dicendo[u] sic: sicut iusticia est in reddendo unicuique quod suum est, sic prudencia in[v] discernendo, fortitudo in[w] sufferendo et cetera. Et in illo[x] modo dilatandi expedit respicere[y] descripciones et interpretaciones, quia[z] una interpretacio aliquando plus facit ad propositum quam alia; et in illo modo vitanda est[aa] obscuritas quia secundum Boicium descripciones, diffiniciones, et interpretaciones[ab] causa innotescendi[ac] fiunt.[ad]

Secundus modus dilatandi fit per divisiones sicut dicit Porphirius:[ae] necesse est dividentem per multitudinem ire (*Liber praedicabilium*, cap. iii, "de specie"); verbi gracia, ut si[af] proponatur virtus in[ag] infirmitate,[ah] perficitur et subdividitur[ai] sic: virtutum quedam cardinales,[aj] quedam theologice et cetera; primis[ak] disponimur ad proximum, secundis ad deum, de quo[al] vide[am] supra, capitulo proximo.

Tercius modus dilatacionis[an] fit raciocinando sive arguendo quod fit[ao] potissime tribus[ap] modis: primo quando de[aq] aliquibus duobus racionatur aliquid ad[ar] approbandum[as] unum[at] sed[au] ad[av] vituperandum[aw] reliquum; verbi gracia, si intendo[ax] approbare continenciam[ay] dicitur[az] sic: luxuria perdit pecuniam, corpus, animam, et famam; ergo continencia que huic contraria est, amplectenda[ba] est.[bb] Alius modus est[75] procedere per[bc] latencia

---

[f] et describitur *om. B1 B2 B3*   [g] q. saum e. *A*   [h] u. qui es t. *A*   [i] ut sic quid *A*
[j] q. instruere *B1*   [k] tamquam *om. B1*   [l] et cetera d. *B1 B2 B3*   [m] istius *B1* eius *A*
[n] opponendum *B1*   [o] vale *B1*   [p] ad declaracionem *A*
[q] et *om. B1* o. sed d. *B1* sic *om. B2 B3*   [r] veritate *B1 B2 B3*   [s] descende *B2*
[t] veritatis *B1* : veritates *B2 B3*   [u] descendo *B1*   [v] p. est in *B1 B2 B3 A*
[w] d. for in *B1*   [x] isto *A*   [y] r. plures d. *A*   [z] i. qui u. *B3* : i. quandoque *B1 B3*
[aa] est obest o. *B1* : abest *B2* : ebest *B3*   [ab] quia una. . .et interpretaciones *om. A*
[ac] innotestescendi *B1*   [ad] fiunt *om. A*   [ae] P. quod n. *A*   [af] ut ly p. *B1*
[ag] in *om. B1 B2*   [ah] v. influit p. *B1*   [ai] subdividatur *A*
[aj] dicit Porphirius. . .quedam cardinales *om. B3*   [ak] primus *B1 B2 A*   [al] do quo *B1*
[am] vi *B3*   [an] dilatandi *A*   [ao] que sit p. *B1*   [ap] p. quibus m. *B1*   [aq] p. modo de *A*
[ar] aliquid ad *om. A*   [as] approbando *A*   [at] unum *om. B1*   [au] sed sed *B2*   [av] ad *om. A*
[aw] vituperando *A*   [ax] sed ad. . .si intendo *om. B1*   [ay] continencia *B3*
[az] dicatur *B1 B2 B3 A*   [ba] applectanda *A*   [bb] est *om. A*   [bc] procedendi scilicet per *A*

---

[75] In MS B2, fol. 98r, line 1 ("si") through line 11 ("mitigavit") is rewritten immediately after "alius modus est" from the chapter *De thematis introduccione* which appears at the beginning of fol. 89v in the same manuscript. A cross in the margin (lines 4-5) and two at

emptimemata[bd] postulando iudicium ab ipsis[be] auditoribus;[bf] verbi gracia, nonne stultus[bg] <foret> qui propriis manibus[bh] texeret[bi] cordam cum qua[bj] suspenderetur ab hoste suo? Talis est peccator sicut dicitur proverbiis 4: funiculis peccatorum suorum quisque[bk] constringitur.[76] Illo[bl] modo usus est Nathan[bm] propheta contra[bn] David[bo] et ipse Christus[bp] in parabolis de agricolis, sicut[bq] habetur in mattheo[br] (cf. Matt. 21:33-44).[bs] [77]

Quartus modus dilatandi est *raciocinari[bt] per exempla; verbi gracia, apostoli[bu] et martires per multas tribulaciones transierunt[bv] ad regnum, ita et nos oportet. Et tunc utendum est antipoforis[bw] [78] et confutasionibus[bx] respondendo[by] ad tacitas[bz] obiecciones[ca] que possent[cb] fieri, ut forte[cc] siquis vellet ostendere quod filius dei debuit[cd] incarnari obiciat[ce] sibi ipsi[cf] nonne per[cg] purum hominem[ch] potuisset mundus redimi: nam si purus homo peccavit, purus homo debuit satisfacere.[79] Set ad hoc dici potest

---

[bd] emptimatica *B1* : emptimematica *A*   [be] ad a. *B3*   [bf] auctoritatibus *B1*
[bg] n. gustus f. *B1* s. est f. *A*   [bh] p. mamanibus t. *B3*   [bi] m. teneret c. *A*
[bj] qua *om. B1*   [bk] quis quis c. *A*   [bl] Isto *A*   [bm] Mathan *B1*   [bn] p. qua D. *B1*
[bo] contra David *om. A*   [bp] Christus om. *B1*   [bq] a. sic h. *B1*   [br] m. 2 *A*
[bt] runari *B2* : ratinari *A*   [bu] apostoli *om. B1*   [bv] tracierunt *B3*
[bw] antiphorum *B1* : antiforis *B2* : antiforum *B3* : antifona *A*
[bx] confucio *B1* : confusionibus *B2 B3*   [by] respendendo *B3*
[bz] tactas *B1 B2* : tectas *B3* t. et o. *B1*   [ca] abiecciones *A*   [cb] potest *B1*   [cc] utpote s. *A*
[cd] debuit *om. B1*   [ce] obviet *A*   [cf] i. aliquando et dicat n. *A*
[cg] i. non dicat per *B1* i. et dicat nonne pro p. *B3*   [ch] purus homo *B1 B2*

---

*raciocinari : runari *H*

---

line 11 indicate that at least part of this interpolation was recognized as a copyist's error.

[76] Eccl. 4:12 mentions the "funiculus triplex" which "difficile rumpitur" but the sentiment here is perhaps more in line with Is. 5:18: "Vae qui trahitis iniquitatem in funiculis vanitatis." It is possible that the whole statement is meant to refer to Prov. 5:22 which Basevorn (Charland, p. 293) quotes: "Funibus peccatorum quisque constringitur."

[77] The interchanges between David and Nathan the prophet are recorded in II Reg. 7 and 12 and I Par. 17. They can be considered enthymemes in their rhetorical, argumentative content. The parable to which Ranulph refers is contained in Matthew 21:33-44 but parables about farmers are also recorded in Mark 12:2-9 and Luke 20:9-15.

[78] "Antipoforis" appears to be the correct reading. Bodley MS. 848, fol. 6v, a copy of the *De dilatacione sermonis* of Richard of Thetford, reads: "Multoties uti antipoforis sive confucionibus"; the *Ars concionandi*, however, (ibid. p. 18) reads "oportet autem ratiocinantem multoties uti anasceve seu confutatione" and the editors note: "'ἀνασχευὴ, id est rei propositae confutatio (ita Forcellini)—sequens definitio confutationis est verbotenus in *Rhetoricis ad Herennium*, Lib. I, n. 3; cf. Cicero, Lib. I, *Rhetorica*, c. 42."

[79] Ranulph's use of this illustration is particularly interesting since it involves the concept of satisfaction, a concept unknown to patristic tradition outside of the doctrine of penance. Although there are many scriptural bases for the doctrine, it was Anselm (*Cur Deus Homo*, I, 20-1) who stated that it was absolutely necessary that Jesus Christ take on the responsibility for this satisfaction. Thomas Aquinas mitigated the "necessity" in Anselm's discussion by investigating the many ways in which satisfaction operated (*Summa Theologica*, Suppl., Q. 12-15)—hence perhaps Ranulph's "debuit." Clement VI in 1343 probably gav⌐

magis[ci] est recreare quam creare, vel saltem non[cj] minus. Si ergo oportuit creatorem esse deum,[ck] multo magis[cl] oportuit recreatorem[cm] esse deum. Set in huiusmodi caveat predicator questionem movere nisi eam[cn] valeat aperte[co] solvere.[cp] Caveat eciam ne[cq] magis[cr] bonum eciam[cs] ita commendet quod[ct] minus bonum videatur deprimere, de[cu] quo vide supra, capitulo quinto.[80]

Quintus modus dilatandi est per concordancias que[cv] aut[cw] concordant in vocabulo ut *beatus vir qui suffert temptacionem* (Iac. 1:12), de quo iob[cx] 38: *accinge sicut[cy] vir[cz] lumbos tuos* (Iob. 38:3), aut eciam[da] concordant in sentencie veritate quamvis non in voce ut ad colossenses[db] secundo: *fides sine operibus mortua est* (Iac. 2:20), de quo dicitur genese 34,[dc] dixit Rachel ad Iacob: *da michi liberos alioquin moriar* (Gen. 30:1); per Rachel fides, per[dd] liberos opera designantur in caritate facta.[de] Aut[df] eciam[dg] quando una[dh] auctoritas expresse[di] dicit illud quod alia[dj] auctoritas dicit latencius, ut si dicitur:[dk] sic[dl] *currite ut comprehendatis* (I Cor. 9:24), quomodo autem currendum sit[dm] determinatur in psalmo: *sine iniquitate cucurri et direxi* (Ps. 58:5), et alibi in psalmo:[dn] *viam mandatorum tuorum cucurri* (Ps. 118:32).

Sextus modus dilatandi est quando ea que[do] conveniunt in radice dilatantur per graduum comparacionem;[dp] verbi gracia, *accingere gladio tuo potentissime* (Ps. 44:4), quidam[dq] accinguntur potenter[dr] ut coniugati, quidam potencius ut continentes, quidam potentissime ut virgines. Vel sic: *inebriamini[ds] karissimi* (Cant. 5:1), cari sunt[dt] incipientes[du] et inperfecti, cariores sunt proficientes qui dampna pro[dv] Christo[dw] paciuntur sed cum

---

[ci] maius *B1 B3 A*   [cj] s. nec m. *A*   [ck] esse dicuntur m. *A*   [cl] maius *A*
[cm] creatorem *B1*   [cn] n. illam *A*   [co] appare *B3*   [cp] solve *B3*   [cq] C. ergo m. *A*
[cr] maius *B1 B3 A*   [cs] eciam *om. A*   [ct] commendat ut m. *A*   [cu] v. depere de *A*
[cv] que *om. B1*   [cw] aut *om. B1*   [cx] job. *om. A*   [cy] a. sic v. *B3*   [cz] s. ubi *A*
[da] aut et c. *B1 B3* : ac et *A*   [db] ad colocatur *B2* ut ibi iacob s. *A*   [dc] g. 30 *B2 A*
[dd] f. et l. *B1*   [de] c. perfecta *A*   [df] Autem *B1*   [dg] eciam *om. B1*   [dh] q. in una *B1*
[di] expresius *A*   [dj] q. una a. *B1 B2 B3*   [dk] dicatur *B1 B2 B3 A*   [dl] sic *om. B1*
[dm] c. si d. *B2*   [dn] sine iniquitate. . .in psalmo *om. B2 A*   [do] que *om. A*
[dp] g. temperacionem v. *B1* : operacionem *A*   [dq] p. quid a. *B1*
[dr] petuntur *B1* : potentar *A*   [ds] ebriamini *B3*   [dt] sunt *om. A*   [du] s. ficientes *B2*
[dv] d. proximo *B1 B3* : d. pro proximo *A*   [dw] Christo *om. B1 B3 A*

---

impetus to further questioning regarding satisfaction in the Bull "Unigenitus Dei Filius" (Denzinger, 550).

[80] Chapter five deals with circumspection in matters connected with all external aspects of the preaching office.

molestia, karissimi sunt qui quasi ^{dx} ebrii irrident ^{dy} inter obprobria. Ad hunc ^{dz} modum ^{ea} spectat dilatare ^{eb} per composicionem; verbi gracia, si dicatur *querite* ^{ec} *faciem eius* ^{ed} *semper* (Ps. 104:4), sic potest dici: queritur ^{ee} deus ^{ef} in baptismo, *requiritur in penitencia, ^{eg} inquiritur ^{eh} meditando in lege divina, exquiritur ^{ei} bene operando, ^{ej} et tandem ^{ek} adquiritur in patria.

Septimus modus est exponendo metophoras per proprietates rerum; verbi gracia, iustus germinabit sicut lilium.[81] Hic dicuntur ^{el} proprietates lilii et ^{em} quod iustus comparatur lilio ^{en} quia sicut lilium candidum est <et> ^{eo} odoriferum et crescit iuxta aquas, sic iustus candens ^{ep} est in ^{eq} continencia, ^{er} odoriferus bona ^{es} fama, et proficit ^{et} in aquis tribulacionis, exemplo ^{eu} de filiis Israelis qui quanto plus premebantur a pharaone, tanto plus ^{ev} crescebant. In illo ^{ew} modo non debet subito mutari ^{ex} methaphora transeundo ad aliarum rerum proprietates, set ^{ey} descendi poterit ad ^{ez} partes subiectivas eiusdem universalis vel ad partes integrales eiusdem integrantis, ut si thema sit: ^{fa} *ego sum* ^{fb} *flos campi* (Cant. 2:1), poterit sermo ^{fc} fieri de rosa, de ^{fd} lilio, et similibus quomodo Christus fuit lilium in nativitate, rosa in passione, viola in sepulchro. Tunc ^{fe} non convenit loqui de Christo quomodo fuit pastor vel petra, sed si thema sit ^{ff} *ego sum pastor bonus* (Ioan. 10:11), posset ^{fg} sermo fieri de pertinentibus ^{fh} ad pastorem, utpote de caula, de ^{fi} ovibus, de cornu, de canibus, de ministris ^{fj} expeditivis seu inpeditivis, utpote de lupo, non in quantum lupus sed ^{fk} in

---

^{dx} s. aut quasi *B1* : s. autem quasi *B3*   ^{dy} rident *A*   ^{dz} Ad huc *A*   ^{ea} modum *om. A*
^{eb} dilare *B1*   ^{ec} queritur *B1*   ^{ed} eius *om. B1*   ^{ee} querite *B1 B2* : quirtur *B3*
^{ef} deus *om. B1*   ^{eg} sic potest. . .in penitencia *om. A*   ^{eh} requirite m. *B2*
^{ei} d. ex consili b. *B1* exequitur *B3*   ^{ej} inquiritur meditando. . .bene operando *om. A*
^{ek} queritur dicitur in principio a. *A*   ^{el} dicantur *B1 B3 A*   ^{em} p. fili et *B3*   ^{en} lilie *B1*
^{eo} cadidum et perficit in aquis tribulacionum et o. *A*   ^{ep} i. candidus *A*
^{eq} in *om. B1 B3 A*   ^{er} continenciam *B1*   ^{es} bana *B1*   ^{et} perficit *B1*
^{eu} tribulancium tribulencium exemplum *A*   ^{ev} premebantur a. . .tanto plus *om. B1 B2*
^{ew} isto *A*   ^{ex} s. ministrari m. *A*   ^{ey} p. si d. *B2 B3*   ^{ez} p. a p. *B3*   ^{fa} sit *om. A*
^{fb} s. egio sine f. *B3*   ^{fc} s. poterit f. *B3*   ^{fd} r. vel l. *B1 B2 B3*   ^{fe} Et tunc *B1 B2 B3 A*
^{ff} t. esset e. *B1 B3 A*   ^{fg} poterit s. *A*   ^{fh} de pertinentibus *om. A*
^{fi} u. si causa de *B1* : de causa de *B2*   ^{fj} de ministrimientis e. *A* : de omnibus *B3*
^{fk} l. sit *B1*

---

*requiritur : quaritur *H*

---

[81] Osee 14:6: "Israel germinabit sicut lilium." The substitution of "iustus" for "Israel" is probably by association with "iustus ut palma florebit." In any case, the quotation is not meant to be completely biblical.

quantum ledit oves et nocet cure pastorali, eo quod oppositorum eadem [fl] est disciplina. Eodem modo negocietur [fm] in partibus integralibus, [fn] ut si thema sit *sumus invicem membra* (Eph. 4:25), non enim [fo] est vicium si [fp] ostendatur quomodo unus [fq] est alteri—oculus in providendo, [fr] brachium in defendendo, pes in [fs] promovendo, [ft] naris [fu] in precavendo [fv] seu discernendo, lingua informando.

Octavus modus dilatandi [fw] est exponere [fx] thema secundum diversos sensus scripture: [fy] historice, allegorice, tropologice, [fz] anagogice. [ga] Est autem historia narracio rei geste; [gb] allegoria est quando per unum factum signatur aliud factum, [gc] ut per hoc quod David vicit Goliam signatur [gd] quod Christus vicit [ge] diabolum; tropologia est quando unum factum signatur ad [gf] aliud faciendum, ut [gg] per hoc quod David vicit [gh] Goliam designatur [gi] quod vir fidelis debet vincere diabolum; [gj] anagogia est quando per [gk] aliquod factum in ecclesia militante signatur [gl] futurum in ecclesia triumphante, sicut patet per [gm] misteria multa [gn] de [go] templo per [gp] quod denotatur ecclesia triumphans sicut per tabernaculum Moysi signabatur ecclesia militans; verbi gracia, de omnibus hiis si dicatur *Ierusalem que* [gq] *edificatur ut civitas* (Ps. 121:3), hic Ierusalem litteraliter [gr] verificatur de quadam [gs] terrestri civitate, allegorice de ecclesia militante, moraliter seu tropologice de anima fideli, anagogice de ecclesia triumphante. Est eciam [gt] notandum quod non omnes allegorie sunt de Christo, sed de sacra scriptura, de ecclesia, de membris eius ac [gu] partibus, ut de [gv] iudeis, [gw] *de gentibus, de sanctis. Item in isto [gx] modo dilatandi [gy] debet pondus verborum considerari: [gz] quare hoc et non aliud, [ha] quare sic et non aliter; [hb] verbi gracia, dicatur [hc] *ego hodie genui te*

[fl] eadem *om. A*   [fm] negocitur *B3*   [fn] integrantibus *A*   [fo] enim *om. A*   [fp] si *om. A*
[fq] unius *B1*   [fr] previdendo *A*   [fs] inde p. *B1*   [ft] pes promovendo *A* : promerendo *B1*
[fu] maris *B2*   [fv] naris precanendo *A* : precando *B1 B2 B3*   [fw] dilatandi *om. B1*
[fx] e. est exponere t. *A*   [fy] s. scilicet h. *A*   [fz] tripologice *B1 B3* et a. *A*
[ga] anagogice *om. B3*   [gb] r. honeste *B1 B3*   [gc] aliud factum *om. A*
[gd] ut per. . .Goliam signatur *om. A*   [ge] vincit *B1*   [gf] per a. *jA*   [gg] ut *om. B1*
[gh] vincit *B1*   [gi] signatur hoc q. *A*   [gj] diabolum *A*   [gk] per *om. A*   [gl] s. ad f. *A*
[gm] p. in *A*   [gn] ministeria *B1* : multis misteriis *A*   [go] m. in t. *B1 B2 B3*   [gp] per *om. A*
[gq] que *om. B1*   [gr] litteraliter *om. B1 B2 B3 A* realiter *A*   [gs] quad *B3*
[gt] eciam *om. B2 A*   [gu] e. hac p. *B1* : e. atque p. *A*   [gv] utpote de *A*
[gw] i. ac de tribus de *B1* : i. de gentibus *A*   [gx] primo m. *B1 B2* : illo m. *B3*
[gy] dicendi *B1*   [gz] c. scilicet q. *A*   [ha] n. aliter *A*   [hb] quare sic et non aliter *om. A*
[hc] dicatur om. *B1*

---

*de : ac *H*

(Ps. 2:7), signanter dicitur "ego"[hd] discretive, quasi diceret non alius et[he] cum substancia[hf] prime persone competat[hg] patri; bene[hh] dicit "genui"—non[hi] creavi, non feci—et bene dicit[hj] "hodie"[hk] —non heri, non cras, non[hl] nocte—"te"—eternaliter, non "tua,"[hm] quia illa feci temporaliter.

Nonus modus dilatandi est per *causas[hn] et[ho] effectus procedere, assignando causas necessarias et essenciales. Nam loquens de causa potest transferre ad oppositum et[hp] econverso; verbi gracia, sit[hq] thema *humiliamini sub manu potenti dei* (I Pet. 5:6), potest sermo fieri de causis humiliandi que sunt imperfeccio corporis et anime nostre, et consideracio perfeccionis[hr] aliene; et[hs] post hoc[ht] possunt[hu] assignari humilitatis affectus[hv] quia illuminat, conservat, exaltat.

Decimus modus dilatandi est per discrecionem,[hw] quando declaratur aliquod incidens preter principale propositum dummodo non[hx] sit nimis remotus[hy] a principali proposito;[hz] verbi gracia, si[ia] dicatur de Iohanne evangelista quod constitutus est matri alter filius propter suam maximam[ib] mundiciam (cf. Ioan. 19:26-27). Tunc ergo[ic] potest sic adiungi: *vero ergo[id] animo[ie] tot exemplaria puritatis intuenti et non imitanti cum in omne fere ecclesia sit; Christus—virgo et[if] mater—virgo a dextris; Iohannes—virgo a sinistris, qui[ig] quidem in loco sublimi ponuntur quasi[ih] ad imitandum, saltem in[ii] castitate etsi non in virginitate. Unde qui post tam valida exemplaria neclecta[ij] vita angelica, spreta[ik] condicione humana, per inmundiciam[il] voluptatis[im] volutatur, certam[in] potest exspectare dampnacionem et forte repentinam,[io] sic[ip] de multis accidit quia proverbiis 22[iq] dicitur: *ruina* proximatur[ir] *malo* (Prov. 12:13), cuius quidem[is] ruine habet malus arram in presenti vita[it] tam per[iu] remorsum quam[iv]

[hd] ego *om. B1* [hd] hodie d. *B2*   [he] et *om. B1*   [hf] c. secunda *B2*   [hg] conveniat p. *A*
[hh] p. cum d. *A*   [hi] non *om. B1*   [hj] dicit *om. A*   [hk] creavi non. . .dicit hodie *om. B1*
[hl] n. in . n. *A*   [hm] tua *om. B1*   [hn] casus *B1 B2 B3*   [ho] percens et *A*
[hp] t. se ad *A* ad effectum et *B1*   [hq] g. si sit *A*   [hr] c. inperfeccionis a. *B1*   [hs] et *om. B1*
[ht] potest hoc *B1*   [hu] possunt *om. B1*   [hv] effectus *B1*   [hw] digressionem *B3 A*
[hx] dicitur modo non *B1*   [hy] remotum *A*   [hz] propsitum *B3*   [ia] ut si d. *B1 B3*
[ib] maximam *om. A*   [ic] ergo *om. A*   [id] ut ergo *B2*   [ie] anime *A*   [if] et *om. A*
[ig] s. quia q. *B1*   [ih] quasi quasi *A*   [ii] i. salutem in *B1*   [ij] e. illecta v. *B1*
[ik] a. specifica c. *B1 B2 B3*   [il] inmundicia *B1*   [im] voluptatis *om. A*   [in] v. ita p. *B1*
[io] reprehsentiam *B1*   [ip] sicut *B1 B3 A*   [iq] q. puerorum d. *B1*
[ir] aproximatur *B1* : proximat *A*   [is] quid *A*   [it] vita *om. A*   [iu] per *om. B3*
[iv] r. qui p. *B1* r. et *A*

---

*causas : casus *H*
*vero : ve *H*

post [iw] reluctam [ix] consciencie. Et [iy] gustat aliquid [iz] hic modo [ja] quod [jb] post [jc] modum bibet ad plenum, [jd] quia [je] secundum Boicium, de consolacione: [jf] hoc [jg] habet [jh] voluptas quod stimulis [ji] agit fruentes et cetera (*De consolatione philosophiae*, Liber III, met. vii), sed habens mundiciam cum Iohanne predicta in comoda evadit secundum illud [jj] proverbiorum: *effugiet [jk] iustus [jl] de angustia* (Prov. 12:13).

XX
De regulis dilatacionum [a]

In adducendo auctoritates ad propositum premittenda [b] sunt alia verba per que [c] auctoritas possit adduci; verbi gracia, si vellimus [d] persuadere quod homines non debent amare terrena sed celestia, et velimus adducere illud apostoli: *nunc [e] autem [f] dico inimicos Christi crucis quorum deus venter est* et cetera (Phil. 3:19). Dicamus tunc sic: non debemus, fratres, [g] terrena nimis sapere, sicut quidam [h] qui non curant nisi de ventris ingluvie. [i] Idcirco [j] quia tales plusquam oportet terrenis sunt dediti merito inimici [k] Christi sunt nuncupati, [l] secundum illud apostoli: *nunc autem [m] dico inimico crucis Christi* et cetera. Et si omnia [n] membra per unicam auctoritatem [o] confirmari possent, decens foret; verbi gracia, sit thema de assumpcione: *hodie extollitur, machabeorum [p] primo* [q] (I Mac. 2:63), dicatur: hic duo notantur: temporis congruitas decenter captata [r] quia "hodie," [s] honoris [t] virginitas [u] virgini collata [v] quia "extollitur," ex [w] quibus duobus [x] adduci possunt [y] illud *iosue [z] 3: *hodie incipiam te exaltare coram omni [aa] Israel* (Ios. 3:7).

[iw] post *om. A*   [ix] per luctum *B1* per r. *B2 B3*   [iy] et *om. A*   [iz] aliquid *om. A*
[ja] hic modicum *A*   [jb] quid p. *B1 B2 B3 A*   [jc] q. prius m. *A*   [jd] bibet ad plenum *om. A*
[je] quod s. *B1 A*   [jf] de consolacione *om. A*   [jg] que hoc *A*   [jh] hec sunt v. *B1 B2 B3*
[ji] quod stimulis *om. B2* q. sancto mulieris a. *B1* stimilis *A*   [jj] illud *om. B2*
[jk] p. 12 effugie *A*   [jl] iustus *om. A*   [a] Regule circa dilataciones *A*   [b] promittenda *B1*
[c] que *om. B1*   [d] volumus *A*   [e] a. non *B2*   [f] autem *om. B1 B2 B3 A*   [g] fratres *om. A*
[h] quid *A*   [i] inalumie *B1 B3* : gluvie *A*   [j] Recirco *B1*   [k] i. crucis C. *A*   [l] nuncupat *B3*
[m] autem *om. A*   [n] omnino *A*   [o] auctoritati *B1*
[p] machabere *B1* : machabeus *B3* : maria *A*   [q] primo *om. B2*   [r] coapta *B1 B2 B3*
[s] hodie *om. B2*   [t] honore *B1*   [u] h. sublimitas v. *A*   [v] collacatur *A*   [w] pro q. *B1 B3 A*
[x] duobus *om. A*   [y] potest *B1 B3 A* p. quod i. *A*   [z] golie *B1* : iosie *B2 B3*
[aa] omni *om. A*

---

*iosue : iosie *H*

Item alia regula est si vocabulum [ab] grecum vel ebraicum [ac] debet [ad] exponi vel interpretari; recurrendum est ad eius interpretacionem magis proposito congruentem, utpote [ae] "Iacob," qui interpretatur [af] "supplantator," [ag] [82] designat [ah] penitentem qui habet supplantare triplicem hostem, scilicet, [ai] mundum, carnem, et diabolum.[83]

Item alia regula est expositio sacre scripture sic: debet moderari [aj] ut non nimis contradicat sensui literali nec articulis [ak] fidei nec approbate veritati.

Item alia regula est [al] cum [am] triplex sit genus [an] predicacionum prout supradictum [ao] est capitulo 7, videlicet dominicalis, festivalis, et ad diversos status. Quando predicatur [ap] de [aq] dominica sumatur thema de evangelio vel de epistola, et [ar] si [as] fuerit de [at] evangelio [au] antequam [av] descendatur ad prosecucionem, narretur historia evangelica, et tunc disseratur de singulis [aw] virtutibus prout exigunt partes evangelii; quod si [ax] festivitas alicuius famosi sancti in [ay] ista [az] dominica occurrerit, [ba] ea que [bb] de moribus alias forent dicenda applicentur [bc] ad ipsum sanctum in specie, et consequenter ad [bd] audiencium [be] edificacionem. Set si occurrat festum in [bf] feria 4 temporum [bg] cinerum sive [bh] pasche [bi] aut in

---

[ab] vocabulam *B1*   [ac] vel obiit et cetera d. *B3*   [ad] debeat *B1 B2 B3 A*
[ae] c. ut quod i. *A*   [af] interpretator *A*   [ag] i. sub plante *B3* : supplantor *B1 B2*
[ah] designet *A*   [ai] scilicet *om. B1 B2 B3*   [aj] mediari *B1*   [ak] arci *B1*
[al] est *om. B1 B2 B3*   [am] dum t. *A*   [an] s. species p. *A*   [ao] p. gracia dictum *B1*
[ap] predicator *B1 B2*   [aq] de *om. A*   [ar] vel de epistola et *om. B1 B2 B3*   [as] e. sic *A*
[at] sit de *A*   [au] si fuerit de evangelio *om. B1 B2 B3*   [av] antichristus d. *B3*
[aw] de multa v. *A*   [ax] si *om. A*   [ay] in *om. A*   [az] ipsa *A*
[ba] occurrent *B1* : occurretur *B2* : contingerit *A*   [bb] illa que *A*   [bc] applicuntur *B1 B3*
[bd] et sequantur ad *A*   [be] audiendam *B1 A*   [bf] f. sancti in *A*   [bg] t. rogacionum c. *A*
[bh] sive *om. A*   [bi] patasseves *B1* : pascheves *B2 A* : paracephes *B3*

---

[82] The "definition" of Jacob derives ultimately from Genesis 27:36: "At ille subiunxit: Iuste vocatum est nomen eius Jacob; supplantavit enim me in altera vice: primogenita mea ante tulit et nunc secundo surripuit benedictionem meam."

[83] The biblical "germ" of this reference is probably I John 2:16: "Omne quod est in mundo concupiscentia carnis est et concupiscentia oculorum et superbia vitae" but the actual enumeration of the threefold enemy is patristic and can be found as early as Augustine in his sermon CLVIII which maintains that after baptism there remains "lucta cum carne, lucta cum mundo. . .lucta cum diabolo" (*PL* 38, col. 864). The triad was not commonplace in theological and monastic writings before 1000, although it was used in the Secret Prayer of a Mass for the Profession of Monks and in the "Regula communis" of St. Fructuosus of Braga which was included in the *Concordia Regularum* of Benedict of Aniane. Jean de Fecamp or Jean l'Homme de Dieu probably established the Three Enemies as a *topos* current from the twelfth century onward. See Siegfried Wenzel, "The Three Enemies of Man," *Mediaeval Studies*, 29 (1967), 47-66. Basevorn also mentions the "triple enemy"; see Charland, p. 285.

vigiliis solempnibus utpote natalis domini,[bj] pentecostes, formetur sermo de[bk] temporali, deinde aptetur[bl] ad sanctum. Quando autem fit sermo absolute de[bm] sancto, principaliter tractetur de sancto[bn] et incidenter[bo] de[bp] morum informacione, verbi gracia, sit thema *pascha domini est* (cf. Ex. 1:11), dividatur sic: hic notatur resurreccionis qualitas sive condiccio[bq] ibi "pascha"[br] quod[bs] interpretatur "transitus"; secundo resurgentis auctoritas sive iurisdiccio[bt] —"domini";[bu] resurreccionis veritas patefacta seculo[bv] —"est" quod est verbum substantivum et veritatis expressivum. Subsequatur divisio sic: hic primo[bw] notatur quod pascha idem est quod transitus, et in[bx] hoc tempore triplicem[by] transitum facit[bz] dominus,[ca] scilicet,[cb] panem[cc] in corpus transsumendo,[cd] mortem nostram per suam dirimendo,[ce] corpus suum post mortem resumendo.[cf] Primum istorum[cg] fecit[ch] die cene quando eukaristiam instituit; secundum in die parascheves[ci] quando[cj] diabolum in cruce devicit;[ck] tercium hodie[cl] quando speciem[cm] resurreccionis nobis contulit. Set et[cn] nos debemus sic[co] transire tripliciter,[cp] scilicet a peccatorum miseriis[cq] ut sacramentis ecclesie reficiamur, secundo a[cr] carnis desideriis ut Christo compaciamur,[cs] tercio ut[ct] a terrenorum deliciis[cu] exuta anima gaudio[cv] perfruamur.[cw] Quod si[cx] predicetur ad[cy] aliquem statum commendetur status ille[cz] per figuras,[da] per exempla canonis[db] et sanctorum, per similitudines rerum visibilium vel per[dc] aliquod miraculum quod in eo[dd] contingit.

Sunt eciam[de] alie[df] regule modernorum[dg] quod non[dh] plures figure quam tres, non plures narraciones quam tres, non[di] plura exempla quam tria in uno sermone[dj] adducantur sic:[dk] videlicet, quod unum membrum[dl] principale non plus[dm] contineat[dn] quam unam[do] figuram, unum exemplum, et unum narracionem; et

---

[bj] d. pasche p. *A*   [bk] s. primo prius de *A*   [bl] captetur *A*   [bm] de *om. B2*

[bn] sancto *om. B2*   [bo] incidunt *B3*   [bp] i. ad m. *B1*   [bq] s. condo i. *B2*   [br] pasch *A*

[bs] quod *om. B2*   [bt] i ibi d. *B1 B2 B3 A*   [bu] i. dem r. *B2 B3*

[bv] p. secundo *B1* : sciendum *B2* : seculo *om. A*   [bw] s. circa primum n. *A*   [bx] in *om. A*

[by] h. ipse triplicem *B2*   [bz] fecit *B1 B3 A*   [ca] dominus *om. A*   [cb] d. sed *B1 B2*

[cc] ponam *B1 B3* : penam *B2*   [cd] transumando *B1* : transmutando *B3 A*

[ce] dormiendo *A*   [cf] redimendo *B1 B2 B3*   [cg] illorum *B1 B3*   [ch] f. in d. *A*

[ci] pascheves *B2* : paracephes *B3*   [cj] p. scilicet d. *A*   [ck] devincit *B1*   [cl] t. die q. *B1*

[cm] specie *B1*   [cn] et *om. B1 B2 B3*   [co] sic *om. A*   [cp] triplici *B1*   [cq] miseris *B1*

[cr] s. autem c. *A*   [cs] ut in quarto compaciantur *B1*   [ct] ut *om. A*   [cu] d. ut e. *A*

[cv] gaudiis *A*   [cw] perfruantur *A*   [cx] Quasi si *B1*   [cy] p. in a. *B1 B2*   [cz] iste *B1*

[da] per filias *B1* : figuram *A*   [db] canonicis *B1*   [dc] v. insuper a. *B1* ut per *B3*

[dd] in illo *A*   [de] S. et a. *A*   [df] alii *B1*   [dg] modernorum *om. B1 B2 B3*

[dh] que non *B1 B2 B3*   [di] plures narraciones quam tres non *om. B1*   [dj] s. vero a. *A*

[dk] sic *om. B1 B2 B3*   [dl] membrum *om. A*   [dm] plus *om. B1*   [dn] continent *B2*

[do] una *B3*

quod aliqui ^{dp} solent ^{dq} probare dictum ^{dr} suum ^{ds} tripliciter, scilicet: auctoritate, racione, et exemplo, secundum illud sapiencie: ^{dt} *funiculus triplex* ^{du} [de] ^{dv} **difficile* ^{dw} *rumpitur* (Eccli. 4:12), hoc ^{dx} aliqui ^{dy} nituntur nunc ostendere tripliciter cum ^{dz} colore **pulcriore,* ^{ea} scilicet ^{eb} per documentum in scriptura, per experimentum ^{ec} in natura, et ^{ed} per exemplum in figura. Alii ^{ee} autem ^{ef} sic ostendunt quia ^{eg} per argumentum insolubile, per experimentum ^{eh} infallibile, per ^{ei} exemplum sensibile. Unde si unum dictum ^{ej} confirmetur per exemplum in natura, decens ^{ek} foret, quod ^{el} aliud ^{em} dictum ^{en} foret ^{eo} confirmatum ^{ep} per exemplum in arte, et secundum Augustinum: si aliquociens ad probandum intentum ^{eq} desit auctoritas, racioni insistendum est sine qua nec auctoritas est auctoritas.[84]

XXI
De coloracione membrorum ^a

Sermo coloratur duobus ^b modis vel per ^c consimilem terminacionem vel per certam ^d sillabarum commensuracionem. Primus illorum ^e modorum fit ^f in antethemate, in themate, in subdivisione, et in fine clausularum. Secundus modus ubique locum ^g habet. De primo ^h nota ⁱ quod aliquando fit ^j similis terminacio secundum unam sillabam ^k ut si sit thema: *corripiet* ^l *me iustus in*

---

^{dp} q. alii s. *A*   ^{dq} solen *B3*   ^{dr} p. factum *B1*   ^{ds} suum *om. B1 A*
^{dt} sapientis *B2* : summe sapiencie *B3* ecclesiastici 4 *A*   ^{du} f. tres d. *A*   ^{dv} de *om. A*
^{dw} difficili *B2 B3*   ^{dx} h. est a. *B1 B2 B3*   ^{dy} alii *A*
^{dz} t. scilicet in auctoritate racione et exemplo secundum c. *A*
^{ea} pulcriores *B1* : pulcriori *B2 A*   ^{eb} scilicet *om. B1*   ^{ec} eximentu *B3*
^{ed} et *om. B1 B3 A*   ^{ee} Alie *B2*   ^{ef} a. vero s. *A*   ^{eg} quia *om. B2*   ^{eh} eximentum *B2*
^{ei} i. pro e. *B2*   ^{ej} dictum *om. B1*   ^{ek} docens *B1*   ^{el} f. per a. *B2*   ^{em} aliquod *B1 B3 A*
^{en} dictum *om. B1*   ^{eo} foret *om. A*   ^{ep} confirmatur *B2* : confirmaretur *A*
^{eq} incensum *B1* : intactum *B2*   ^a colleracione *B1* De coloracione membrorum *om. A*
^b tribus *A*   ^c per *om. B1*   ^d per rectam s. *B3*   ^e istorum *A*   ^f sit *B1 B2 A*
^g ubi locus h. *B1*   ^h primi *B1 B2 B3*   ⁱ nota *om. B3*   ^j sit *B1*   ^k solebam *B3*
^l corupiat *B1*

**difficile : difficili *H*
**pulcriore : pulcriori *H*

---

[84] Augustine studies the meaning and justification of authority and its relation to reason most clearly in the *De vera religione*, chapters 24:45 ff., 26:48, 27:50, 28:51; see *PL* 34:141 ff.

misericordia (Ps. 140:5) describitur[m] prelatus quantum[n] ad statum[o] —"iustus," quantum ad[q] actum[r] —"corripiet,"[s] quantum ad medium[t] —"in[u] misericordia." Quandoque fit coloracio secundum duas sillabas ut si[v] in predicto themate dicatur: hic ostenditur de prelato[w] qualem[x] se deberet[y] exhibere ibi[z] "iustus," qualem[aa] actum exercere[ab] ibi "corripiet," qualem medium[ac] *tenere —"in[ad] misericordia." Item quandoque fit coloracio secundum tres sillabas sic: premittitur hic status prudenter prelibandus—"iustus";[ae] adiungitur hic[af] actus[ag] frequenter exercendus[ah] —"corripiet";[ai] et tandem[aj] exprimitur[ak] modus clementer moderandus quia "in misericordia." Et attenditur hic[al] ista[am] coloracio penes diccionis[an] qualitatem.

Alius modus penes[ao] quantitatem et vocatur cadencia, habens locum tam in simplici pausacione[ap] que vocatur punctus[aq] flexus, quam in maiori pausacione[ar] que vocatur[as] punctus medius seu acutus, quam eciam in plena pausacione[at] que vocatur finis versus. Illa quoque cadencia quamvis olim multipliciter exerceretur[au] tamen[av] apud modernos tribus modis[aw] celebratur; nam una vocatur dactilica quia continet duos dactiles,[ax] id est,[ay] sex sillabas ad[az] instar duorum dactilicorum cadentes ut "francis[ba] origine";[bb] secunda cadencia est dactilica et[bc] spondayca ut "genere francus";[bd] tercia est dactalica et dupliciter[be] spondaica ut "schemate generoso." Prima cadencia istarum[bf] apcius ponitur in primo punctu, secunda in secundo et in media distinccione,[bg] set[bh] tercia quamvis ubique poni posset,[bi] apcius tamen[bj] in fine ponitur.[bk]

---

[m] d. hic *A*   [n] quantum *om. B2 B3*   [o] ad finem *B1 B2 B3*   [p] quantum *om. B2*
[q] i. quomodo ad *B1*   [r] quem c. *B2*   [s] correpcio *A*   [t] ad modum *B1 A*
[u] m. in m. *B1 A*   [v] si *om. B1*   [w] de prolate q. *B2*   [x] quale *A*   [y] debet *A*
[z] ibi *om. A*   [aa] quale *A*   [ab] excercere *B1*   [ac] quale modum *A*   [ad] in *om. B1*
[ae] p. preliabundus ibi iustus *A*   [af] hic *om. A*   [ag] ac actus *B1*   [ah] excercendus *B1*
[ai] corripit *B1*   [aj] et tandem *om. A*   [ak] exivitur *A*   [al] hic *om. A*   [am] illa *B2 B3 A*
[an] dicciones *B1 B3*   [ao] m. ponet q. *B1*   [ap] pausacionem *B1* : pausa *A*
[aq] punctus *om. B3*   [ar] m. pausa *A*   [as] flexus quam. . .que vocatur *om. B3*   [at] pausa *A*
[au] exercetur *B2 A*   [av] tam a. *B1* cum a. *A*   [aw] modus *B2*   [ax] dactilos *B3*
[ay] d. secunda scilicet s. *A*   [az] ad *om. A*   [ba] francis *om. B1*   [bb] ordine *B1*
[bc] d. qui continet et *B2* et *om. A*   [bd] fractus *B2*
[be] spondayca ut. . .et dupliciter *om. B1*   [bf] illarum *B1 B3*
[bg] distinccione *om. B1 B2 B3*   [bh] set *om. A*   [bi] possit *B1 B3 A*
[bj] temen *B2* : tam *B3* : cum *A*   [bk] ponitur *om. A*; et cetera *B2 A*

---

*tenere "in misericordia" : "in misericordia tenere" *H*

Explicit ars componendi sermones. Nota quod litere capitanee huius artis sillibatim, invicem tantum sonant: Ars Ranulphi Cestrensis. [bl]

[bl] *om. B1 B2; A* :Explicit tractatus artis predicatorie de compilacione domini ranulphi de ordinacione sermonum.

APPENDIX:

An outline of the Ars componendi sermones *from chapter 2 to chapter 21 and an indication of the major sources within the preaching tradition from which Higden compiled his material.*

(It should be borne in mind that even in places where Ranulph's borrowing follows the source quite closely, there is rarely a verbatim transcription. In the tabulation of sources, Charland's editions appear as **C**, *the Franciscan Ars concionandi as* **AC**, *the Ars praedicandi of John of Wales as* **AP**, *Thomas Waley's De modo componendi sermones as* **Waleys**, *the Forma Praedicandi of Robert Basevorn as* **Basevorn**.)*

II. *De intencionis rectitudine* [1]
    A. Proper motives in preaching (glorification of God, edification of neighbor, bringing forward of truth)
    B. Motives to be avoided (favor, profit, ostentation)
    C. Characteristics to be avoided
        1. Dicendi subtilitas
        2. Fabulosa vanitas **[Waleys, C p.337]**
        3. Puerilis scurilitas

III. *De conversacionis sanctitudine*
    A. Holy life makes for sound preaching
    B. Example is more efficacious than words

IV. *De prolacionis aptitudine*
    A. One should preach "alte, prompte, mature"
    B. Maturity consists of
        1. appropriate motion of the body
        2. proper address of the ear
    C. Illustration of and exhortation to "maturitas" **[Basevorn, C p.320]**
    D. Opportuneness of time and place in the preaching apostolate

---

[1] Chapters II-V appear to be culled from several authors and texts, chiefly from Waleys, C pp.329-41, the *Distinctiones* of Nicolas Byard in B.N.Lat. 12424, fol. 249, and general guides such as that of Guibert de Nogent and that of Add. MS. 38818, fol.232. Ultimately, these chapters are related to Augustine's *Regula ad servos dei* [*PL* XXXII] and to the early medieval treatise on preaching by Humbert of Romans.

V. *De dicendi circumspeccione*
    A. Sermons must be made according to the audience and take into account
        1. the "quid" or the necessary meaning of the material
        2. the "cui" or the status of the hearers
        3. the "qualiter" or the *modus* dicendi
        4. the "quantum" or the *mensura perorandi*
    B. The matter should be the vices, the virtues, the pains of hell or the joys of heaven as they are manifested in scripture
    C. The status of the audience ought to determine the particular focus of the matter in condemning vice or lauding virtue
    D. The sermon matter must be adequately divided and discussed in order that it will not be tedious, obscure, ostentatious, etc.
    E. The *mensura perorandi* refers to the necessity that the matter be set out simply for the uneducated and profoundly for the well-instructed

VI. *De thematis congruitate*
    A. Names of the five requirements for a suitable theme which are the subject of this and the four following chapters **[Basevorn, C p.249]**
    B. Discusses the first of these: "quod ipsum thema non sit obscurum sed plenum impartet intellectum" **[Basevorn, C p.250]**
        1. A perfect theme has congruent apposit and supposit
        2. A theme is imperfect when apposit or supposit is missing
        3. A theme is proper when it accords with the feast celebrated
        4. A theme is accomodated when it affords both literal and mystical meanings
        5. An abused theme is one that literally refers to the reprobate but is turned allegorically to refer to a saint

VII. *Quod thema congruat materie proponende*
    A. Three species of sermon "penes materiam" **[AP]**[2]
        1. *sermo dominicalis*
        2. *sermo festivalis*
        3. *sermo ad diversos status hominum sive ad diversa negocia rerum* (e.g. for visitations, synods, elections, processions)
    B. Illustrations of themes to be used at certain times of the year, for special saints, or in "negociis" **[Basevorn, C pp.249-50, 253]**

VIII. *Quod thema sit de biblia*
    A. Abuses such as the use of non-biblical texts, inaccurate readings, and substitution of translations are illustrated and condemned **[Basevorn, C pp.250-1]**
    B. Unimportant adverbs, conjunctions, and interjections may be omitted from a theme if they do not impair the biblical meaning **[Basevorn, C pp.251-2]**
    C. Certain parts of the text, such as prepositional phrases, the time of a verb, the mode of statement, the personal attribution of a biblical

---

[2] In a volume attributed to Albert the Great (?Ulm, 1480), fol.xxii.

citation, the special signification of a word, and the order of one part to another may not be changed **[Basevorn, C pp.252-3]**
D. Illustrations given of the few instances when alteration of a text is permissible **[Basevorn, C p.253]**

IX. *Quod thema sufficienter dividatur*
A. Rule for and illustration of the manner in which the theme should have three meaningful words **[Basevorn, C p.254]**
B. Illustration of the manner in which a theme may be divided into three significant phrases and a warning that these divided parts must correspond with the original text and be artistically confirmed **[Basevorn, C pp.254-55]**
C. Illustration of how a theme of two words may be explicated in three parts **[Basevorn, C p.255]**
D. Comment on modern usage which does not countenance a prolixity of division yet it is possible and "utile pro plebe" to follow the example of James of Genoa and explicate a long text in pieces without formal sub-division
E. An example of the foregoing method with twelve separate parts **[Basevorn, C p.255]**
F. How a compound theme may be divided into two sections
G. A theme may be composed of one exhortative word, but a word like *lumen* does not convey sufficient understanding **[Basevorn, C p.256]**

X. *Quod thema concordancias admittat*
A. Recommendation of verbal and real concordance
B. Illustration from *ambulate* to an Isaian text *ambulat in ea* (i.e. *recta via*) which is not verbal concordance, but whose division is concluded through one authority with *ambulate* and this suffices **[Basevorn, C p.258]**
C. For preaching in English, "convertible," or substantially synonymous, texts like "to go" and "to walk" may be translated identically; but this practice should be used with caution, especially if the audience knows scripture and the corresponding Latin verb *ire* and *ambulare* which are not in vocal concordance **[Basevorn, C p. 258]**

XI. *De prothematis extraccione*
A. Ancient practice was to select a protheme different from the theme **[Basevorn. C p. 258]**
B. Moderns favor the extraction of the protheme from the theme according to four aptitudes
  1. that the circumstances of the person preaching be touched on there; i.e. *vita sancta, solida sciencia, congrua loquela* **[AP, fol.xx]**
  2. that the circumstances of the auditors be handled: these being a *sedulitas verbum dei audiendi*, an *auditum retinendi*, and a *retentum exequendi* **[AP, fol.xx]**
  3. that the circumstances of the sermon itself be considered, since it is founded on sacred scripture and implores divine help because of its lofty eminence and of the necessities of the preacher and

                    hearer
            4. that only the imploring of divine aid be made
    C. Illustration of the extraction of a protheme from a theme of one
       word **[Basevorn, C p.256]**
    D. Method of eliciting a protheme from a theme of several
       words **[Basevorn, C pp.257, 259]**
    E. Critique of this illustration **[Basevorn, C pp.259-60]**
    F. Further illustration of the extraction of a protheme from the text:
       acceptus est regi minister intelligens
    G. Protheme may also be introduced by a common saying **[AP, fol.xx]**
    H. Protheme may also be "eclipsed," or omitted entirely in some cases
       where prolixity would impair the effectiveness of the whole

XII. *De oracionis premissione et gracie impetracione*
    A. Offering prayers is a customary action **[Basevorn, C pp.262-3]**
    B. Examples of those who offered a prayer in the initial section of their
       sermons **[Basevorn, C p.263]**
    C. Moderns seem to propose theme and elicit antetheme before invoking
       peace and grace **[Basevorn, C p.263]**
    D. Example given of the proposing of the theme immediately followed by
       the prayer **[Basevorn, C p.264]**
    E. Precept concerning the dependence of the *oratio* on the matter preceding
       it and an illustration of this rule which forms the *modus
       Oxoniensis* **[Basevorn, C p.264]**
    F. Illustration of the Parisian mode which places the prayer first and in
       which divine aid is thus immediately invoked **[Basevorn, C p.264]**

XIII. *De auditorum alleccione*
    A. Ciceronian definition of exordium
    B. Methods of insuring a favorable attitude in the audience **[Basevorn, C
       pp.260-1]**
            1. Begin with something either subtle or curious (example given)
               [Basevorn, C p.261]
            2. Frighten an audience with a terrifying tale or *exemplum*
               (illustrated) **[Basevorn, C p.261]**

XIV. *De thematis introduccione*
    A. Cautions concerning the proper resume of the theme **[Basevorn, C
       p.268]**
    B. Modes of introducing a theme
            1. *per scripturam*
                a. Historical, tropological, allegorical, anagogical approaches **[AP,
                   fol.xx]**
                b. Through scriptural precept
                c. Through the writings of the saints
                d. Through poetical and/or philosophical writings
            2. *per argumentum*
                a. Induction **[Basevorn, C pp.269, 272]**
                b. Syllogism **[Basevorn, C p.270]**
                c. Enthymeme (plus commendation of Parisian use of

confirmatory authorities) **[Basevorn, C pp.271-2]**
    d. Example
      i. *per exemplarem manuducionem* (illustrated)
      ii. *per similem in natura* (illustrated)
      iii. *per exemplum in arte* (illustrated) **[Basevorn, C p.270]**
      iv. *per exemplum in historia* (illustrated) **[Basevorn, C p.270]**
      v. *per vulgare proverbium* (illustrated)
C. Mode of introducing a theme of one word
    1. Employ an authority from which three members may be elicited **[Basevorn, C p.272]**
      a. Lengthy illustration of the above plan (on *intellige*) **[Basevorn, C pp.272-3]**
      b. Short illustration on the theme: *ambulate* **[Basevorn, C p.273]**

XV. *De thematis divisione*
  A. Divisions are formed according to the significance of words and do not permit that the same word be both divisor and dividend nor that a practically synonymous word be employed **[Basevorn, C p.274]**
  B. Illustrations of faults in divisions which use unacceptable likenesses in words and possible corrective measures
  C. Terms placed in a division ought to be quite clear in the confirming authority (illustration given)
  D. The corcording texts should also agree in derivations (example provided)
  E. If significant, congruent words cannot be found for the division, recourse can be had to consignifications like case, genus, number, and circumstances (*quis, quid,* etc.)
  F. A division may be made according to an order other than the verbal one and two illustrations are given **[Basevorn, C pp.274-5]**
  G. Propriety must be observed in advancing from the theme to its division; i.e. logical thematic conclusions must be drawn from the theme
  H. Every significant word in the theme must come under the processes of division (examples of good and bad form given)
  I. In a theme of one word, the division may fall in a variety of places (example and secondary divisions given)
  J. In a theme of two words, the first division must be two-fold; but the following separations may divide these two parts in several ways
  K. In a theme of three words, it is fitting that the division and subdivisions follow along the triple pattern
  L. Themes may be divided according to verb and noun forms (i.e. by person and case). Several examples are given **[AC p.12]**[3]

XVI. *De clavibus divisionis*
  A. Purpose of these keys is to elucidate the sense of the divisions *sub ratione propinquintatis, sub ratione communitatis, sub ratione generalitatis* **[AC, p.9]**
  B. Examples given of the use of keys in *extra* and *intra* divisions **[AC, p.9]**

---

[3] In the Quaracchi, *Bonaventurae Opera Omnia,* IX.

C. Short method of introducing divisions and keys illustrated
D. Recognition that the ancients also asked the questions "quis, quid, **[AC, p.14]** qualiter," but that it is more subtle to describe a thing "quoad substanciam, quoad accidenciam, et quoad modum" **[Basevorn, C p.279]**
E. Keys or declarations may be made according to diverse sciences
    1. By grammar through nouns, verbs, particles, and adverbs (gives lengthy illustrations of modes of verb: person, time, voice, and particle usages) **[Basevorn, C pp.277-8]**
    2. By logic according to whether parts of the whole are virtual, universal, or integral **[Basevorn, C p.275]**
    3. By philosophy through determinations of the *termini* and *medius* **[Basevorn, C p.279]**
F. Illustration of the *clavis* method in a copulative theme
G. Recommendation that here and in most themes so "declared" the confirmation be added immediately to the parts **[Basevorn, C p.280]**

XVII. *De sermonis dilatacione*
A. Dilation is accomplished through two methods: by the subdivision of the members; by exposition through authoritative modes
B. Lengthy illustration and analysis of a division and dilation of the theme: *habitabit iuvenis cum virgine*
    1. Scriptural citations for whatever is detestable, imitable, and admirable in the state of virginity and notice taken of the imperative, commendatory and highly laudatory modes of discourse used in these illustrations
    2. Subdivision of the commendatory section into the possible oppositions of the virtues extolled in order that their nature may be explored in triplicate patterns **[Basevorn, C p.299]**
    3. Illustration of manner whereby members of this subdivision can have interrelationships among themselves or "per correspondenciam membrorum ad invicem coaptare" **[Basevorn, C p.301]**
    4. Warnings that circular correspondences are not useful to the majority of the people; yet illustrations of this type and of pyramidal and linear constructions are given **[Basevorn, C pp.302-5 passim]**
    5. Recommendation of the linear as "clarus et utilis ad populum" with admonition against the extended treatment of one member to the detriment of the others **[Basevorn, C p.306]**

XVIII. *De membrorum subdivisione*
A. Statement of the equation of methods in division and subdivision **[AP, fol.xxi]**
B. Six modes of division according to Boethius' *De divisione* (division of the universal into subjective parts [genera and species]; division of the whole into integral parts; division of words into their various significations [literal and allegorical senses]; division of a substance into accidents; division of the accidents into substance; division of the accidents into accidents) and a seventh mode which implies the division of the potential whole into its potential parts **[AP, fol.xxi]**

C. Advice concerning subdivision: consider the sense of the member and the reason for the subdivision and employ the method(s) described accordingly in sequence and with due respect for verbal consonances **[AP, fol.xxi]**

D. Illustration of the process in the development of *transire* **[AP, fol.xxi]**

E. A warning about using the division of words into their various significations because this process is more pertinent to lecturing and disputation than to the function of preaching **[Basevorn, C p.292]**

XIX. *De dilatacione facienda per auctoritates*[4]

A. First mode: Discussion of a noun as it appears in definitions, descriptions, interpretations, and notifications—with illustrations

B. Second mode: by division as discussed in the previous chapter and illustrated briefly here and through the cardinal virtues

C. Third mode: through ratiocination or argumentation, in particular by contrarieties and hidden enthymenes

D. Fourth mode: to reason by examples; illustrations provided and warnings against any foolhardy or excessive use of this method

E. Fifth mode: by concordance either in vocabulary or in meaning or in direct and indirect reference

F. Sixth mode: by comparison of things which agree in their root; and also through compositional variants such as *queritur, requiritur, inquiritur,* etc.

G. Seventh mode: devising metaphors through the proprieties of things: as for example those of a lily and a just man; this metaphor cannot be indiscriminately changed since it is better to proceed to the universal or integral parts than to completely revise (example provided)

H. Eighth mode: to expound a theme according to various senses of scripture; although the allegorical meaning of many passages is different, the weight of meaning of the words used must always be considered

I. Ninth mode: by causes and effects, i.e., by necessary and essential causes and consequent reasoning to their effects and the reverse (example given)

J. Tenth mode: digression, which implies saying something incidental to the principle proposition but not terribly remote from it; example given through St. John the Apostle's purity of life

XX. *Regule circa dilatacionem*

A. Some words are more easily able to be confirmed through authority than others (illustration given) **[AP, fol.xxi]**

B. If all members are confirmed by one authority, it is necessary that they be confirmed in a proper manner (example given from a theme on the

---

[4] A discussion of the sources of this chapter presents a special problem since Ranulph extends the treatment of Basevorn, C pp.291-5, by using a fuller "Thetford" MS. He divides Basevorn's third class into two and condenses Basevorn's 41st chapter on Digression (C pp.297-8) as his tenth mode. The manner in which a fuller text treats these modes of dilation can be seen by a consideration of the third part of the Franciscan *Ars Concionandi*, pp.17-21. Actually, the Thetfordian treatment of the modes of dilation was the most widely known sermon aid in the Middle Ages.

Assumption) **[AP, fol.xxi]**

C. If a Greek or Hebrew word is to be expounded or interpreted, it must be done according to the commonly-accepted interpretation (e.g. Jacob=supplantor) **[AP, fol.xxii]**

D. Exposition of sacred scripture should not contradict the literal sense **[AP, fol.xxii]**

E. Ground rules for the necessary exposition of a biblical text and the occasions on which it may be directed toward a particular saint (illustrated) **[AP, fol.xxii]**

F. Recommendation that preaching to a particular *status* be accompanied by figures, canons, examples from saints' lives, and similitudes to invisible things; but should not (according to moderns) be in excess of three of any particular kind in one sermon because a member ought not to contain more than one figure or example triply proved by authority, reason, and illustration **[AP, fol.xxii]**

G. Authority, reason, and illustration may take the forms of scriptural documentation, natural reasoning, and figurative example or indissoluble argument, infalible demonstration, and sensuous testimony—but appropriateness must be observed

XXI. *De coloracione membrorum*

A. Two modes of rhetorical coloration: through similar terminating syllables; through syllabic commensuration. The first may ensue in theme, protheme, divisions, and clause endings; the second in all places where it is suitable **[Basevorn, C p.321]**

B. First mode illustrated: resemblance to rhyme stressed and characteristic reference to the "quality" or syntactical condition of the words used **[Basevorn, C p.321]**

C. Second mode shown to be more concerned with the quantity of particular syllables; consequently, called cadence **[Basevorn, C p.322]**

 1. *punctus flexus, medius,* and *finis versus* defined **[Basevorn, C p.322]**

 2. Three methods employed by the moderns discussed **[Basevorn, C p.322]**

 3. Positions in which these cadences might be used suggested **[Basevorn, C p.322]**

GLOSSARY

Note: references are to page and line number

adiacens (-ere) lie next to 21/8, 21/11

antiqui (antiquus) sermon theorists who did not use thematic form, e.g. Augustine 24/4, 25/2

appositum epithet or adjective agreeing with the subject or, by extension, the whole phrase in which the adjective lies 15/12

clavis restatement of the parts of a division to clarify them 47/3

colore (color) a rhetorical device specifically describing the similar termination of statements made about the division or subdivision 59/7, 69/14 etc.

cotandum see *quotare*

deordinacionis (deordinacio) definite identification of a type or class 46/21

disconveniencia lack of agreement, inconsistency 20/8

enthymematice (enthymema) a condensed or rhetorical syllogism 37/19, a conclusion drawn from the contrary 38/8

exemplariter (exemplar) precedent, model 37/18

fingere to make or fashion in a fictitious manner 18/5

glossa an explanation of a biblical word or a collection of such explanations from various church authorities 27/6

gnarrat (-are) relate, report 40/10

guerra war 38/19

induccione (induccio) reasoning from known particulars to generals 37/8

latencia hidden, concealed 60/28, 62/15

levita Levite (specifically the one described in Jud. 19:27) 20/21

manduccionem (manuduccio) introduction 35/2

maturitas modesty, gravity 10/4

misticam (mistica) non-literal, allegorical 15/23

modernus sermon theorist who espouses thematic construction 22/26

moralem (moralis) moralistic or tropological interpretation of scripture 20/23

oracio theme, subject 3/20; prayer, invocation 30/7 etc.

particulas (particula) item, detail, individual instance 23/2

precellentivum (precellentivus) surpassingly excellent 54/20

predicabilibus (predicabilis) any of the various kinds of predicates that may be affirmed or denied of a subject, as genus, species, property, accident, difference 12/11

proposiciones (proposicio) assumption, statement 18/20
quantitatem (quantitas) extent, range 12/2
quotare repeat or cite for authority or illustration 34/21
reales (realis) genuine, representing the true or actual 24/3
sensum (sensus) understanding, perception 3/9, 3/10
subsannarent (-are) deride, mock 25/1
suppositum (suppositus) subject, topic 15/12
syllogistice (syllogisticus) argument by three propositions 37/18
tempus tense 19/9
truffas (truffa) fraud, crime 27/3
uniformitas sameness 21/13
vocem (vox) language, speech 3/8, 3/10
vocales (vocalis) verbal 24/3
vocabula (vocabulum) word 21/3, 21/4
ydemptitas identity, oneness 21/13

DAVIS MEDIEVAL TEXTS AND STUDIES

Scholarly Editions and Studies devoted to those aspects of the European Middle Ages that include English, Germanic, Latin, and Romance languages and literatures; music; philosophy; and rhetoric.

PUBLISHED:

I.   Hugo Bekker. *The Poetry of Albrecht von Johansdorf.*

II.   John J. Hagen, O.S.A. Translator. *Gerald of Wales, Jewel of the Church: A Translation of Gemma Ecclesiastica by Gilardus Cambrensis.*

III.   Norris J. Lacy. *The Craft of Chrétien de Troyes: An Essay on Narrative Art.*

IV.   Margaret Winters. Editor. *The Romance of Hunbaut: An Arthurian Poem of the Thirteenth Century.*

V.   Henry Ansgar Kelly. *Chaucer and the Cult of Saint Valentine.*

VI.   Margaret Jennings. Editor. *The Ars Componendi Sermones of Ranulph Higden, O.S.B.: A Critical Edition.*

VII.   Katharina M. Wilson. *Hrotsvit of Gandersheim: The Ethics of Authorial Stance.*

FORTHCOMING:

VIII. Emil J. Polak. *Medieval and Renaissance Letter Treatises and Form Letters: A Census Of Manuscripts Found in Eastern Europe and the U.S.S.R.*

E.J.Brill — P.O.B. 9000 — 2300 PA Leiden — The Netherlands